Guns and Guerilla Girls

Guns and Guerilla Girls
Women in the Zimbabwean National Liberation Struggle

Tanya Lyons

Africa World Press, Inc.

P.O. Box 1892
Trenton, NJ 08607

P.O. Box 48
Asmara, ERITREA

Africa World Press, Inc.

P.O. Box 1892
Trenton, NJ 08607

P.O. Box 48
Asmara, ERITREA

Book Design: 'Damola Ifaturoti
Cover Design: Ashraful Haque

Library of Congress Cataloging-in-Publication Data

Lyons, Tanya.
   Guns and guerilla girls : women in the Zimbabwean national liberation struggle / by Tanya Lyons.
     p. cm.
Includes bibliographical references (p.) and index.
   ISBN 1-59221-166-6 (hardcover) –ISBN 1-59221-167-4 (pbk.)
   1. Zimbabwe–History–Chimurenga War, 1966-1980–Women. 2. Women revolutionaries–Zimbabwe. 3. National liberation movements–Zimbabwe–History–20th century. I. Title.
   DT2988.L96 2003
   968.91'04'082–dc22   2003015796

Until lions have their own historians,
tales of hunting will always glorify the hunter.
- African proverb

Table of Contents

List of Illustrations

Plate 1: Map of Zimbabwe

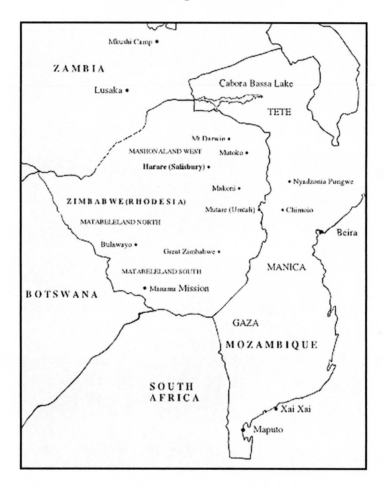

Preface

Women in the Zimbabwe Revolution
Women revolutionary militants fought and died
alongside their male compatriots in the heroic struggle
to free the motherland. The war of national liberation
proved the greatest equaliser of sexes in Zimbabwe.
- Poster at the National Liberation War Museum Display
at the Zimbabwe National Archives

What were women doing in the Zimbabwe National
Liberation War, this ambiguous and contradictory
revolution and liberation struggle that spelled the end for
white Rhodesia and the beginning of an independent, postcolonial
Zimbabwe? Women in the Zimbabwean National Liberation Struggle
are recognized at the National Liberation War Museum Display at the
Zimbabwe National Archives in a poster depicting six women training
to shoot guns. I had read about the heroic African women fighters and
seen images of them carrying babies on their backs and a gun over their
shoulders. Who were these women? This research uncovered a more
complex history of women's involvement in the liberation war than
these simple images.

Zimbabwean women's roles in the liberation war were unique in
many ways, yet their experiences also share commonalities with women
in other liberation wars in southern Africa. I was fortunate to have had
the opportunity to spend twelve months in Harare during 1996 and
1997. This book was written at a time in Zimbabwe when some women
ex-combatants were negotiating financial security for themselves by
threatening to expose male *chefs* (leaders or commanders), who are

now high ranking officials within the government, as rapists of women guerillas during the war, fathering their children, and leaving them with no compensation or financial support. In early 1998, the majority of registered ex-combatants, including many women, were paid Z$50,000 (US$2,500) in compensation for their wartime service as guerilla fighters. At the time of writing, no threats of exposing alleged rapists have been carried out. This investigation of representations and experiences of guerilla girls and women in Zimbabwe's liberation war is an attempt to open up the discourse of war in Zimbabwe to include the experiences of women who acted in the nationalist struggle for independence as guerilla fighters. My research was influenced by the political climate and current events of the day, which involved women ex-combatants. Any preconceived ideas I had about my research and my time in Zimbabwe were soon dispelled by the people I met, the places I saw, and the situations I found myself in. I had hoped that my journey would be a learning experience and that in return I could share my findings. I did not realize that I would learn quite so much. I hope that the presentation of this book will do justice to the many people who contributed their time and enthusiasm to my research.

Acknowledgements

My research in Australia and Zimbabwe was made possible by the financial support of the Australian Postgraduate Award, 1995-98; the Walter and Dorothy Duncan Trust, 1995 - 96; the George Murray Travel Grant, 1996; the Overseas Travel Grant, 1996: and the Politics Department, the Faculty of Arts, Scholarships Office, and Graduate Studies at the University of Adelaide.

I spent one year in Zimbabwe and could not have completed my research without the generous support of the following institutions: The Department of Political Science and Administration, at the University of Zimbabwe, where I was a Visiting Research Associate, 1996-97; the National Archives of Zimbabwe; the ZANU Archives; the Zimbabwe National Liberation War Veterans Association; the Zimbabwe Women's Resource Centre and Network; and the Feminist Studies Centre, Harare. Special thanks go to Colonel Emile Munemo; Wilfred and Wilbert; Sekai Nzenza-Shand; Melanie Mugamu; Prudence Uriri; Irene Staunton; Simon Bright; Ingrid Sinclair; Bev Mathison; Jane Taylor; Alison Goebel, and Amy Kaler. Thanks also to Kassahun Checole and Damola Ifaturoti of Africa World Press and the anonymous proof reader for valuable comments on this manuscript. I would also like to sincerely thank all of the women ex-combatants who gave of their time to meet and talk to me. This book is dedicated to them.

List of Abbreviations

ANC	African National Congress
AK-47	Russian Assault Rifle
BSAC	British South Africa Company
BSAP	British South Africa Police
CCJP	Catholic Commission for Justice and Peace
CYL	City Youth League
MPLA	Movement for the Popular Liberation of Angola
PF-ZAPU	Patriotic Front of the Zimbabwe African People's Union
NDP	National Democratic Party
SRANC	Southern Rhodesian African National Congress
UDI	Unilateral Declaration of Independence (1965)
V.C.	Victory/Victoria Camp (ZAPU Base in Zambia)
ZANLA	Zimbabwe African National Liberation Army (armed wing of ZANU)
ZANU	Zimbabwe African National Union
ZANU(PF)	Zimbabwe African National Union Patriotic Front
ZBC	Zimbabwe Broadcasting Commission
ZTV	Zimbabwe Television
ZIPA	Zimbabwe People's Army
ZIPRA	Zimbabwe People's Revolutionary Army (armed wing of ZAPU)
ZNLWVA	Zimbabwe National Liberation War Veterans association

Introduction

Hope for the nation is born out of the
intensity of newly created memory.
- Yvonne Vera in *Nehanda*

In April 1980 Zimbabwe (formerly Rhodesia) gained independence
from Great Britain and Ian Smith's white minority rule. One of
the most significant features of the anticolonial struggle was the inclusion
of women in the nationalist guerilla armies. This book is about those
women. Representations and rhetoric from the liberation war, fought mainly
in the 1970s, evokes an image of the heroic woman warrior fighting for
political independence, wielding a gun in one hand and holding a baby
with the other. Investigating the representations of "women warriors" in
Zimbabwe's anticolonial national liberation war, reveals certain
glorifications, which have obscured the roles and experiences and silenced
the voices of the thousands of young girls and women who were involved
in the struggle for independence.

This book challenges these representations by juxtaposing them with
the voices of Zimbabwean women ex-combatants' own versions of their
involvement as guerilla fighters. Documenting a women's history of the
Zimbabwean liberation war, set against the backdrop of the representations
of "guerilla girls," serves several purposes. First, it clarifies some feminist
issues of women's equality with men based on women's participation in a
traditionally male domain - war. Second, it provides an analysis of the
activities preceding the disappointment felt in some feminist circles in
Zimbabwe and internationally. Soon after independence it became apparent
that many of the alleged gains made by women during the struggle would
not be automatically transferred into public policy designed to liberate
women or make them more equal with men. As a result, many analyses

of women's involvement in the struggle have focused on these post-independence disappointments for women without analyzing the events of the war and women's roles and experiences of them. Third, it focuses in particular on the roles and experiences of women in the Zimbabwean National Liberation Struggle (1964-80) in order to bring to the foreground a women's history of the struggle which has to a large extent been silenced in popular discourse of the war.

In doing this, the relationship between the representations of women's roles and the voices of women ex-combatants discussing their roles will be examined. This will bring us back to the many assumptions made about women's roles during the war, often based on representations rather than connecting them to women's own voices. For example, in 1995 when a group of Zimbabwean women delegates traveled to Beijing for the Fourth International Women's Conference, the aim was to report on the situation of women in Zimbabwe since the first conference held for the United Nations Decade for Women in 1975. They took with them a glossy publication prepared especially for the Beijing conference detailing *Zimbabwe Women's Voices.* The book aimed

> to allow the silent voices of many Zimbabwean women to be heard. The book will facilitate dialogue between Zimbabwean women and other participants at the conference in Beijing as well as creating a forum for Zimbabwean women to communicate with each other.[1]

While this book has been important for acknowledging the voices of Zimbabwean women who talk about their lives from varied perspectives, one can also trace some interesting trends in the discourse of women in Zimbabwe that culminate in this volume. For example, when the chairperson of the Zimbabwe Women's Resource Centre and Network, Thoko Ruzvidzo, discusses the "national machinery for women" in Zimbabwe, she suggests that

> [h]istorically, the first post-Independence changes resulted from the pressure mounted by women before Independence. There was a meeting in Mozambique, the Xhai Xhai meeting, where the women met as women within ZANU to map out their strategies to improve the status of women after Independence. The women exerted pressure on ZANU to make women visible within the new

government of Zimbabwe. This is how the Ministry of Women's Affairs came to be.[2]

This First ZANU Women's Seminar, held in 1979, has often been seen as the turning point not just for the national organization of women but for women's liberation in Zimbabwe. This common view is interesting because it tacitly complies with previous views on women's roles in the liberation war in Zimbabwe. That is, that women fought side by side with their men in the struggle, but as soon as the war was over they did not receive the sexual equality they had fought for. Like the publication *We Carry a Heavy Load,* a report written for the Zimbabwe Women's Bureau, *Zimbabwe Women's Voices,* continues the evolving trend in post-independence publications on women's roles in Zimbabwe, in ignoring the differences between "women in Zimbabwe" and "women ex-combatants" who joined the guerilla fighters in the anticolonial struggle.[3]

There is a difference between women who did and did not join the freedom fighters. The women who joined up as guerilla fighters and trained in cross-border camps, came back to independent Zimbabwe with different experiences than those of women who stayed behind. Perhaps because of these differences the women ex-combatants were also treated differently than other women. Women's roles are defined as different than men's, and, as a result, some inconsistencies, contradictions, and glorifications in the representations of women are revealed here.

We will examine the interconnections between feminism, nationalism, and the war of independence in Zimbabwe. Feminist fieldwork faces a dilemma of approach and methodology in representing the Other, or "subaltern" (in Gayatri Spivak's phrase) or third world woman. The role of women in wars in general is contextualized with the debate on feminist connections with nationalism, in particular in relation to the First and Second *Chimurenga* (anticolonial struggles) in Zimbabwe (1896-97 and 1965-80). How are women situated within the war literature? What is the connection between socialism and feminism in Zimbabwe, which ultimately led to the feminist disappointment in the national struggle for not resulting in women's emancipation.

What is the historical role of women in the struggles against colonization and white minority rule? We will see the (non)visibility of women in the histories of military-style anticolonial activities, nationalist political action, and ultimately armed struggle in the late 1960s and 1970s. The rare appearances of women in nationalist and academic discourse (about the history of nationalist struggle in Zimbabwe) demonstrates the necessity of re-presenting the stories of women involved in the Second *Chimurenga* in their own voices. The personal stories of some women ex-combatants express their reasons for joining the nationalist guerilla fighters and their experiences in the training camps and the war. Privileging their voices above standard historical accounts of the war reveals a feminist historical account dissimilar to the latter.

The roles of African women in the struggle are juxtaposed with the roles and expectations of white Rhodesian women during the war. This exploration allows for a balanced view of women in war, because in the liberation struggle the racial divisions between white minority rule and anticolonial struggle were not always figuratively or literally black and white.

One of the most important roles performed during the war was by the "mothers of the revolution," those women who remained inside Rhodesia and found that the war front came to them on a regular basis. Some of these mothers performed the most heroic tasks during the war, and indeed suffered immeasurable pain at the hands of Rhodesian forces (and some guerilla fighters). Yet, their role in the war has not been fully recognized, and in most cases they have been left uncompensated for their sacrifices and losses during the struggle.

There was a range of actions in anticolonial struggle, in printed historical accounts, in women's own voices, and through fiction. From these accounts a more substantial history of the liberation war is possible and analysed as to some of the problems associated with (officially) including women in a national war of liberation.

The "problems of women" that emerged during the final years of the war can be compared to the positive images and glorifications of women guerilla fighters that emanated from nationalist propaganda. Ambiguities, misrepresentations, and contradictions surround not only the role of women in the struggle but the way in which they have been represented. The problems, glorifications, propaganda, and stereotypes of women that developed during the struggle must be deconstructed, the differences between men's and women's actions established. When Rhodesian propaganda is separated from nationalist rhetoric, the real problems for women emerge. The differences between women in the two main nationalist parties, ZANU and ZAPU, are then established. The significant issue of equality between the sexes can be seen in the issues of "sex for soap," *lobola* (bride-wealth) and family planning.

Finally, there are repercussions to the representations of women in the struggle. Women often symbolize the nation, but in the case of Zimbabwean national independence, women were blatantly reinscribed into the domestic sphere. This reinscription is important for understanding the attempts to ban a film made in Zimbabwe sixteen years after independence, which told the stories of two women involved in the struggle. The controversy surrounding the film *Flame (1996)* reveals the "silences and lies" in the history of the liberation war in Zimbabwe. It is essential to get the history of the war told from as many perspectives as possible.

Endnotes

1. Ciru Getecha and Jesimen Chipika, eds., *Zimbabwe Women's Voices*, (Harare: Zimbabwe Women's Resource Centre and Network, 1995) p. 8
2. Ibid, p. 16.
3. Kate McCalman, coordinator and compiler, "We Carry a Heavy Load: Rural Women in Zimbabwe Speak Out," Report of a survey carried out by the Zimbabwe Women's Bureau, December 1981.

PART ONE:
FEMINISM, NATIONALISM, AND THE STRUGGLE FOR INDEPENDENCE

Chapter One

Dilemmas in Feminist Fieldwork in Africa[1]

T here are dilemmas and contradictions that face Western women researching women in Africa. These dilemmas apply not only to women's issues but to an array of research and development issues between the West and the "rest." It is argued here that feminist theory and inquiry are well placed to question the locations of the researcher and the researched. In my reading of the debate between Third World women and Western feminists there appears to be very little space for the Western, feminist-Africanist to locate her work without being situated within the neo-imperial or Africanist/Orientalist discourse.[2] One perspective lays blame on Western feminist theorists for silencing the African woman in the very speech intended to liberate her from oppression. The other perspective authorizes the voice of Western feminists within the discourse of "women in/and development."[3] Although some respect may be paid to one's identity, falling into the trap of "speaking for others" is quite frequent.[4] As Gayatri Spivak has said, declaring your identity and position as a gesture "can never suffice."[5]

I wish to locate my research outside of a neo-imperial discourse that, however subtly or implicitly, purports to speak for others, while remaining in a framework of feminist methodological fieldwork. This position could be considered unstable in its attempt to find a balance between feminism and postcolonialism. Postcolonialism does not mean only "after independence" or "after colonization" or "postindependence." Postcolonialism begins with the responses to first colonial contact and has developed into a theoretical framework that exposes "the inadequacies of conventional accounts of the past by attempting to include what these accounts tended to leave out."[6] By scrutinizing "the foundations of the structure of knowledge" postcolonial writers and scholars have enabled the oppressed to be included as actors in the historical record. [7] By weakening the orientalist discourse the voices of the subaltern, in this case African women, can be better heard.[8]

A dialogue between African women theorists and Western feminists will illustrate the need for a stable relationship between feminism and postcolonialism. Sekai Nzenza-Shand critiques Western women researching African women, [9] Christine Sylvester outlines strategies of "empathetic co-operation"[10] and Jayati Lal discusses the dilemmas of doing feminist fieldwork.[11] The dilemmas of doing feminist fieldwork in Zimbabwe arise from the "politics of identity."[12] The foreign, white, Western, middle-class, feminist might appear to have many advantages, such as access to funding. Yet such advantages are negated when she is met by the "scepticism, defensiveness, and ambivalence" of some Zimbabwean women who have argued that this kind of research only serves to "silence" the African woman.[13]

Sekai Nzenza, a Zimbabwean/Australian author and academic, has argued that when white women speak their voice is valued but when black women speak their "speech is denigrated in academic circles because [they] lack the language of theory."[14] She explains that there are culturally insensitive "obstacles to understanding," which contribute to the silencing of African women.

> The difficulty is compounded by the problems and possibilities of high theory, which at the present is the chosen mode of articulation. On the one hand, I recognize its enabling potential and the fact that it cannot be shut out of African thinking. On the other, it is very distant from our experience, and it is, after all, understood only by a small elite, largely in the Western world.[15]

Academic theories are usually generated for academic audiences. It is not simply high theory that uses and thus silences African women's experiences. The position from which the white woman researcher speaks can guarantee some kind of an audience. Her work is more likely to be read in academic circles where African women are rarely located. The African woman might speak in other ways within their communities, but perhaps in the Western world we are incapable of hearing. Nzenza suggests that the

> future [for] feminist methodologies rel[ies] on oral forms of evidence. The only problem is how this data should be collected and how it is presented ... The researcher still retains the power to select questions, and to silence those words she feels are not important to her research. Clearly her ideological position also determines the way conclusions are drawn from raw data. The African woman remains a static, silent object of research, while her life is "spoken for," and about, in feminist academic circles.[16]

Nzenza concludes that "the issue is not that the women have been silent, but that they were not heard or understood."[17] As Spivak has noted, regarding the subaltern, they *can speak*, it is just that no one is listening.[18]

In searching for the subaltern voice, Reina Lewis defines it as the "embryonically counter hegemonic" voice that "may contest and to varying extents transform the power relations of hegemonic discourse."[19] Lewis argues that the subaltern voice can be found with "orientalist discourse" if we consider that to be as Lisa Lowe argues "an uneven matrix of orientalist [sic] situations across different cultural and historical sites in which each orientalism is 'internally complex and unstable.'"[20] Therefore, the subaltern voice is audible within hegemonic discourse, appearing in the cracks. If we search in the cracks of hegemonic discourse until we hear the voice of the subaltern woman, how can we then project her voice to ensure it is heard by a wider audience, both inside and away from academia? John Beverly questions whether we can actually represent the subaltern either mimetically - speaking about - or politically and legally - speaking for - without confronting the dilemma of subaltern resistance to elite conceptions and without ignoring the ways she can speak, if she is just "spoken for."[21] Beverly asks "what would be the point after all of representing the subaltern as *subaltern*?"[22] The aim here is not to represent the *subaltern* women guerilla fighters as subaltern, but to re-present them as a subject of history from the "welter of documentary and historiographic discourses that deny the subaltern that power of agency."[23] In this case it is about the Zimbabwean liberation war, which has denied women ex-combatants a right to be acknowledged for their experiences of war. Here Zimbabwean women guerilla fighters are the subaltern for the sake of the argument, and as the subaltern they cannot speak, as Spivak has "paradoxically" claimed, because by doing so it would mean they are no longer subaltern. By letting the voices of women ex-combatants be heard here, we are representing them as subaltern no longer. How can a fieldworker claim to represent the subaltern?

> [W]e do not claim to represent ("map," "let speak," "speak for") the subaltern. We seek to register instead the way in which the knowledge we construct and impart is structured by the absence, difficulty, or impossibility of representation of the subaltern.[24]

I do not claim to *represent* the subaltern but to acknowledge the absence of subaltern representation. To be unrepresented means to be unheard. To be heard means to be no longer subaltern. To represent the subaltern in this way means that they can become actors and agents of their own history. The point here is not to be the voice of the subaltern but to engage in a dialogue with her, thus privileging her voice in the context (and restraints) of academic research. As Lal warns,

> [T]his tendency to silence the subjects of our research is made even more disturbing in light of the fact that the conditions under which we produce and labor as intellectuals tend to push us into being more accountable to the Academy than the communities we study.[25]

In creating a dialogue between the subject and the researcher, however, steps can be made to overcome this silencing and to ease the dilemmas of accountability.

The ultimate aim of this kind of research and reportage by the postcolonial scholar is to "deconstruct the discourses that constitute the subaltern as such."[26] The various discourses and representations of women in the struggle for Zimbabwean independence must be analyzed The subaltern here are not simply the women guerilla fighters, though. If subaltern refers to various subordinated attributes, such as caste, class, or gender, then the subaltern here are also the voices of women's experiences of war, which have been subordinated to the discourse of war in Zimbabwe.

Although she has reservations about such an analysis, Nzenza-Shand has admitted that,

> I ... now feel that once the power relations between black and white women have been acknowledged, a dialogue on specific issues can begin. But I still cannot help wondering why these middle-class, public-school-educated young women from London choose to study African women.[27]

This ambivalence about white women's interest in African women locates any research within colonial discourse. Nzenza points here to her perceived position as the exotic Other under the gaze of Western eyes. It has been the case that some recent academic literature that questions how Orientalism exoticized the Other, has instead represented the same images, voyeuristically retelling the same colonized stories, recapturing the same exotic images for the Western gaze.[28] By simply revisiting the site of Orientalist images, can we acknowledge and deal with the power relations between the West and the rest, or is our power of academic representation used instead to repossess the Other?

Nzenza is concerned that we are continuing the Western gaze upon the Other, and thus she offers a critical methodology for the white Western woman to research the African woman.[29] Firstly, she explains how "I" will be perceived in the field as coming from a position of power:

> As African women occupying a marginal space, we have yet to claim our subjectivity in psychological terms. Without any form of direct exposure to the Western world on a personal level, African women's interpretation of a white woman's life is that of privilege and power.[30]

As an Australian woman going to Zimbabwe to experience Africa on a personal level it was necessary to consider Nzenza's critique of my potential action as a white woman. My position of perceived power combined with my alleged perception of the African woman as being oppressed, needed to be challenged. Christine Sylvester has suggested "empathetic cooperation"[31] for the Western feminist doing research about African women. In this mode of "world-traveling" Sylvester suggests some travel tips derived from Norma Alarcón: "Learn to become unintrusive, unimportant, patient to the point of tears, while at the same time open to learning any possible lessons."[32]

Jayati Lal has suggested some strategies to deal with this dilemma in doing feminist fieldwork. In an approach similar to Nzenza, Jayati Lal asks, "What are the implications [of the researcher's identity] for the politics of field-based research?"[33] She realizes that for her "identity and notions of self influenced [her] choices, access, and procedures in research and also permeate the representation of research subjects in [her] writing."[34] Lal warns feminist scholars not simply to pay lip service to our positionings. She argues that there is a

> trend for women's studies scholars to make obligatory pronouncements of their positioning into the analysis without ever actually contending with their differences *in* the analysis, toward a mere invoking of what has been called the "mantra" of self-positioning vis-à-vis the axes of race-sex-class-sexuality. This lip service to difference does not inform an assessment of how such positionings are implicated in one's analysis, and as such it is a politically disengaged response.[35]

To be politically engaged in one's analysis, a critical approach to the study of African women within postcolonial discourse, requires more than lip service to one's position of power.

Women in/and Development
A sizable number of Western women academics and activists spend some time in Africa researching women's issues.[36] Giving their voices authority to speak within the discourse of women and development enables them to pursue the needs of African women, perceived by the West and paid for by the West. The researcher speaks on behalf of the African woman taking for granted that it is better to *speak for*, rather than to ignore. In this way, for example, it could be possible to contribute to the fight against Third World women's oppression by channeling international development assistance to women's needs and concerns in Africa.

Marjorie Mbilinyi has argued that the Women in Development (WID) discourse "is the dominant discourse about 'women' and/or gender in African countries, and other perspectives find it increasingly difficult to be heard or to get funding."[37] As Sylvester has argued, "WID has flown to

Africa in non-world-traveler class and is now sympathetically but not empathetically located there."[38] She recognizes that most WID experts *are* indigenous women now, but it remains the women in the West who control or monopolize the "global funding and resources such as publications and consultancy work."[39]

Although the research reported here was not conducted with those resources or aims, the critics of WID are salutary reminders of how feminist theory and research can easily shift into colonial gear despite efforts to highlight resistance to colonial power relations.

Women's Oral History

The dilemma of colonizing African women's voices can be avoided if we consider the importance of oral histories in the telling of significant historical and current events.[40] In general, historical writing has diminished or excluded women's lives and history. While women's voices have sometimes been documented by feminist historians trying to reclaim their past, often these volumes remain unpublished or lost to history as they gather dust on archival shelves because they are deemed to be irrelevant to the wider political debate. Zimbabwean women's experiences have thus been excluded from mainstream history in Zimbabwe. Yet when consulted, their stories provide valuable insights into history.[41] The feminist researcher can then justifiably collect the oral histories either from previous documentation or fresh sources and centralize them in the discourse of war.[42]

Yet Lal is "uneasy" about using the voices of the subject to "buttress" sociological or political arguments. She wonders

> to what extent such a narrative serves to whet the readers' or audiences' desire to know, and the narrators need to prove, that one really was "There!." In a reflexive mode, there is thus always a danger that "the people studied are treated as garnishes and condiments, tasty only in relationship to the main course, the sociologist."[43]

I have no desire to be anyone's "main course." While I am slightly uncomfortable in light of Lal's critique about using as a garnish the voices of women ex-combatants, without their voices the research would be like an aperitif with no main course. However, there is a need to seriously consider how to approach this research. The *garnish* approach to feminist fieldwork outlined by Lal has been labeled "feminist tourism" by Sylvester.[44] Sylvester has argued that if we become preoccupied with proving that we have been there and done that,

> leaving us with baseball caps affixed with tourist decals - "I climbed Mt. Kilimanjaro with Tanzanian National Feminists"- ... [we will only end up with] exotic images appended to stationary self-travel-ing locked up safe from intrusive provincialisms.[45]

This kind of travel or fieldwork only "encourages arrogant perceptions of others as having only the interests the traveler assigns."[46] The contradic-tions for any fieldwork emerge here since we cannot center the subject's voice to the exclusion of theory. However, in using the voices of women to explain theory, we are not simply "capturing" the Other, as Lal explains, "via new technologies of inscription: tapes, surveys, interviews, word pro-cessing."[47] Through the ability to represent themselves within the re-search activity and documentation, the "research subject ... [can] shape [her] own self-representation."[48] That is, the researcher cannot begin to claim that she can control the subject's response. For example, interviewees may decide to *misrepresent* their socio-economic situation or embellish the truth of their stories in some way. In my research in Zimbabwe, I had a distinct impression that some women recreated their own histories either by not mentioning, avoiding or denying some painful aspects of the war. Lal argues that we need to take into account the agency of our research subjects since this kind of situation is mostly

> underplayed ... in discussions about the politics of representation. The fact is that our subjects are often not just responding to our agendas and to our questions, but they are also engaged in actively shaping their presentations to suit their own agendas of how they wish to be represented.[49]

Collecting women's oral histories for any research on women in/and de-velopment is thus central to the discourse, which then becomes shaped by both African and Western women.

Representations
The juxtaposition between women ex-combatants' voices (their stories

10

and re-presentations of their experiences) and the representations of women as guerilla fighters in the discourses of the liberation war needs to be examined. Their voices are the signifiers of their no longer being the subaltern. By representing themselves the women ex-combatants challenge their status (subordinated) in the discourse of war. The representations that these women are juxtaposed with are those that portray the women guerilla fighters in the context of the liberation war. To represent is "to present an image through the medium of a picture or sculpture"[50] or, indeed, as McKenzie has stated, a "representation is the manifestation of an idea or ideas through diverse media."[51]

In Zimbabwe, representations of women guerilla fighters appear in a wide spectrum of mediums, including newspapers, magazines, novels, film, public monuments, and in language use. Their appearance in these representations has not meant that they have been portrayed accurately. However, the women ex-combatants have been associated with the characteristics ascribed to them through the process of representation. An idea of them has been represented. As such, the representations have accrued a certain degree of power over the actual lives of the women being represented. As Bill Nichols has argued, it is the images "that represent (re-present) something else ... To represent images is to symbolize ... [and] symbols ... act as delegates, standing for, or in place of, that to which we refer."[52] The representations of women guerilla fighters have come to symbolize something other than the women ex-combatants to whose lives, histories, and experiences they refer. Until women ex-combatants can counter these representations with their own, the process of representing women as symbols (in this case of the nation) will continually silence their histories, and their voices. But how do we assess the relationship between their voices and the representations? How can a non-power relationship be facilitated?

Desiree Lewis has contended that it is more important to understand the power of representations between subject and audience.[53] Lewis uses the difficult case of Winnie Mandela-Madikezela to make this point. She argues that "black women," particularly in South Africa, have "little control over how they are represented in hegemonic naming systems, and for whom dominant groups' interpretations have far-reaching effects."[54]

Mandela-Madikezela epitomizes the black African woman freedom fighter, mother of the nation, and the passionate rebel. However, after allegations of corruption and murder she fell from grace after thirty years of struggle, but maintained popular support in her own right. Now divorced from Nelson Mandela, the first democratically elected president of South Africa, she has been subjected to continued public scrutiny and scandal. These scandalous representations portray Winnie Mandela-Madikezela as a bad role model for women in South Africa. Therefore, because Lewis had formed an opinion about her based upon these representations, she decided that it was necessary to reconsider her opinions. Lewis argues that

> "commonsensical" way of beginning a reclamation [of Winnie Mandela] would be to access the "real facts," to subvert the pattern of misrepresentation surrounding her, to interview her extensively and to construct a discourse which links her voice to my own. But this would end up as another misrepresentation: *My* autobiography filtered through *my* representation of Winnie Mandela, flawed by *my* inevitable situation in dominant discourses - irrespective of *my* "best of intentions." Another unauthentic and appropriative account of Winnie Mandela.[55]

Can we simply see through the representations by assuming we can know someone or something, by engaging in dialogue with them? Lewis argues that we cannot easily do this because it would become another representation that misses the point - a misrepresentation. Hence, Lewis decided that "rather than write about Winnie Mandela ... [it is better] to write about how she has been talked about: what she has 'meant,' how and why interpretations of her have ranged so dramatically from the extreme idealization to vilification inside South Africa and beyond."[56] Thus it is preferable to analyze (and deconstruct) the way women guerilla fighters have been portrayed in the discourse of war, to ask what these images meant, to whom they have meant something and how they been misinterpreted and by whom, for what purpose. However, diverging from Lewis's resolve not to interview Winnie Mandela-Madizekela, I argue that these meanings and misrepresentations cannot be understood if we do not at least attempt to engage in dialogue with the subject in order to facilitate a non-power relationship. Any further misrepresentations can be avoided by representing the voices of the women involved with consideration to the dilemmas of feminist methodology.

Just as Lewis could have invited Winnie Mandela-Madizekela's comments on how she feels about the misrepresentations about her (which could throw some light on the political and historical details of the position of the black African woman in public discourse in Africa), this research has benefited from some women speaking out about how they have been represented, misrepresented, and portrayed in their roles in the liberation war. Some women ex-combatants used this research to re-represent their situation and thus to reinvent themselves as heroines of the liberation struggle. Others simply took the opportunity to discuss their roles in the war, perhaps for the first time since independence.

Methodology

The fieldwork for this book was conducted in 1996-97 in Zimbabwe. When I began interviewing women ex-combatants in Harare, my aim was to get a better understanding of what the liberation war meant to them, how they fought differently than men, and how they now represent themselves, especially in their roles as "guerilla girls." What I found was that they had very different interests. Most of the women were concerned with getting access to financial compensation grants, funding, and rehabilitation programs for their liberation war activities. They were rather less worried about how they have been and are being represented in the mass media, novels, or by academics. As Sekai Nzenza has argued, it is clear "that while the Western feminist is concerned with the oppression of African women, *they* are much more concerned with the urgent needs of day-to-day living."[57]

Taking account of the "politics of identity," and my own position within (academic) Africanist/feminist circles, it is possible - indeed, it is essential - to remain accountable to the academy and to the research subject(s) by creating dialogue and striving for "empathetic cooperation." While the present research is academic, this does not preclude other objectives. One of these has certainly been to contribute to the wider discussion about women and war in Africa, in particular the debates concerning the position of women ex-combatants in Zimbabwe, who have been disadvantaged (or advantaged) economically, socially, and politically through their roles in the liberation war. Without the feminist tools discussed by Nzenza, Sylvester, Geiger, and Lal, and without any sense of accountability to the subject, it might be necessary to "stay at home." With them, it is possible

13

to confront and begin to resolve the dilemmas of feminist fieldwork in Africa. Some of the women had not had an opportunity before they came into contact with me to discuss their experiences, not even with their husbands or children. As Monica stated, "I have never talked to anybody about this [it] is very difficult for me to relate because it was very difficult."[58]

There are pressures upon and against representations and also the pressure of silence, and consequently the need to listen to the voices of women ex-combatants sixteen years after the end of the war. In 1980 they were talking about "the *shit* of war," but as late as 1996 these same women had still not been recognized or compensated for their suffering. Indeed, they had disappeared from public discourse.

Chimurenga, Chimurenga is the chant whispering on the hem of skirts, in the rustle of thigh. *Chimurenga*, the Liberation War. Many of the women cannot talk about it. The young peasant girls, the 15- and 16-year-old schoolgirls and the young women from all walks of life who fought cannot talk about it. Or they refuse to or they cannot find the words. They stutter over phrases in Shona and English; improvise gestures and sentences, to make one understand *the metallic smell of killing and chaos: the dismemberment of life; the silence and shit of war.*

The ones who *do* talk will tell you of napalm bombs dropped on village huts, splattered blood and massacred hundreds in the early morning hours. They speak of white men who raped them. Of the noises of neighbours and kin ripped by bullets, pile by the roadsides in the dry heat or bloated from the rains - dumped there by white soldiers as a public warning to the living. They speak haltingly of dying elders ... The women tell you of watching other women die; the blood of children. Of their own menstrual blood, stiff and caked to their legs and clothing for days, for there was no water to wash with, or no sanitary napkins on the battlefields. And of their feet and ankles and the never-healing sores they contracted walking, running, crawling through backlands and narrow escapes.[59]

The story of women's experiences, women's history of the liberation war in Zimbabwe is not just one story. There are thousands of stories to be told. My eighteen interviews with women ex-combatants are but small pieces of the historical puzzle. They do not make up the authoritative history of women's experiences, nor do they have more authority than other collections of oral histories in Zimbabwe. Most of these women were interviewed in Harare in 1996, sixteen years after the end of the war. For many, the memory of war was an individual and painful experience. Most preferred to discuss their stories in private and anonymously. There was no collective identity for a group of people called *women ex-combatants*. For example, there has been no women's section within the Zimbabwe National Liberation War Veterans Association (ZNLWVA) or outside of it, although the term *women ex-combatant* does exist in public discourse. Most women did not benefit from postindependence rehabilitation programs designed to integrate women ex-combatants into society. While some of the women I interviewed had made it economically, socially, and politically, others had not. Some were happy with what little they had, others were frustrated and disappointed in independent Zimbabwe. My interviews were conducted prior to the demand and payment of extensive compensation to ex-combatants through the War Victims Compensation Fund.[60]

The ZNLWVA provided much assistance and enthusiasm for my project and introduced me to a small but vocal group of women ex-combatants. Each woman ex-combatant I interviewed was given a copy of the questions before the interview and a description of my research objectives and university affiliation. Each woman was also offered the choice of remaining anonymous and most preferred this.

In many cases the women did not stick to the prepared questions but talked freely of their experiences. They were asked why they joined the struggle and to describe their experiences of war as women. Most women did not feel comfortable talking about the political situations that occurred during the war, either because it is still too politically sensitive to discuss or they were unsure of the facts, so the interviews relate personal experiences. These experiences, however, do reflect the political and emancipatory strategies that concerned or involved women.

Endnotes

1. This title is taken from Diane Wolf, ed., *Feminist Dilemmas in Fieldwork*, (Colorado: Westview Press, 1996). See Tanya Lyons,"Gender and Development: African Women and Western Feminisms, and the dilemmas of doing

feminist field work in Africa" in *Outskirts: Feminisms Along The Edge*, Vol. 4, May, 1999, Online: http://mmc.arts.uwa.edu.au/chloe/outskirts/

2. See Gwendolyn Mikell, *African Feminism: The Politics of Survival in Sub-Saharan Africa*, (Philadelphia: University of Pennsylvania Press, 1997); Edward Said, "The Scope of Orientalism," *Orientalism*, (London: Routledge, 1978); V.Y. Mudimbe, *The Invention of Africa: Gnosis, Philosophy, and the Order of Knowledge*, (Bloomington: Indiana University Press, 1988), pp. 1-23. Mudimbe examines the cultural and political economy of Africanism is light of Said's *Orientalism*

3. See Shahrashoub Razavi and Carol Miller, *From WID to GAD: Conceptual Shifts in Women and Development Discourse*, (Geneva: United Nations Research Institute for Social Development, February 1995), for the Fourth World Conference on Women, Beijing, 1995.

4. See Linda Alcoff, "The Problem of Speaking for Others," in *Cultural Critique*, 20, Winter 1991-92, pp. 5-32.

5. Gayatri Spivak, "Can The Subaltern Speak?" in Gary Nelson and Lawrence Grossberg, eds., *Marxism and the Interpretation of Culture*, (Chicago: University of Illinois Press, 1988), p. 271.

6. Stuart Hall, "Marxism and Culture," *Radical History Review*, 18:514, 1978, p. 9, cited in Angela Gilliam and George Bond, eds., *Social Construction of the Past: Representation as Power*, (London: Routledge, 1994), p. 3.

7. Angela Gilliam and George Bond, eds., *Social Construction of the Past: Representation as Power*, (London: Routledge, 1994), p. 3.

8. Reina Lewis, *Gendering Orientalism, Race Femininity, and Representation*, (London: Routledge, 1996), pp. 3-4.

9. Sekai Nzenza-Shand, "Women in Postcolonial Africa: Between African Men and Western Feminists," in Phillip Darby, ed., *At The Edge of International Relations: Postcolonialism, Gender, and Dependency*, (London: Pinter, 1997).

10. Christine Sylvester, "Africa and Western Feminisms: World Traveling the Tendencies and Possibilities," *Signs*, 20:4, Summer 1995, pp. 941-76.

11. Jayati Lal, "Situating Locations: The Politics of Self, Identity, and 'Other,' in Living and Writing the Text," in Diane Wolf ed., *Feminist Dilemmas in Fieldwork*, (Colorado: Westview Press, 1996).

12. See Nira Yuval Davis, *Gender and Nation*, (London: Sage, 1997), pp. 119-20.

13. See Sekai Nzenza-Shand, *Songs to an African Sunset: A Zimbabwean Story*, (Melbourne: Lonely Planet, 1997), pp.170-1. Also, Chandra Mohanty, "Under Western Eyes: Feminist Scholarship and Colonial Discourses," in *Feminist Review*, 30, Autumn 1988, pp. 61-88: and see Trinh T. Minh-ha, *Woman, Native, Other: Writing Postcoloniality and Feminism*, (Bloomington: Indiana University Press, 1989).

14. Sekai Nzenza, "Who should Speak for Whom? African Women and Western Feminism," in Penny Van Toorn and David English, eds., *Speaking Positions: Aboriginality, Gender and Ethnicity in Australian Cultural Studies*, (Melbourne: Department of Humanities, Victorian University of Technology, 1995), p. 103.

15. Sekai Nzenza-Shand, "Women in Postcolonial Africa: Between African Men and Western Feminists," p. 215.
16. Sekai Nzenza, "Who should Speak for Whom? African Women and Western Feminism," p. 104.
17. Sekai Nzenza-Shand, "Women in Postcolonial Africa: Between African Men and Western Feminists," p. 216.
18. Gayatri Spivak, "Can The Subaltern Speak?".
19. Reina Lewis, *Gendereing Orientalism, Race Femininity, and Representation,* p. 4
20. Ibid.
21. John Beverly "Theses on subalternity, representations and politics," in *Postcolonial Studies,* 1:3, 1998, pp. 305-19.
22. Ibid, p. 306.
23. Ibid.
24. Ibid.
25. Marcus, 1994, cited in Jayati Lal, "Situating Locations," p. 206.
26. John Beverly "Theses on subalternity, representations and politics," p. 316,
27. See Sekai Nzenza-Shand, *Songs to an African Sunset,* p. 171.
28. For example see Chilla Bullbeck's, *Re-Orienting Western Feminisms: Women's Diversity in a Postcolonial World,* (Cambridge: Cambridge University Press, 1996); Edward Said, *Orientalism,* 1978.
29. Sekai Nzenza, "Who should Speak For Whom? African Women and Western Feminism," pp. 100-6.
30. Ibid., p. 100.
31. Lugones, 1990: 396, cited in Christine Sylvester, "Africa and Western Feminisms," p. 954.
32. Norma Alarcón, 1990: 363, cited in ibid, p. 957.
33. Jayati Lal, "Situating Locations," p. 190.
34. Ibid.
35. Ibid, p. 197.
36. See Jane Parpart, *Women and Development in Africa,* (Lanham: University Press of America, 1989); Geeta Chowdhry, "Engendering Development? Women in Development (WID) in International regimes," in Marianne Marchand and Jane Parpart, eds., *Feminism/ Postmodernism/ Development,* (London: Routledge, 1995); Jane Parpart and Marianne Marchand, "Exploding the Canon: An Introduction/Conclusion," in Marianne Marchand and Jane Parpart, eds., *Feminism/ Postmodernism/ Development,* (London: Routledge, 1995).
37. Marjorie Mbilinyi, 1993: 47-48, cited in Christine Sylvester, "Africa and Western Feminisms," p. 956. This includes critiques of Women and Development (WAD) and Gender and Development (GAD) perspectives. See for example Shahrashoub Razavi and Carol Miller, *From WID to GAD: Conceptual Shifts in the Women and Development Discourse.*
38. Christine Sylvester, "Africa and Western Feminisms," p. 956.
39. Ibid.
40. Susan Geiger "What is so Feminist about doing Women's Oral History?" in

Cheryl Johnson-Odim and Margaret Strobel, ed., *Expanding The Boundaries of Women's History: Essays on Women in the Third World*, (Bloomington, Indiana University Press, 1992). Also see Belinda Bozzoli, *Women of Phokeng: Consciousness, Life Strategy, and Migrancy in South Africa, 1900-1983*, with the assistance of Mmantho Nkotsoe, (London: James Currey and Porstmouth: Heinemann, 1994).

41. See, for example, Teresa Barnes and Everjoyce Win, *To Live A Better Life: An Oral History of Women in the City of Harare, 1930-70*, (Harare: Baobab Books, 1992).

42. Irene Staunton, eds., *Mothers of the Revolution*, (Harare: Baobab,1990).

43. Jayati Lal, "Situating Locations," p. 205.

44. Christine Sylvester, "Africa and Western Feminisms," p. 945.

45. Ibid.

46. Ibid.

47. Jayati Lal, "Situating Locations," p. 204.

48. Ibid.

49 Ibid.

50. *Collins English Dictionary*, Australian Edition, HarperCollins, Sydney, 1992.

51. Darlene McKenzie, "Looking at Them, Looking at Us," in *Racism, Representation, and Photography*, Sandra Phillips, eds., compiled by Andrew Dewsney, (Australia: Inner City Education Centre, 1994), p.180.

52. Bill Nichols, *Ideology and the Image: Social Representation in the Cinema and Other Media*, (Bloomington: Indiana University Press, 1981).

53. Desiree Lewis "Winnie Mandela: The Surveillance and Excess of 'Black Woman' as Signifier," in *Southern African Feminist Review,* 2:1, June 1996.

54. Ibid, p.7.

55. Ibid.

56. Ibid.

57. Sekai Nzenza, "Who Should Speak for Whom? African Women and Western Feminism," p. 102.

58. Interview with Monica, Harare, August, 1996. The names I use in this study have been changed when anonymity was requested. The women already in the public eye have been named.

59. Alexis DeVeaux, "Zimbabwe Woman Fire!" in *Essence*, July 1981, pp. 72, 111-12.

60. In late 1997, after much protesting by the ZNLWVA, the government agreed to pay up to 50,000 war veterans a total of Z$50,000 in a lump sum payment and $Z2,000 a month, plus free education, health services, and tax-free loans of up to $Z20,000. These payments led to massive protests, riots, and demonstrations in Harare after the government was forced to increase taxes to cover the costs.

Chapter Two
Women in War

In times of war ... women are permitted to enter the arena of violence
- up to a point.... But as soon as the war [is] over they [a]re glad,
we are led to believe, to go back to their "natural" roles.
- Eileen MacDonald in *Shoot The Women First*

Citizenship with Arms

The view of women's roles in war vis-a-vis their perceived natural roles in the domestic sphere has dominated the perceptions, assumptions, and stereotypes of women in war. The discourse about war often fails to mention women's wartime roles, whether they are pro-war or antiwar. This in part reflects the social dichotomy that isolates women in the private, household, and family spheres and men in the public, political, and military spheres. This gendered division "is commonly treated as a natural function of the physical differences between men and women, although it is in reality no more than a man-made device."[1] These beliefs about the function of gender differences are pervasive in all societies. However, events throughout the world have shown that the realm of socio-political war activities is less gendered than much of the popular and academic literature would have us believe. Women have always participated in and been affected by war.[2]

Gender-sensitive lenses are a useful theoretical tool for highlighting the role of women in the contemporary discourse about war.[3] The problem facing a gendered analysis of war is that "[w]ar is an activity and an event of such cataclysmic, existential significance that it has always been 'above' questions of gender identity."[4] Gender-sensitive lenses "enable ... us to 'see' how the world is shaped by gendered concepts, practices, and institutions."[5] These gender-sensitive lenses work like other lenses, as Spike Peterson and Anne Runyan explain:

> Whenever we study a topic, we do so through a lens that necessarily focuses our attention in particular ways. By "ordering" what we look at, each lens enables us to see some things in greater detail or more accurately or in better relation to certain other things. But this is unavoidably at the expense of seeing other things that are rendered out of focus - filtered out - by each particular lens.[6]

Despite the previous analytical distances between gender and war, since the 1980s this area of research has become of increasing interest to academia. Much of this interest, however, has focused on Western European or American experiences, and thus on Western women.[7] Exceptions to this rule include Arlene Bergman's, *Women of Vietnam*,[8] Tessa Cleaver and Marion Wallace's study of women and war in Namibia,[9] Stephanie Urdang's *And Still They Dance: Women, War, and the Struggle for Change in Mozambique*,[10] and Miriam Cooke's analyses of Middle Eastern and Arab women and war.[11] Frantz Fanon's essay "Algeria Unveiled,"[12] is an earlier example of a gendered analysis of war and anti-colonial struggle, but these studies cannot be adequately dealt with here.

Nonetheless, gender analyses of war have been predominantly Eurocentric, and have made general claims about all women, despite cultural and political differences. For example, during the 1990 Gulf War, American women soldiers appeared on the front lines, and it was treated by some as if it were the first time in the history of the world that women have fought at the front.[13] Such a perspective negates the experiences of women in non-Western countries, who have not had the choice of staying at home during a war or who live in the war zone. This also negates the experiences of women who have been at the front in various roles, in particular during many of Africa's liberation struggles.[14]

Jacklyn Cock writes that the relationship between women and war is obscured and mystified by sexism, which maintains that women are physically inferior and hence unsuitable for combat roles, and (at least) "one variant of feminism," which claims that women are "innately nurturers" with a flare for "pacifism."[15] Judith Wagner Decew argues that there has been a "long tradition of antiwar and antimilitarist sentiment among many women and feminists,"[16] who

> find it bizarre or sick or at least misguided for women even to seek an equal right to fight, to kill, or to participate in the institutions of the military on a par with men. These feminists believe that women should strive for a much more meaningful equality, one that would empower women to prevent war, to make military combat obsolete.[17]

In contemporary discourses of war and in (some) feminist perspectives, the question of women's equal right to participate in the military is often avoided. It is assumed that women should not want to have anything to do with "the destructive enterprise of war."[18] This is often based on the stereotypes that women are incapable of fighting or are essentially nurturers and should therefore only be involved in life-supporting rather than life-destroying activities.

Yet, over the centuries women have always been involved in the wars that have forged new nations, destroyed kingdoms, liberated countries from oppressors, and protected their land and labor from invasion.[19] If recognition is granted to the role of women in war, the view that war remains the exclusive domain of men becomes fallacious. Whether or not glorifying women's participation in wars becomes a victory for feminism is another question.

To understand the ways in which women are involved in the war process, a brief outline of the ways in which women have been historically incorporated into war and the war story will illuminate perceived natural differences used to justify different actions and different positions. As Eileen Macdonald has pointed out, it is not seen as natural for women to be involved in war. Assumed differences between genders are typically reinforced in the war effort even though women are often needed in the public (war) sphere. At the end of a war women are encouraged to return to the private domestic sphere to facilitate a return to normality. Women are told to reproduce (for) the new nation in their capacity as mothers and wives to compensate for lives lost in the struggle. Women's lives become flexible in this arrangement. After women are sent back home "war is understood as a totally male affair."[20] As Rebecca Grant notes, "[w]ars have been fought by men, resolved by men, and chronicled by men," so it is no surprise that war is understood as an-all-male domain.[21] However, she sees some change in the way war is perceived and described and how war stories may be told in the future:

> By the end of the twentieth century ... female soldiers will reach higher rank and play an increasingly important role in the military in several nations. Journalists, scholars, and eventually the historians who write on contemporary warfare will include women in their ranks. In practice, warfare and the process behind the decision to go to war are no longer the exclusive domains of men. Surely this is a quiet triumph for feminism.[22]

This process has taken hold in recent media coverage of warfare, exposing the human face of war and soldiers. Women soldiers are increasingly being accepted as normal, however there is still a long way to go for both feminism and the military.

The chivalrous and patronizing message evoked in the practice of getting "womenandchildren"[23] out of danger first rests upon the ancient belief that men go to war to defend their women, because men indeed sometimes go to war to get them. This view leaves very little room for independent female action that is not directed by men.[24] In any case, women become the passive reasons for war. When women are needed to support the war they are assigned roles designed to serve male participants, such as wives, prostitutes, entertainers, and sympathetic nurses. More subversively, women can become the seductive spies or the cheerleaders, cheering on the men going off to the front. Also, importantly they are the mothers reproducing the male soldiers and they are the cooperative citizens willing to take over men's roles in field and factory work, but only until the men return.[25] Within these supportive and nurturing roles women's activities are portrayed as secondary to the main event.

Mary Ann Tétreault points out that it is "autonomous female participation in revolutions [that] underlies the legitimacy of postrevolutionary demands for women's liberation."[26] This idea goes back to the thoughts of Bruni and Machiavelli, who emphasized the need for all citizens to be soldiers. To be the former, one had to be the latter: "It is the possession of arms which makes a man [sic] a full citizen."[27] Tétreault takes this further to suggest that equality of citizenship is often linked to blood payments. That is, a group's claim to legitimacy after a revolution is in part associated with, or perceived to be concerned with, the extent of earning this by "the blood of its members."[28] Tétreault argues that "women's blood payments are entitlements to power, but this is not normatively preferable to a gender neutral entitlement to liberty as the result of revolutionary transformation."[29] That is, being involved in war is the most obvious way that women can earn their demands for equality of access to the resources of the state. In this way their roles are not easily covered up, reinscribed, or redefined into the domestic and private sphere.

Feminist Connections with Nationalism

There are direct links between nationalism and feminism. During various national liberation struggles in Africa, many women realized that the root cause of their oppression was not capitalism and colonization alone but also patriarchal.[30] Allison Drew points out the connections made by many analysts between nationalism and feminism and the struggle for women's emancipation alongside national liberation. She has argued that feminism results from the inability of nationalism to liberate women from the shackles of domesticity after wars of national liberation:

> Feminism is transformed from a set of ideas to a social movement ... when the contradiction between sexual division of labour and what women are capable of doing becomes particularly apparent, for example, when women participate in national liberation and armed struggles only to find themselves relegated to subservient roles after national independence or when they achieve unprecedented educational levels, as in the post-war advanced capitalist countries, only to find themselves ghettoized in domestic or clerical work.[31]

Drew uses the common assumptions made about women's participation in liberation wars which represent women's roles as *not* subservient to men's in the struggle, but as *equal*. To be disappointed in women's lowered status after national independence is hence not surprising when these feminist links are made to national liberation.

Kumari Jayawardena has made the most substantive links between feminism and nationalism in the Third World.[32] According to Geraldine Heng, Jayawardena "repeatedly attests, [that] feminist movements in the Third World have almost always grown out of the same historical soil, and at a similar historical moment, as nationalism"[33]. That is, women's participation in liberation wars will result in their emancipation. The expectation within nationalist movements is that a feminist movement will emerge as a matter of course. Feminism does not have to always be a Western import. Jayawardena argues that in the Third World countries she studied,

> struggles for women's emancipation were an essential and integral part of national resistance movements. In all these countries, the 'woman question' forcefully made its appearance during the early 20th century. The debate on the role and status of women had of course started earlier, but in the era of imperialist and capitalist expansion the question assumed new dimensions ... In short the issue was one of democratic rights.[34]

Jayawardena emphasizes the participation of women "in revolutionary and democratic movements" because "the role of women in such struggles has not been given adequate attention; one hears only of the 'heroes' and little of the numerous 'heroines' of Asia."[35] She therefore stresses "the movement towards women's emancipation ... [as] acted out against a background of nationalist struggles aimed at achieving political independence, asserting a national identity, and modernizing society."[36] That is, home grown women's liberation will result from women's participation in nationalist struggles. If feminism is only conceived as a foreign ideology, this would imply a continuation of the subordination of women in the Third World.

In the African context, Gwendolyn Mikell has contributed to the connection between feminism and nationalism when she argues that women's oppression and

> declining political status was directly related to the oppressive control of the colonial regime. African women took strength from the fact that their participation was essential if their countries were to end the colonial experience and achieve independence.[37]

Women could fight against colonialism through nationalist struggle, but without the development of some kind of feminism the fight against patriarchy would be short lived. Thus,

> after independence, male suppression of African women's political

autonomy increased, despite the contributions women had made to nationalist politics and despite state claims to equitable approaches in education, policies, and laws.[38]

Again, Mikell brings us back to the common assumptions about women's roles in war and their postrevolutionary demands for equality that often resulted in disappointment - because patriarchy was not thwarted alongside colonialism. It is necessary here then to review the literature on Zimbabwe's liberation struggle in order to establish a basis from which to critique these views.

A Gender-sensitive View of the Literature of the Zimbabwe Liberation War

Jean Bethke Elshtain has argued that women are mainly absent from the war story, or from definitions of war, in fiction and history. This is partly due to the definition of what constitutes the "front," who decides where this is located, and "who is authorized to *narrate*."[39] Zimbabwe's anticolonial struggle has been labeled "a dirty little war," and there are many narratives of the transition from Rhodesia to Zimbabwe.[40] Most of these studies exemplify the traditional masculinized version of history, focusing on the *big* male events and the leadership of the nationalist parties ZAPU and ZANU.[41] The story that will be told here is not about the leaders of the struggle but an investigation into the roles, experiences, and representations of a particular category of people involved in the guerrilla war - women.

Hundreds of thousands of pages have been printed about the Zimbabwe Liberation War from many different perspectives: white Rhodesian,[42] black Zimbabwean,[43] foreign scholar,[44] foreign journalist, diplomatic missions and non-governmental organizations such as the Catholic Commission for Justice and Peace and Amnesty International. The Zimbabwean struggle for independence is a story that fascinates and continues to be told in various forms, with various repercussions. The plethora of fictitious and so-called objective, factual discourse about the war has been conducted in the language of men. As Elshtain has argued:

Because women are exterior to war, men interior, men have long been the great war-story tellers, legitimated in that role because

25

they have "been there" or because they have greater entree into what it "must be like." The stories of women resistance fighters and soldiers have sometimes been told but have not attained the literary status of the great war novels by men.[45]

In Zimbabwe there are some examples of women participating in the discourse about war through both historical narrative and fiction. Yet, as Irene Staunton a Zimbabwean publisher, has suggested, one reason why women's literary voice is seldom heard is because "men finish a novel and submit it immediately, thinking it's the greatest novel in the world. Women are more modest."[46] What women choose to write about is another matter.

Most popular fiction about the war has been written by men. Nonetheless, since independence, Zimbabwean women have spoken and written about their experiences of war. They have represented their history in various forms, much of it as quoted interviews by Western academics and journalists and as detailed oral histories by local Zimbabwean scholars. Yet, it is another struggle altogether for women to attain the literary status that men have in Zimbabwe. Some women have managed to publish their work because of the support of local publishers and an increasing interest in postcolonial writers in the West. For example, Sekai Nzenza's autobiography, *Zimbabwean Woman: My Own Story*,[47] records her experiences of war as a school student in Rhodesia; Irene Ropa Rinopfuka Mahamba's *Woman in Struggle*[48] describes the processes of how she became involved in the struggle; and Freedom Nyamubaya's collection of poems in *On the Road Again: Poems During and After the National Liberation of Zimbabwe*,[49] evokes the pain, trauma, and adventures of the war for Zimbabwean women in Mozambique. These books have only had limited circulation, but they represent a small body of literature available to the discerning researcher within Zimbabwe. More recently, Nozipo Maraire has published her novel *Zenzele: A Letter To My Daughter*. It offers a detailed representation of women spanning three generations, showing them in a romanticized and glorified way as the spies and cheerleaders of the liberation war.[50]

These female writers' stories and books are not yet as popular as the male versions of war, such as Chenjerai Hove's *Bones*,[51] Charles Samupindi's *Pawns*,[52] Shimmer Chinodya's *Harvest of Thorns*[53] (which has a schools edition), and Alexander Kanengoni's *Effortless Tears*[54] (which appears on university reading lists in Zimbabwe and internationally). In comparison, Nzenza's autobiographical story was not distributed in Zimbabwe. Mahamba's and Nyamubaya's works were published in Zimbabwe but do not appear on many curriculum course guides. While Maraire's novel might change this pattern as it compares favorably with Tsitsi Dangarembga's *Nervous Conditions*,[55] *Zenzele* was published in South Africa, the author lives in the United States, and the book is not available in Zimbabwe in an inexpensive edition.[56] The representations made by female authors are particularly significant in examining the discourse of war in Zimbabwe. Nzenza questions how a young woman copes after seeing a dead guerrilla fighter being dragged from a body bag by Rhodesian soldiers who then ask her to identify him. Mahamba investigates why young women joined the "boys in the bush," and Nyamubaya's writings examine the experiences of women in the training camps outside of Zimbabwe in Mozambique.

It is also notable that a discussion of women as fighters is mostly absent from the discourse about war by both male and female writers. Women's stories have been told, but mainly within the context of women's issues rather than of war. This is significant when we are seeking to represent the voices of women in the discourse about war. Such a gender view simplifies a complex situation, because women are *present* in the stories of war but they are mainly *represented by* men, as biologically determined and socially constructed wives, mothers, or sisters.[57]

A handful of feminist scholars have attempted to describe the military role of women in Zimbabwe's armed struggle for independence. While there has been an emerging interest in the role of Zimbabwean women in the National Liberation War over the last fifteen years, most of these works remain unpublished Masters and PhD theses.[58] To be sure, there has been interest in women's war roles and their postindependence experiences by international feminist scholars as well as Zimbabwean women activists and scholars. This interest may be, in part, a reaction to the lack of recognition of women's war service by the state.[59] What all of these works have in common is an unquestioned acceptance of what is in fact a very limited range of evidence about women's involvement in the war. Upon reflection the "facts'" have mainly been provided by a handful of leading men and women within Zimbabwe's ruling party ZANU(PF), both during the struggle and after liberation. For example, Joyce Mujuru, Sally Mugabe, Naomi Nhiwatiwa, and Robert Mugabe, are often cited in these texts for their "authoritative" opinions on women's roles.[60] Jane Ngwenya from ZAPU is one exception to this rule, as her voice was often heard on the topic of women in the war.

Yet, some foreign and local researchers have consulted other women about their experiences of the war, and their voices come to us in volumes such as Kathy Bond-Stewart's *Independence Is Not for Only One Sex*, and *Young Women in the Liberation Struggle*; and Irene Staunton's *Mothers of the Revolution*. These were published in Zimbabwe and made available cheaply through various women's organizations, although none of the women interviewed for this book had read any of these works. Apart from the published books there was the *None But Ourselves Oral History Project*, which is now housed in the National Archives of Zimbabwe.[61]

One attempt to record the voices of women guerrilla fighters was made by a woman. However, there is no evidence to suggest her efforts survived. A letter to the editor of *Moto*, by Madeleine Mattarozzi, described how she had become aware of a

conspiracy of silence, surrounding the return of ex-combatants, particularly female ex-combatants. Recently I visited the Museum of Revolution in Maputo and was delighted to find that a large proportion of the exhibits on display concerned women's activities during the struggle for Independence in that country. Photographs showed women training with weapons, on patrol and transporting arms, as well as tending the sick or preparing food. Yet in this country there has been virtually no mention made of the role of women played in the struggle. Where references do exist, they are vague and often inaccurate. One history text designed for primary school states that women cooked food for the comrades and carried weapons for them. In the interests of historical accuracy I have been talking to women who were actually combatants, and have been recording their own personal stories. Eventually I hope to be able to publish a collection of such anecdotes. If any of your readers who are female ex-combatants would like to contribute their stories, contact Madeleine Mattarozzi, Box 4745, Harare.[62]

However, apart from this and the other references above, the rhetoric from government ministers, ZANU(PF) officials, and the leaders of the nationalist movements during the war has predominated. Also, there has been a sustained and growing ambiguity as to what it was that women actually did in the liberation war. On the other hand, scholars Bhebe and Ranger argue that "there have been too many attempts to produce a heroic 'herstory' of the war; attempts which have overestimated the number of female guerrillas and overstated the emancipatory mobilization of women."[63]

Their two volumes dedicated to *Soldiers and Society in Zimbabwe's Liberation War* does not deal in any way with women soldiers or the woman question - despite its often vociferous presence during the war. As Kriger has criticized the predominant focus on the leaders of the war,[64] Bhebe and Ranger also acknowledge criticisms of the way historical accounts of the war have emphasized the leaders. Instead they highlight the importance of 'voices' in the history of war, including peasant voices. They quote Teresa Barnes to the effect that

> Wars are often summed up as the decisions of leaders and the movements of armies. It is often forgotten that all of these depend on ordinary soldiers, who personally sacrifice to achieve advances and victories, and physically suffer the consequences of retreats and victories. But their experiences are usually obliterated in the manufacture of histories, and may even be lost to popular memory. The result is a propagation of an official mythology of war.[65]

The histories of the Zimbabwean liberation war are however different from that of other wars because, after Ranger's example, they have focused on "the people" and how their lives were affected by the ravages of war. Much of Ranger's work has been concerned with giving peasants a voice in history.[66] Ranger and Bhebe argue that more gender analysis is needed, but they seem convinced that gender exists only in the realms of civilian or cultural life.[67] They argue that there has not been "any fully satisfactory gendered accounts of the war and its aftermath"[68] that can compare with the gendered analyses of earlier periods in Southern Rhodesia.[69] Hence, further research needs to be done in order to understand issues of gender and generation, and they indicate which topics deserve priority.[70]

To their credit Ranger and Bhebe acknowledge that there is no simple way of dealing with "the woman question," including women's mobilization during the war or women's emancipation in Zimbabwe. Eschewing an overtly political stance, they argue that "we cannot discuss the legacy of war for gender relations simply in terms of the fulfillment or non-fulfillment of the emancipatory promise."[71] Indeed it is not realistic to view postindependent Zimbabwe as successful in its liberation of women as a direct consequence of promises made during the struggle. This is despite the new regime's establishing a Women's Ministry and enacting various legal provisions such as the Legal Age of Majority Act, which gave all people over the age of eighteen years the right to vote and to determine their own futures, including getting married without the permission of parents. It is likewise not useful to view "so far as gender relations are concerned, [that] the revolution has been betrayed."[72]

The Revolution

In Zimbabwe the revolution was intended to overthrow white minority rule, and some elements aimed for a socialist society. Tétreault offers a concept of revolution, which helps to understand the case of Zimbabwe:

> Revolutions are attempts to guide the process of political change along a preferred path of system transformation. This is not to say that revolutions actually achieve any or all of the outcomes desired by revolutionaries. Revolutions are neither unitary nor static. Different participants hope for different outcomes or different emphases among a set of shared goals.[73]

In Zimbabwe it has been well documented that there were many different political agendas at work at various times within the nationalist movement.[74] However, radical voices of continued revolution were suppressed after political independence was negotiated at Lancaster House in late 1979. For these reasons much of the Zimbabwean literature about the war has concerned itself with how far the nationalist revolution went and how far it failed. These arguments conclude that there was not even "a revolution that lost its way,"[75] let alone a revolution that "brought about fundamental changes in political institutions, social structures, and government activity."[76] Sita Ranchod-Nilsson generalizes the term *revolution* and argues that there were possibilities for revolution in Zimbabwe, but "petit bourgeois interests of the nationalist leadership" thwarted any attempts made by the "rank-and-file military forces and their supporters inside the country."[77] Sylvester argues, based on a Gramscian model of revolution, that there were four simultaneous revolutions that unfolded in Zimbabwe, between 1945 and 1979, none of which succeeded or failed completely. "Each transformed some aspect of consciousness, social structure, state, and economy,"[78] and one revolution gave women a voice in the history of the revolution, if only briefly.

The question of a potential women's revolution is mainly restricted to feminist authors and researchers and has not been part of the mainstream discussion of Zimbabwe's liberation or revolution. Hence, the "revolution" that will be of concern here will be the one that has involved women. Bringing to the foreground the differences in experience and action between women and men will provide an understanding of the role of women in war. Tétreault argues that from a normative perspective the study of women and revolution is important because

[n]ormatively, women, as human beings whose social role is always defined at least in part by their reproductive capabilities, experience revolution and its outcomes differently to men. To classify revolutions so that their microsocial impacts may be ignored in the analysis of paradigm cases reflects a philosophical bias that is not simply sexist but also rigidly masculinist and ahistorical.[79]

For the case at hand, the impacts on women will be of concern because, as Tétreault argues, to consider revolutions "from the perspectives of women and families" and the connections they have to revolution reveals a substantial contribution by women. This is so because

[u]nless a revolution can topple an old regime within a very short period of time, its ultimate triumph depends upon successful appeals to women and families to supply resources to nourish it. As primary producers, women are essential for a sustained challenge to the state to be successful. However, their cooperation is not free.[80]

For example, in Zimbabwe the "mothers of the revolution" who fed and clothed the guerrilla fighters during the war expected not only respect from "the boys" (*vakomana*) but also improvements in their socio-economic conditions after the war.[81]

Women who fought in Zimbabwe have a central role in all aspects of the war story. Based on their presence in the war there is a feminist expectation that they will also appear in the histories and stories of war. Such a presence demands that women also benefit from any changes made to the system that is overthrown. Citizenship may depend upon being able to take up arms and fight for independence, and the nationalist struggle enshrined such expectations when it was connected with feminist development.

Endnotes

1   Michelle Rosaldo, "Women, Culture, and Society: A Theoretical Overview," in Michelle Rosaldo and Louise Lamphere, eds., *Women, Culture and Society*, (Stanford: Stanford University Press, 1974), cited in Rosemary Ridd, "Powers of the Powerless," in Rosemary Ridd and Helen Callaway, eds., *Caught Up in Conflict: Women's Reponses to Political Strife*, (Oxford: Macmillan, 1986), pp. 1-2.

2.   The roles of women in anti-war and peace activism will not be covered here. See Dorothy Thompson ed., *Over Our Dead Bodies: Women Against The Bomb*, (London: Virago, 1983); and Sara Ruddick, *Maternal Thinking: Towards a Politics of Peace*, (Boston: Beacon Press, 1989).

3.   V. Spike Peterson and Anne Sisson Runyan, *Global Gender Issues*, (Boulder: Westview Press, 1993), p. 1.

4.   Miriam Cooke, "Wo-man, Retelling the War Myth," in Miriam Cooke and Angela Woollacott, *Gendering War Talk*, (New Jersey: Princeton University Press, 1993), p. 177.

5.   V. Spike Peterson and Anne Sisson Runyan, *Global Gender Issues*, p. 1.

6.   Ibid.

7.   For example, Jean Bethke Elshtain, *Women and War*, (New York: Basic Books, 1987); Margaret Higonnet, et. al., *Behind the Lines: Gender and the Two World Wars*, (New Haven: Yale University Press, 1987); see Jan Jindy Pettman, *Worlding Women: A Feminist International Politics*, (St. Leonards: Allen and Unwin, 1996); and see Marilyn Lake and Joy Damousi, *Gender and War: Australia at War in the Twentieth Century*, (Cambridge: Cambridge University Press, 1995), p. 1.

8.   Arlene Eisen Bergman, *Women of Vietnam*, (C. A: People's Press, 1975); Barbara Evans Clements, *Daughters of the Revolution: A History of Women in the U.S.S.R.*, (Illinois: Harlan Davidson, 1994); Kumari Jayawardena, *Feminism and Nationalism in the Third World*, (London: Zed Books, 1986).

9.   Tessa Cleaver, and Marion Wallace, *Namibia Women in War*, (London: Zed

Books, 1990).

10. Stephanie Urdang, *And Still they Dance: Women, War and the Struggle for Change in Mozambique,* (London: Earthscan, 1989).

11. Miriam Cooke, "Wo-man, Retelling the War Myth": Also see Miriam Cooke, "Arab Women Arab Wars," *Cultural Critique,* Winter, 1994-95, pp. 5-29.

12. Frantz Fanon, "Algeria Unveiled," in *A Dying Colonialism,* translated by H. Chevalier, (New York: Grove Press, 1965), (original French 1959); see Anne McClintock, *Imperial Leather: Race, Gender and Sexuality in the Colonial Conquest,* (New York: Routledge, 1995), pp.360-67.

13. Elisabetta Addis, Valeria Russo and Lorenza Sebesta, eds., *Women Soldiers: Images and Realities,* (New York: St. Martins Press, 1994).

14. See special issue on "African Women and Conflict," *African Woman - Biannual Development Journal,* issue 10, March - September 1995; Meredeth Turshen and Clotilde Twagiramariya, eds., *What Women Do in War Time: Gender and Conflict in Africa,* (St. Martins: Zed Press, 1998); Liki Mani Muthoni, *Passbook Number F47927: Women and Mau Mau in Kenya,* (London: MacMillan, 1985); Cora Anne Presley, "The Mau Mau Rebellion, Kikuyu Women and Social Change," in *Canadian Journal of African Studies,* 22:3, 1988; and Jacklyn Cock, *Colonels and Cadres: War and Gender in South Africa,* (Oxford: Oxford University Press, 1991).

15. Jacklyn Cock, "Keeping the Fires Burning: Militarization and the Politics of Gender in South Africa," in *Review of African Political Economy,* 45/46, 1989.

16. Judith Wagner Decew, "The Combat Exclusion and the Role of Women in the Military," *Hypatia,* 10:3, Winter 1995, pp. 56-73.

17. Virginia Held quoted in ibid, p. 58.

18. Rebecca Grant, "The Quagmire of Gender and International Security," in V. Spike Petersen, ed., *Gendered States: Feminist (Re)Visions of International Relations Theory,* (Boulder & London: Lynne Rienner Publishers, 1992), p. 89.

19. Reina Pennington, ed., *Military Women Worldwide: A Biographical Dictionary,* (Boulder: Greenwood Press, forthcoming).

20. Jacklyn Cock, "Keeping the Fires Burning: Militarization and the Politics of Gender in South Africa."

21. Rebecca Grant, "The Quagmire of Gender and International Security," p. 83.

22. Ibid.

23. Cynthia Enloe, "Womenandchildren: Making Feminist Sense of the Persian Gulf Crisis," in *The Village Voice,* 25 September 1990.

24. See Frantz Fanon, "Algeria Unveiled," pp. 49-51.

25. Nancy Huston, "Tales of War and Tears of Women," *Womens Studies International Forum,* 5:3/4, 1982, cited in Jacklyn Cock, "Keeping the Fires Burning: Militarization and the Politics of Gender in South Africa," p.52.

26. Mary Ann Tétreault, "Women and Revolution: A Framework for Analysis," in Mary Ann Tétreault, ed., *Women and Revolution in Africa, Asia, and the New World,* (Columbia: University of South Carolina, 1994), p.19.

27. J.G.A Pocock, *The Machiavellian Moment: Florentine Political Thought and the Atlantic Republican Tradition,* (Princeton University Press, 1975), p.90;

Also see ibid, p.19.

28. Mary Ann Tétreault, "Women and Revolution: A Framework for Analysis," note 75, p.30.

29. Ibid.

30. See for example Pepe Roberts, "Feminism *In* Africa: Feminism *And* Africa," in *Review of African Political Economy*, 27/28 1983, pp. 175-84.

31. Allison Drew, "Female Consciousness and Feminism in Africa," in *Theory and Society*, 24:1, 1995, pp. 1-33.

32. Kumari Jayawardena, *Feminism and Nationalism in the Third World*; See Geraldine Heng, "A Great Way to Fly": Nationalism, the State, and the Varieties of Third-World Feminism," in Jacqui Alexander and Chandra Talpade Mohanty, eds., *Feminist Genealogies, Colonial Legacies, Democratic Futures*, (New York and London: Routledge, 1997), pp.30-45.

33. Geraldine Heng, "A Great Way to Fly": Nationalism, the State, and the Varieties of Third-World Feminism," p. 31.

34. Kumari Jayawardena, *Feminism and Nationalism in the Third World*, p. 8.

35. Ibid, p.ix.

36. Ibid, p.3.

37. Gwendolyn Mikell, "African Feminism: Toward a New Politics of Representation," in *Feminist Studies*, 21:2, 1995, p. 407.

38. Ibid.

39. Jean Bethke Elshtain, *Women and War*, p. 213.

40. Peter Godwin and Ian Hancock, *Rhodesians Never Die: The Impact of War and Political Change on White Rhodesia, 1970-1980*, (Harare: Baobab Books, 1995).

41. Norma Kriger, *Zimbabwe's Guerrilla War: Peasant Voices*, (Cambridge: Cambridge University Press, 1992; Harare: Baobab, 1995), p.170.

42. See for example, David Maughan-Brown, "Myths on the March: The Kenyan and Zimbabwean Liberation Struggles in Colonial Fiction," in *Journal of Southern African Studies*, 9:1, 1982, pp. 93-117; Peter Godwin and Ian Hancock, *Rhodesians Never Die: The Impact of War and Political Change on White Rhodesia, 1970-1980*; and Peter Godwin, *Mukiwa: A White Boy in Africa*, (London: Macmillan, 1996).

43. Stanley Nyamfukudza. *The Non-Believer's Journey*, 1980, was the first novel to focus directly and critically on the liberation war: See also Solomon Mutswairo, *Mapondera, Soldier of Zimbabwe*, 1978; and Wilson Katiyo, *A Son of the Soil*, 1976. For an analysis of all of these novels see Preben Kaarsholm, "Coming to Terms with Violence: Literature and the Development of a Public Sphere in Zimbabwe," Seminar Paper, IDS, University of Zimbabwe, January 1993.

44. See Ngwabi Bhebe and Terence Ranger, eds., *Soldiers in Zimbabwe's Liberation War*, vol. 1, (Harare: University of Zimbabwe Publications, 1995) and Ngwabi Bhebe and Terence Ranger, eds., *Society in Zimbabwe's Liberation War*, vol. 2 (Harare: University of Zimbabwe Publications, 1995).

45. Jean Bethke Elshtain, *Women and War*, p. 212.

46. Irene Staunton, quoted in "SADC Women Writers Coming into their Own,"

aiacan@web.net, internet news, 1986, (960806). Flora Veit-Wild's survey of Zimbabwean writers reveals for example that by 1987 only 31 women had been published while 179 men had been published by the same time; see Flora Viet-Wild, *Teachers, Preachers and Non-Believers: A Social History of Zimbabwean Literature*, (Harare: Baobab, 1993), p. 355.

47. Sekai Nzenza, *Zimbabwean Woman: My Own Story*, (London: Karia Press, 1988).

48. Irene Ropa Rinopfuka Mahamba, *Woman in Struggle*, (Harare: Mambo Press, 1986).

49. Freedom Nyamubaya, *On the Road Again: Poems During and After the National Liberation of Zimbabwe*, (Harare: Zimbabwe Publishing House, 1986); also see Freedom Nyamubaya *Dusk of Dawn*, (Harare: Zimbabwe Publishing House, 1995).

50. Nozipo Maraire, *Zenzele: A Letter to My Daughter*, (Johannesburg: Ad Donker Publisher, 1996).

51. Chenjerai Hove, *Bones*, (Harare: Baobab, 1988).

52. Charles Samupindi, *Pawns*, Schools Edition, (Harare: Baobab, 1992).

53. Shimmer Chinodya, *Harvest of Thorns*, (Harare: Baobab, 1989).

54. Alexander Kanengoni, *Effortless Tears*, (Harare: Baobab, 1993).

55. Dangarembga's novel has won a few awards and deals with women and generations in Rhodesia and Zimbabwe, but does not deal with the war of liberation at all, so I will not discuss this book here; Tsitsi Dangarembga, *Nervous Conditions*, (Harare: Zimbabwe Publishing House, 1988).

56. Zenzele costs Z$138.95 (approx US$7) compared to Z$39.75 for a locally published book such as Yvonne Vera, *Nehanda*, (Harare: Baobab, 1993).

57. See Chenjerai Hove, *Bones*; and Charles Samupindi, *Pawns*. Also notable is Rudo Gaidzanwa's *Images of Women in Zimbabwean Literature*, The (Harare: College Press, 1995), which does not mention women guerilla fighters.

58. See Leda Stott, *Women and the Armed Struggle for Independence in Zimbabwe (1964-1979)*, Edinburgh University, Centre of African Studies, Occasional Papers, 25, 1990; also see Alison Momeyer, "Inside the Struggles: Voices of Women Coming of Age in the War for Independence," (unpublished independent project, University of Zimbabwe, 1990). It is noteworthy that each year more foreign students come to Zimbabwe to research the role of women in the struggle. For one exception to the rule see Josephine Nhongo-Simbanegavi, *Zimbabwean Women in the Liberation Struggle: ZANLA and its Legacy, 1972-1985*, PhD Thesis, Faculty of Modern History, University of Oxford, 1997. Her research offers some new insights and challenges to the study of women in the liberation war. However, permission from the author was sought, but not granted for use in the present study. Accordingly, her research has not been cited here.

59. Sita Ranchod-Nilsson, "This Too Is a Way of Fighting: Rural Women's Participation in Zimbabwe's Liberation War," in Mary Ann Tétreault, ed., *Women and Revolution in Africa, Asia, and the New World*, (Columbia: University of South Carolina, 1994): And see for example, Kathy Bond-Stewart, *Young Women*

in the Liberation Struggle Stories and Poems From Zimbabwe, (Harare: Zimbabwe Publishing House, 1984); and Kathy Bond-Stewart, *Independence is Not Only for One Sex,* (Harare: Zimbabwe Publishing House, 1987); Miranda Davies, *Third World-Second Sex: Women's Struggles for National Liberation: Third World Women Speak Out,* (Zed Press, London, 1983); Norma Kriger, *Zimbabwe's Guerrilla War: Peasant Voices.*

60. For example see Sharon Macdonald, "Drawing the Lines - Gender, Peace and War: An Introduction," in Sharon Macdonald, Pat Holden and Shirley Ardener, eds., *Images of Women in Peace and War: Cross-Cultural Perspectives,* (Wisconsin: The University of Wisconsin Press, 1987), p. 10.

61. The "None But Ourselves Oral History Project" by the Oral Tradition Association of Zimbabwe, housed in the National Archives of Zimbabwe is an important example, although none of the tapes have been transcribed. See Julie Frederiske, *None But Ourselves: Masses vs. Media in the Making of Zimbabwe,* (Harare: Otazi and Anvil Press, 1982). See also Irene Staunton, ed., *Mothers of the Revolution.*

62. Madaleine Mattarozzi, "What about Women," Letters to *Moto,* 1:2, August 1982. Unfortunately, the box number no longer exists, and there were no Mattarozzi's in the Zimbabwe phone books. There was also no trace of any publications by her.

63. Ngwabi Bhebe and Terence Ranger, eds., *Society In Zimbabwe's Liberation War,* p. 26.

64. Norma Kriger, *Zimbabwe's Guerilla War: Peasant Voices.*

65. Teresa Barnes criticizing the work of David Martin and Phillis Johnson in their book *The Struggle for Zimbabwe: The Chimurenga War,* (London: Faber and Faber, 1981) cited in Ngwabi Bhebe and Terence Ranger, eds., *Soldiers in Zimbabwe's Liberation War,* p. 6.

66. Terence Ranger, *Peasant Consciousness and Guerrilla War in Zimbabwe: A Comparative Study,* (London: James Curry, 1985); and Terence Ranger, *Revolt in Southern Rhodesia: 1896-7,* (London: Heinemann, 1967; second edition 1979).

67. Ngwabi Bhebe and Terence Ranger, eds., *Soldiers in Zimbabwe's Liberation War,* p.5.

68. Ibid p.26.

69. For example, Diana Jeater's, *Marriage, Perversion, and Power: The Construction of Moral Discourses in Southern Rhodesia, 1894-1930,* (Oxford: Clarendon, 1991); and Elizabeth Schmidt's, *Peasants, Traders, Wives: Shona Women in the History of Zimbabwe,* (Harare: Baobab, 1992).

70. Ngwabi Bhebe and Terence Ranger, eds., *Society In Zimbabwe's Liberation War,* p. 5.

71. Ibid, p.28.

72. Ibid.

73. Mary Ann Tétreault, ed., *Women and Revolution in Africa, Asia, and The New World,* (Columbia: University of South Carolina Press, 1994), p. 8.

74. See, for example, Christine Sylvester, "Simultaneous Revolutions: The

Zimbabwean Case," *Journal of Southern African Studies*, 16:3, 1990, pp.452-75; Ngwabi Bhebhe and Terence Ranger, *Soldiers in the Liberation War*; Janice McLaughlin, *On the Frontline: Catholic Missions in Zimbabwe's Liberation War*, (Harare: Baobab Books, 1996). Moore argues that the *Vashandi* or ZIPA movement, if it had not been 'pacified,' might have taken the war along a different revolutionary path. See David Moore, "The Contradictory Construction of Hegemony in Zimbabwe: Politics, Ideology and Class in the Formation of a New African State," PhD dissertation, York University, 1992.

75. Andre Astrow, *Zimbabwe - A Revolution that Lost its Way?* (London: Zed Press 1983); See Christine Sylvester, "Simultaneous Revolutions and Exits: A Semi-Skeptical Comment," in Mary Ann Tétreault, ed., *Women and Revolution in Africa Asia, and The New World*, p. 416.

76. Sita Ranchod-Nilsson, "This Too is a Way of Fighting: Rural Women's Participation in Zimbabwe's Liberation War,"p. 63.

77. Ibid, note 2, p. 84.

78. Christine Sylvester, "Simultaneous Revolutions: The Zimbabwean Case," p. 454. Also see Quintin Hoare and Geoffrey Nowell Smith, eds., *Selections from the Prison Notebooks of Antonio Gramsci*, (London: Lawrence and Wishart, 1971, reprinted 1986), pp. 44-118.

79. Mary Ann Tétreault, ed., *Women and Revolution in Africa, Asia, and the New World*, p. 20.

80. Ibid, p. 4.

81. Sita Ranchod Nillson, "This Too Is a Way of Fighting"; and see Irene Staunton, ed., *Mothers of the Revolution*.

Chapter Three

Zimbabwean Nationalism and Feminism

In the struggle the women had a chance to demonstrate their potential. Their support was essential when we were in crisis. If women were comrades and equal in the struggle, then we should be comrades and equal in reaping the fruits of that struggle. That is the objective of our mission [in the Ministry of Community Development and Women's Affairs].
- *The Herald*, March 6, 1981

The demand for women's equality today is as much a threat to humanity as nuclear weapons are.
- Letter to the Editor in *Moto*, May 1984

Disappointment

The potential for women's emancipation alongside national liberation has clearly dominated studies of women's roles in national liberation wars in Africa. As a result, many of these studies conclude that nationalism and political independence did not translate into any particular feminist benefits for women. Despite the socialist rhetoric of women's emancipation as a fundamental prerequisite for national liberation, not only did women's emancipation not follow from independence, but it was never really intended. Most feminist analyses of women in war in Africa have not questioned socialist rhetoric about women's war roles, and as a result these analyses become lamentations on broken promises and feminist hopes diminished in the postindependence periods. For example, Rukweza Prisca Borerwe has stated, "Although women participated in the liberation struggle to the same extent as males, it is very difficult for them to get into politics. The most important obstacles women have to deal with are male prejudices."[1] These assumptions of women's equality with men in the war need to be understood in the context of there being very little evidence to support socialist claims of women's emancipation.[2]

Like Prisca Borerwa, others have noted the lack of benefits Zimbabwean women gained as a group in the post-independence period, especially in regard to their lack of legal rights pertaining to land acquisition, marriage, and *lobola* (bride-wealth). The sense of betrayal and disappointment for women is based on the assumption that women fought *equally* with men in the nationalist struggle for liberation.[3] For example, The *Zimbabwe People's Voice* stated in 1979 that

> [i]t should be noted that Zimbabwean women are participating equally well as their male counterparts in the struggle against colonialism, fascism, and imperialism. In Zimbabwe, women's role in the struggle for national liberation is unquestionable.[4]

However, as Amina Mama has argued, "Regrettably, the treatment of women in several of the independent states proves that participation in military activity does not necessarily translate into progressive gender politics."[5]

Anticolonial nationalism "defin[es] the nation against the nonrepresentative colonial power, trying to build a nation to claim a state."[6] The physical borders of this state often replicate the arbitrary colonial boundaries established without consideration for precolonial communities, cultures, or identities. Zimbabwean nationalism operated on the physical boundaries of Rhodesia, although the nationalist movement itself existed in an international arena. Both men and women were mobilized by being made aware of how the inherent oppressions of colonialism, capitalism, and minority rule negatively affected them. The demands for a new social and political order - majority rule - were inspired in part by socialism, which in turn fueled parts of the nationalist movement.[7] After political independence, however, the influence of colonialism lingered on. Neocolonialism, traditional customs and laws, and a patriarchal heritage continued in the newly independent nation.

This result was disappointing to many ex-combatants, who had fought to liberate Zimbabwe from the shackles of oppression.

Zimbabwean women guerilla fighters were heralded internationally as women who rose above traditionally subordinated gender positions in order to fight equally with men in the struggle for national independence.[8] This view has carried through to the 1990s. Angeline Shenje-Peyton offers a typical example as she argues that in Zimbabwe "women fought in the war for independence on equal footing with men."[9] This statement in the *Harvard Human Rights Journal* became an authoritative representation of what women did in the war.

The international spotlight on Zimbabwean women coincided with the United Nations Decade for Women, culminating in the mid-term World Conference on Women in Copenhagen in 1980. Richard Lapchick and Stephanie Urdang[10] spearheaded the research on the role of women in southern African liberation struggles.[11] Their work, based on the UN Conference Report, drew attention to the socialist connections between national liberation and women's emancipation, focusing on women in South Africa, Namibia, and Zimbabwe. Amilcar Cabral had argued in Guinea-Bissau that a revolution would not be complete without the social transformation of both men and women, and that women had to fight for and earn their right to equality with men.[12] Samora Machel in Mozambique argued that "[t]he liberation of women is a fundamental necessity for the revolution, the guarantee of its continuity, and the precondition for its victory."[13] Influenced by the successes in Mozambique and Guinea-Bissau, Robert Mugabe, leader of ZANU, explained how "[w]e learned through the liberation struggle that success and power are possible when men and women are united as equals."[14]

As a result of the international socialist-feminist hope for the liberation of southern African women, interest in the role of African women in liberation movements has focused more on why equality with men was *not* gained after national independence[15] than on the actual experiences of women guerilla fighters during the war.[16] The experiences of women in Zimbabwe's liberation struggle gathered here provide the key to understanding why African women in national liberation struggles could not consolidate their wartime independence and relative equality with men, and extend that equality after national independence. Compared to women in Namibia, Angola, Mozambique, and Guinea Bissau,[17] Zimbabwean women were more actively involved in military guerilla formations, and yet this did not ensure automatic equality or access to the fruits of independence for women.[18]

The disappointment and betrayal felt by Zimbabwean women is often reflected among Western feminist theorists who glorified the role of African women in military and guerilla action.

> The African countries cited as most progressive on "the woman question" have tended to be those that have involved women in military action, and not coincidentally women across the globe have adopted posters of women carrying guns as icons of revolutionary feminism.[19]

As Urdang has noted, "Many a photo taken by visitors to the [Mozambican] liberated zones during the war show the unusual sight of a young woman with an AK-47 rifle slung across her back."[20]

Nationalist and feminist analyses - that women fought equally and heroically with men during the war but gained little compared with men afterwards - need to be challenged as a theoretical perspective. Basing women's claims for equality on poorly documented assumptions about women's roles in the liberation war results in an interpretation of women's status in Zimbabwe that is theoretically narrow and empirically shallow. It is more useful to examine how women actually experienced the liberation war and to investigate the many ways women were involved in nationalism and the nationalist struggle for independence,[21] because as Urdang has pointed out, "most of the women fighters actually performed inglorious but necessary tasks (catering, porterage, etc),"[22] so it is difficult to distinguish *equal actions* between men and women in the struggle. Nonetheless, women did experience a different status while they were involved in the guerilla armies. The question is, why do they lose that status after national liberation has been won?[23]

Amina Mama has asked if " African women experienced greater liberation since the demise of colonial regimes, or have the nationalists merely continued the trajectories of contempt and disempowerment? What has been the role of women in antiimperialist struggles, and how has this affected their position in postcolonial states?"[24]

Betrayal

In Zimbabwe, it would appear that the nationalists continued the traditional patterns of patriarchy despite women's role in the struggle and the socialist promises of women's liberation. As Enloe has argued, after wars of national liberation there is usually some kind of drive toward normality, and the family is most often the significant social unit in which to develop and maintain social stability; it also reproduces and replenishes the population. Therefore, what happens is that "eventually even [women's] political leverage as liberation army veterans may dissolve."[25] This depoliticizes women's war actions.

> Women who fought in the revolution expected that the gender as well as racial order would be reorganized as a result of warfare and their part in it, but a kind of participation that perpetuated a sexual division of labour could delay such expectations being fulfilled by a new state now short on resources, under attack, and reliant on its new state military.[26]

In the case of Zimbabwe, one cannot understand women's status and role in society today without understanding what women actually did in the liberation struggle. What kind of status did they enjoy during the liberation war? How did women want to be involved? What were they allowed to do within nationalist action and discourse? What happened to them? Were they fighting against colonization or patriarchy? These questions arise from what Amina Mama has pointed out as the sense of betrayal felt by women over the nation states' inability to live up to their expectations. Is it simply that "men have reneged on their promise to share the fruits of independence"?[27] As we shall see in many cases such a promise was never made.

Zimbabwean Feminist - Nationalist Rhetoric

Women were crucial in the struggle in order to support the male guerilla fighters' actions. Women in the villages provided food, clothing, and shelter, often risking their lives, to assist the guerillas.[28] Young women and men became *chimbwidos* and *mujibas* (messengers and carriers) providing information on the whereabouts of Rhodesian soldiers to the guerilas. Many women took on the jobs of cooks, medical personal, and teachers. When the armed struggle began in earnest after 1972 one of the most significant decisions was to accept women to be trained as guerilla fighters.[29] They worked and struggled alongside male nationalists and guerilla fighters, supporting the revolution from both inside Rhodesia and the military training camps across the border. Through their involvement in nationalist action these women challenged many traditional gender roles. Through political education in the guerilla training camps and throughout the rural areas, women were taught by nationalists that "black Zimbabwean women are further exploited than their menfolk,"[30] in order to secure their active support for national liberation.

> Through their participation in the struggle for national liberation, however, women have learnt a new strength, and a new conviction of their rights and creative potential. It will be the releasing of this potential, and the linking of women's emancipation to the struggle for genuine economic independence that will finally free Zimbabwe and with it the women from their history of oppression and exploitation.[31]

The nationalists were told that national liberation would benefit both African women and men. The rhetoric of women's emancipation thus entered the discourse of nationalism in the mid to late 1970s, encouraging women to see the potential for their own liberation within nationalism. Interestingly enough, the height of the armed struggle coincided with the beginning of the UN Decade for Women in 1975. Was there a connection?

> In 1975 the United Nations Decade for Women was declared in Mexico City. Women gathered from every continent to discuss goals and strategies for nationally based women's liberation. For many it seemed like a new beginning: in the West, discussion was moving from purely feminist circles to take on a more global dimension, while women in the Third World who were struggling for national independence and development were beginning to demand substantive changes in the role of women in society.[32]

While the UN Decade for Women coincided with Mozambican Liberation (on June 25 1975 - after more than ten years of armed struggle), international attention to the experiences of both women and men in neighboring Zimbabwe's Liberation Struggle. The view that the involvement of African women in national liberation struggles was a necessary evil during the UN Decade needs to be recognized. Women's liberation could not be achieved while women and men were both fighting for freedom and colonialism.

Nonetheless, it was during the Zimbabwean anticolonial struggle that questions of women's liberation were first raised. Teurai Ropa, a senior ranking woman in ZANU said, "The 1975 decade for women ... further strengthened our ideas of changing the laws."[33] Women's emancipation was discussed and the seeds of women's liberation were planted in the imagination of many women, when an eight-member delegation from the nationalist parties ZAPU and ZANU, headed by Jane Ngwenya (from ZAPU), attended the opening conference of the UN Decade for Women.[34] Here they began the discourse about women's liberation with national liberation.

After national liberation it was claimed by senior women in ZANU that women were involved in legislative changes to encourage their emancipation. There were substantial attempts to encourage the liberation of women in line with national liberation. Teurai Ropa has stated that

> [w]e held several seminars right through the country getting feedback from women themselves, and wrote a paper to the Cabinet which was passed ... we want to see women appearing in each and every government department. [We changed] the Income Tax [laws], the Age of Majority Act, the Inheritance Law, the Matrimonial Causes Act ... and labor regulations.[35]

It is surprising that women guerilla fighters, whose actions spearheaded the debates on women's equality, were not considered separately during the consultation process, and as a result they were not differentiated between other women who did not become guerilla fighters.[36] The following type of rhetoric was not uncommon:

> The emancipation of women is a must and not an act of charity. Women are an indivisible part of society. Their struggle is part of society's struggle for progress. Women should enjoy equal rights

with their menfolk. No progress can be reached without the effective participation of women. Women must now totally dedicate themselves to the revolution. Only through conscious participation in the revolutionary struggle will Zimbabwean women gain the confidence of their men.... The progressive world is aware women are in the forefront of the antiimperialist fight. Women have scored great achievements ... Recognition of the role of women in the struggle for men's emancipation is of importance by all progressive forces [sic].[37]

The conclusion was that women's emancipation would result from national independence. Therefore, women must fight for independence, from the racist regime that could not offer emancipation to men or women. As one nationalist magazine stated it:

In their active participation in the liberation of Zimbabwe the women have always been very clear about the objectives of the struggle. As they see it, they are fighting for national independence and sexual equality. To them the two things are inseparable and they insist that simply to fight for improved status within the framework of the racist oppressive system, as some "successful" progressive women have tried to argue, is quite meaningless. The achievement of independence to them is the best guarantee for changing the situation they are in and for guaranteeing the establishment of equal rights for all, irrespective of race, colour or sex. The priority is independence and not "women's rights."[38]

The socialist rhetoric continued and women's emancipation appeared to become central to the discourse about socialist-style revolution. ZANU's idea of emancipation for women claimed to follow a stringent socialist political line:

Emancipation requires action on several levels. First of all, a political line must be laid down. Women must be politically conscious. They must be engaged in the battle for political mobilization and organization of the masses. Their commitment to the liberation struggle will then become concrete action, leading them to take part in making decisions affecting the country's future. In this way, women will gradually be in a position of influence at all levels of decision making, that is, organizing affairs of the state, for example, politics, armed forces, diplomacy, factories, art, science, culture, and so on.... It is the task of women to reorientate the male-folk out of their chauvinistic minds so that they realize that women's emancipation is an integral part and precondition to a successful revolution ... Women should educate children of both sexes stressing what the emancipation of women is? [sic] This enables the young generation to grow being conscious of the necessity of liberating women.[39]

Women's equality with men was thus held to be highly desirable for the revolution, and women should therefore emancipate themselves because "love can only exist between free and equal people who have the same ideals and commitment in serving the masses and the revolution."[40] Robert Mugabe, the leader of the Zimbabwe African National Union (ZANU), argued in 1979 that

as a Liberation Movement with a socialist programme we are particularly interested in the role and position of women in Socialist countries, so we can, by comparison, judge our progress or lack of progress in the process for the advancement of our own women.[41]

Mugabe cited examples from Lenin who said that "[i]f women are not drawn into the public service, into militia, into political life, women are not torn out of their stupefying house and kitchen environment, it will be impossible to build even democracy, let alone socialism."[42] Quoting from Mao, Mugabe repeated that "[w]hen women all over the country rise up, that will be the day of the victory of the Chinese revolution."[43] In Vietnam, where women fought against American imperialism, Mugabe quoted the leader of the liberation movement Ho Chi Minh: "[I]f the women are not emancipated, socialism is only half established."[44] In Mozambique, president Samora Machel, another influence on Mugabe, also "emphasized the need for the emancipation of women as a fundamental necessity for the Revolution."[45] Mugabe argued that in Zimbabwe "[t]he national struggle, therefore, especially at its higher level, when it became the armed national struggle, became as much a process towards the liberation of the nation as towards the emancipation of the woman."[46] One document on *The Role of Women*

Before and After Liberation by the ZANU Department of Women's Affairs, written in 1977,[47] is of particular importance. It confirms that women's liberation, hand in hand with the revolution, was a useful device:

> It should be emphasised that women's emancipation in Zimbabwe is coexistent with and complimentary to the overall struggle for emancipation and liberation from the settler-capitalist state and socio-economic system in Zimbabwe today.[48]

In 1981 the Zimbabwe Women's Bureau outlined the feminist pathway for women:

> With the independence of Zimbabwe this year, and a popularly elected government now in power, the women are looking to a redressing of the oppressive and unequal situation that they have long suffered under. Their expectations for a genuine improvement in their daily lives has at last the possibility of being met. Both ZANU(PF) and the Patriotic Front (ZAPU) have pledged themselves to the full incorporation of women into the new society. It will require determination on the part of both women and men to face this challenge and bring about the new order. Economic relations and oppressive attitudes will not change overnight. The long and painful struggle for the genuine emancipation of women lies ahead.[49]

This statement emphatically stresses the "long and painful struggle," and that "it's not yet a revolution, but the seeds are there."[50] But in fact the harvest has been very poor and the weeds have been profuse. There has been limited emancipation for women along feminist principles. As seen above, the government's support for women's emancipation waned significantly after 1981, leaving it entirely in women's hands.[51] The "seeds" of the revolution were planted by the elite, educated, ruling party women working outside of Zimbabwe, in London and Los Angeles, coinciding with the United Nations Decade for Women 1975-85. The germination period was supposed to be a decade, not just in Zimbabwe but elsewhere. As we have seen with the 5th International Women's Conference in Beijing in 1995, the birth of this movement has been delayed, although some advances have been made, illustrated profoundly by the publication *Zimbabwe Women's Voices* (1995).

Nonetheless, it was the connection that had been made between nationalist action and feminist agendas that resulted in the (feminist) expectation that women should be emancipated at the same time as their countries were liberated, especially during socialist-style revolutions. In early 1978 Mabel Mudondo, ZANU's member in London, wrote about "the emancipation of women and their role towards liberation struggles."[52] Inspired by socialist philosophy, she argued that "women will never be emancipated without a working class led revolution."[53] Mudondo drew links between women's emancipation and women's involvement in political mobilization and national liberation struggles. Mudondo planted the seeds of a socialist-inspired feminist dream of a revolution for women, to harmonize with the liberation of the Zimbabwean nation. Mudondo wrote enthusiastically of Zimbabwean women's capabilities in nationalism, feminism, and the feminine:

> Today, Chimurenga ... prosecuted by ZANU has seen the emergence of a new type of Zimbabwean woman, free from the servant mentality of the communal/feudal society and from the slave mentality of colonialism. The new Zimbabwean woman would have to liberate herself from the chains which bound her to a life of depravity and degradation. Through her part in the struggle *fighting with the bazooka in her hand*, working side by side sharing the burden of labor equally with her man, the Zimbabwean woman today would have transformed herself from a slave to a free woman who can hold her head up proudly. Her influence in society will be constructive, creative, and *beautiful* [emphasis added].[54]

Mudondo concluded that only through women's full mobilization in the revolution as "mothers, responsible for child bearing," and in other various roles, would more women be emancipated.[55] The "various" roles women performed during the war held potential for women to challenge traditional stereotypes and establish some kind of feminism, which could overturn to oppressive cultural and political traditions. However, it did not take long for Mudondo's heroic women to put down their *bazookas* for babies, both because they were forced and voluntarily.

Zimbabwe Women's Perceptions of Emancipation

During the national liberation war ZANLA women comrades requested literature on women's emancipation. In a transcript of a meeting discussing women's problems within the party some women comrades spoke out about their needs:

> **Comrade Rumbidzai:** "Gossiping which brings about disunity [in the party structure] is a result of being unoccupied so if we could get something to do (games or books to read) especially to some who cannot do manual work, and the like."
> **Comrade Catherine:** ... "it is in the process of being accomplished."
> **Comrade Pronica:** "What sort of books are these? Is it something on women's emancipation or something else?"
> **Comrade Rumbidzai:** "We like those on women's emancipation but it would also be good to have others to improve our English.".
> **Comrade Teurai Ropa:** "You want novels and comics (NO) [sic] Books which do not concern the revolution can never be brought here. Long back we never read comics and novels. I cant give you such stuff. *I will give you books on women's emancipation and the revolution.* Don't tell me you are not interested in sewing etc. or other things in the revolution. You cannot be interested in the war then have no other interests." [emphasis added][56]

This request for books on women's emancipation was clearly supported but it is not clear whether any books were distributed among the women cadres.[57] Furthermore, Teurai Ropa's comments also suggest that women had to be more interested in sewing and other supportive tasks for the revolution, than in their own emancipation. Considering that there is no evidence of the distribution of books on women's emancipation in the women's training it is noteworthy that some women ex-combatants from ZANLA stated that the topic of women's emancipation was rarely discussed among the rank and file. Nyarai stated that, "They were talking about women's liberation, but we wanted to liberate Zimbabwe."[58] "They" were the educated elite, like Teurai Ropa and Naomi Nhiwatiwa. Nyarai continued:

> If you are a boy you can come to liberate Zimbabwe. If you are a girl you can come to liberate Zimbabwe. It was not difficult for

women to liberate Zimbabwe because we were working together.[59]

Sekai agreed that women's liberation was not discussed; "As head of security I had no time to discuss women's liberation during the war. The idea was to liberate Zimbabwe first."[60] However she admitted that after she met Teurai Ropa, some of women's needs began to be addressed within the war:

> I met Teurai Ropa.... Myself and others elected Teurai to be the chair of the women's group. Already Teurai and the other women would discuss grievances like women's needs to get cotton wool, the needs of children. If it wasn't for Teurai many women would have died.[61]

Teresa said:

> We did not specifically talk about women's liberation. We were not highlighting on women at all, because remember I was saying we were treated as equals, so we were appealing to all Zimbabweans to just feel there is a challenge.[62]

Rudo said that

> women's liberation wasn't discussed. I think this just came about, whether this was discussed somewhere, where I didn't attend, but otherwise it just came about.[63]

For Rudo, just participating in the struggle created the situation where she could be equal with men:

> Even when you were doing training, some groups were training together with men. The same training. And the duties we were doing were just almost the same. We had no feeling of "that because I am a woman ... not because I'm a woman, I would just ask him, why are you doing this to me? Not because I am a woman. I never felt like that.[64]

Yet, as Freedom Nyamubaya stated, "liberation for women was not discussed, not until the end of the war."[65] Women's liberation was mainly promoted around 1979 in conjunction with the first ZANU Women's Seminar at Xai Xai in Mozambique, where international attention was focused on the plight of women in the struggle, and ZANU women attempted to put pressure on the new Zimbabwean government to liberate women. However, the following remarks by Teurai Ropa point to the ambiguities in what was considered to be women's liberation and how this could fit with traditional gender roles:

> Yes, women did discuss women's emancipation; actually we were having social talks. How do we perceive ourselves as mothers, as the sole custodian of custom, as leaders in society. Customarily how should we behave, how should we be portrayed, and so on. But this was just said in the dark. We didn't know that there were these things like the laws that needed changing.[66]

It was only after independence that women could attempt to change the laws that excluded or oppressed women. During the war, challenges to women's treatment seem to have been limited.

Feminism Based on Nationalist Revolution
However, while the rhetoric and promise of women's emancipation appeared at the height of the armed nationalist struggle, it became clearer after the war that the goal of women's liberation was only relevant for some. In 1981 Teurai Ropa claimed that women's aims for the liberation of Zimbabwe also included their own liberation, simply because of women's involvement in the nationalist struggle.

> Participation in the struggle changed our way of thinking, our behavior and self conceptualization. In our culture combat is not for women. Only men used to go hunting. But in the struggle both men and women participated equally in the battlefield. Our participation in the struggle for liberation was also the participation for liberation for all women, within and without struggle. We, faced with similar disabilities, proved that these disabilities could be overcome and that our performance could be just as good as man's ... We fought so that our voice could carry as good a weight as anybody else's.[67]

Normally then, women were perceived as "disabled" compared to men, but nationalist ideology provided a window of opportunity for women to prove they could overcome these "disabilities" and be more like men. Women could then argue for the benefits that came with political independence in a postcolonial state. The Zimbabwe Women's Bureau in 1981 pointed out that

> women are looking to a redressing of the oppressive and unequal situation that they have long suffered under. Their expectations for a genuine improvement in their daily lives has at last the possibility of being met. Both ZANU(PF) and the Patriotic Front (ZAPU) have pledged themselves to the full incorporation of women into the new society.[68]

These pledges quickly met their demise in the legislative void of empty promises. Yet, as the Zimbabwe Women's Bureau linked women's emancipation to Zimbabwe's economic independence and placed its hopes within the new ZANU(PF) government, it also had to remind women that there was still a "long and painful struggle for the genuine emancipation of women ... ahead."[69] They could not rely solely on the government.

Canaan Banana, the first democratic president of Zimbabwe, spoke about women's emancipation at a workshop on women in 1982. He said that Zimbabwe's economic independence required women's liberation, just as women's participation in the struggle was a crucial component in the success of the revolution:

> The importance of women in the socio-economic transformation of any society, cannot be over emphasised ... The liberation of women is a fundamental necessity for the revolution, the guarantee of its continuity and the precondition of its victory. Coming to our situation here in Zimbabwe, the success of the armed struggle was to a large measure due to the active participation of women, and I am convinced that the protracted struggle for national transformation will depend upon the extent to which we can utilize the resources of our women. The participation of women in the armed struggle, no doubt created the necessary conditions for transforming their consciousness, enabling them to discharge their

responsibilities and to have a clearer perception of liberation as a total human process involving both men and women.[70]

Banana placed much emphasis on women's participation in the liberation war as the equalizer of the sexes:

The women combatants, peasant mothers and young girls, known in "Chimurenga" terminology as "*zvimbwido*", clearly demonstrated that women should never be underestimated. The women cadres fought side by side with their male counterparts, displaying the same spirit of determination and courage until final victory. In the rural areas, peasant women brushed aside threats of reprisals from the Smith regime and threw all their weight behind the armed revolution. They protected our gallant freedom fighters, nursed the wounded and fed the hungry. Even little girls were also in the forefront of the war. As *zvimbwido* the young girls showed unbreakable determination and revolutionary spirit by transporting equipment for the comrades, by mobilizing the population and providing vital intelligence on enemy manoeuvres. The war was thus won through concerted action by both men and women. There was total unity in action. Both men and women were taught to relate to each other as human beings and not as sexual stereotypes. This experience freed our men and women from narrow perceptions so that there was no longer any meaning to the concept of "women's rights" anymore than there was to "man's rights," but only "human rights."[71]

Women as cadres, peasants, and *zvimbwido* were able to free themselves to fight for human rights. The focus of the revolution here shifts from just women's concerns to everybody's concerns.

The Acting Minister for Community Development and Women's Affairs, Mr. Kumbirai Kangai, told a group of women at a workshop in 1981 that they had

earned [in] the hardest possible way recognition of your inherent right to equality with men by virtue of the contribution you made during the war of liberation of our country. The women's struggle had now attained a more peaceful but nevertheless important objective of equality of treatment and opportunities.... Men and women should keep fighting shoulder to shoulder as we did in the struggle.[72]

The pursuit of equality for women was rooted in their wartime activities according to Banana and Kangai, and since independence men and women should continue the combined struggle.

This commitment had already begun to wane by 1980. Socialist rhetoric espousing the liberation of women in conjunction with national liberation had little effect on most women's lives and experiences during the struggle, and provided only minimal benefits for women after the struggle. The rhetoric was there, but it appeared almost as an afterthought in a small paragraph on the fifteenth page of a short pamphlet of the *1980 ZANU(PF) Election Manifesto.*

> Under a ZANU(PF) government, women will enjoy equal rights with men in all spheres of political, economic, cultural and family life. Men and women will enjoy equal pay for equal work. Men and women shall marry of their own free will. The state will protect marriage, the family, and the mother and the child.[73]

In 1985 women's emancipation from both traditional practices and colonial oppression was still appearing on the ZANU(PF) agenda. Proof of its interest in seeing through the emancipation of women the "Zimbabwean Way," lay in the establishment of the Zimbabwe Women's League and the National Council of Women both within the structures of ZANU(PF) and the Ministry of Community Development and Women's Affairs, with Teurai Ropa as minister and Naomi Nhiwatiwa as deputy minister.[74] The original Ministry of Women's Affairs itself also remains a legacy of ineffectiveness in changing the lives of women, despite often cited self-congratulations on securing legislative changes like the Legal Age of Majority Act. However, until there are major changes in the customary laws based on the patriarchal control of women, especially in relation to *lobola*, these achievements mean very little. Not until there is equal representation of women in government, in leadership roles and in decision making positions, can it possibly be said that women gained equality from their roles in the liberation war. In 1997 in Zimbabwe there were only twenty-one women out of 150 parliamentarians: three women out of sixteen ministers: and eight women out of sixty-seven city councilors. This suggests that there was no real direct political success from the so-called women's revolution. [75]

Not Western Feminism, Please!

Not surprisingly, when Teurai Ropa was promoted to Minister of Community Development and Women's Affairs, she announced that there was not going to be a revolution for women after all in Zimbabwe. Directly after independence the discourse about women's emancipation in Zimbabwe was based on nationalist experiences. Any suggestion that the concept and ideology of feminism was involved continues to annoy many of the women who participated in the war. Feminism has been considered as a racist Western import, irrelevant to black women in the Third World, including Zimbabwe. The nationalist movement is credited with any gains made for women. By November 1981 Teurai Ropa quickly put an end to any radical speculation that women might have got their socialist education in the military training camps in Mozambique. She stated that there was not going to be a revolution for women - there would not be a complete overthrow of patriarchy, just as colonialism and capitalism were not completely overthrown. Revealing the tensions between African women's liberation and Western feminism she

> urged Zimbabwean women to remain realists and avoid extremes in their search for liberation from oppression by the male sex, [especially warning them against the developed countries' women whose] ideals had become incompatible with even the laws of nature [like wanting men to become pregnant]. This type of women's liberation was spreading like a virus. Zimbabwe's women must keep it at bay if they wished to maintain their usefulness in society.... The liberation we seek is equal opportunities for both sexes socially, politically and economically, and a recognition of women as adults, with justiciable [sic] rights in decision-making.... We must not seek to be men. Neither do we seek that our husbands become housewives. [76]

Teurai Ropa said that Zimbabwean women would not aspire to "wearing trousers" and "smoking cigarettes." Definitions of emancipation attempted to reduce the challenge made to women's traditional roles in

Zimbabwe, while challenging Western feminist ideals of liberation:

> First of all, we must understand the meaning of women's emancipation. In the capitalist state the meaning of women's emancipation is distorted. They think that an emancipated woman is one who smokes, drinks, wears trousers, who indulges in sexual intercourse, who refuses to have children etc. While others think that emancipation is accumulation of diplomas etc. All these are erroneous ideas and superficial concepts, they do not really suggest a correct revolutionary line that will emancipate women.[77]

The ruling party's commitment to women's emancipation formed part of the discarded rhetoric. By 1985 the ruling party ZANU(PF) was still reminding women that their emancipation was not going to be Western in character. They made the necessary qualifications as to what kind of emancipation Zimbabwean women could gain:

> The Party does not encourage the so-called women's liberation movement popular in the United States and other capitalist countries, which tries to set women against men based on crude and superficial analysis. We want to promote real *equality* at the level of work, economic opportunity, and social status ... to be equal partners with men in development.[78]

Although women's liberation was spoken about during the war it was a brief and passing phase. Since independence some attempts have been made to silence what remained of it in the discourse. The problem for feminism (and women) associated with national liberation was that the liberation movement usually followed a patriarchal agenda, which did not feel obliged to emphasize women's liberation, except when the international spotlight forced (verbal) concessions to be made. The discourses of disappointment, betrayal, feminist expectations based on socialist rhetoric and nationalist revolution, and the repulsion against Western feminism expressed more loudly after independence, have all contributed to an understanding of the context within which women ex-combatants in Zimbabwe experienced the liberation war. We now turn to these experiences and to the place of women in the struggle.

Endnotes

1. Rukweza Prisca Borerwe, quoted in Ciru Getecha and Jesimen Chipika eds., *Zimbabwe Women's Voices*, (Harare, Zimbabwe Women's Resource Center and Network, 1995), p.67.

2. Robert Mugabe, *Our War of Liberation: Speeches, Articles, Interviews 1976-1979,* (Gweru: Mambo Press, 1983). There are quite a few copies of the original speech filed away in the ZANU Archive, Box of Women's Affairs.

3. See Christine Qunta, ed., *Women in Southern Africa,* (London: Allison and Busby, 1987), "Interviews with Teurai Ropa Nhongo and Ntombelenga Takawira," pp.146-57.

4. "Women Indispensable in Struggle," in *Zimbabwe People's Voice*, March 17, 1979.

5. Amina Mama, "Sheroes and Villains: Conceptualizing Colonial and Contemporary Violence Against Women in Africa," in Jacqui Alexander and Chandra Talpade Mohanty, eds., *Feminist Genealogies, Colonial Legacies, Democratic Futures*, (New York and London: Routledge, 1997), p. 54.

6. Jan Jindy Pettman, *Worlding Women: A Feminist International Politics*, (St. Leonards: Allen and Unwin, 1996), p. 54.

7. See Partha Chatterjee, *Nationalist Thought and the Colonial World: A Derivative Discourse?* (London: Zed Books, 1986), pp. 40-1.

8. See Miranda Davies, ed., *Third World - Second Sex: Women's Struggles and National Liberation: Third World Women Speak Out*; Alexis DeVeaux, "Zimbabwe Woman Fire!" p. 111: Jan Jindy Pettman, *Worlding Women: A Feminist International Politics,* (NSW: Allen and Unwin, 1996); Also see Sharon Macdonald, "Drawing the Lines - Gender, Peace, and War: An Introduction," p.10.

9. Angeline Shenje-Peyton, "Balancing Gender, Equality, and Cultural Identity: Marriage Payments in Postcolonial Zimbabwe," in *Harvard Human Rights Journal*, vol.9, 1997, p.115.

10. Richard Lapchick and Stephanie Urdang, *Oppression and Resistance: The Struggle of Women in Southern Africa,* based on materials prepared for the world conference of the United Nations Decade for Women Copenhagen, 1980, (Westport: Greenwood Press, 1982).

11. In 1995, fifteen years after independence, Terence Ranger and Ngwabi Bhebe argued that there have not been any "satisfactory gendered accounts of the war and its aftermath." See Ngwabi Bhebe and Terence Ranger eds., *Soldiers in Zimbabwe's Liberation War*, p.5; and Ngwabi Bhebe and Terence Ranger, *Society in Zimbabwe's Liberation War*.

12. Stephanie Urdang, *Fighting Two Colonialisms: Women in Guinea-Bissau,* (New York and London: Monthly Review Press, 1979), p. 17. In Guinea-Bissau Amilcar Cabral promoted the equality of women with men in the struggle for national liberation from Portuguese colonization, yet he realized it was not necessary to train women specifically for guerilla warfare because there was

enough men. Women's involvement was based on traditional gender roles supporting men, as nurses, teachers, and cooks.

13. Samora Machel, (the late president of Mozambique), *Sowing the Seeds of Revolution*, (Harare: Zimbabwe Publishing House, 1981), p.20: Also see Stephanie Urdang, *And Still They Dance: Women, War and the Struggle for Change in Mozambique*, (London: Earthscan, 1989).

14. Robert Mugabe, "Message to the World Conference of the United Nations Decade of Women," delivered by Sally Mugabe, Copenhagen July 1980, cited in Richard Lapchick and Stephanie Urdang, *Oppression and Resistance: The Struggle of Women in Southern Africa*, p. 108.

15. Kathy Bond-Stewart, *Independence Is Not Only for One Sex*, (Harare: Zimbabwe Publishing House, 1987); Elinor Batezat, et al., "Women and Independence: The Heritage and the Struggle," in Colin Stoneman ed., *Zimbabwe's Prospects: Issues of Race, Class, State, and Capital in Southern Africa*, (London: MacMillan, 1988), pp.153-73.

16. Both Stephanie Urdang's study on Mozambique and Cleaver and Wallace's study on women in Namibia focus on the effects of war on women in general, and on how women cope during crisis. Both studies admit that only limited numbers of women became active guerilla fighters, hence their research has not focused specifically on women guerilla fighters, but women in general. See Stephanie Urdang, *And Still They Dance: Women, War and the Struggle for Change in Mozambique*; and see Tessa Cleaver and Marion Wallace, *Namibia Women in War*, (London: Zed Books, 1990).

17. See Stephanie Urdang, *And Still They Dance: Women, War and the Struggle for Change in Mozambique*; Tessa Cleaver and Marion Wallace, *Namibia Women in War*; Miranda Davies, ed., *Third World - Second Sex: Women's Struggles and National Liberation: Third World Women Speak Out*.

18. Richard Lapchick and Stephanie Urdang, have argued that Zimbabwean women's roles were "responsible for the increased acceptance of women as equals in all areas by Zimbabwean men." However, their research published in 1982 pre-empts that any gains made for women in the early independence excitement would be continued. See Richard Lapchick and Stephanie Urdang, *Oppression and Resistance: The Struggle of Women in Southern Africa*, (Westport: Greenwood Press, 1982). While a Ministry of Women's Affairs was established in 1980, it was subsumed into various other ministries and portfolios by the early 1990s. Changes to the legal status of women under the Legal Age of Majority Act, which gave all people over eighteen years of age the right to vote etc., are currently under threat in Zimbabwe. Some parliamentarians want to change the age for women's legal age of majority to twenty-one years. The Zimbabwe Women's Resource Centre and Network is protesting these moves (March 1998).

19. For example, the SWAPO poster of a woman with a gun over her shoulder and a baby on her back. See ibid, p.55.

20. Stephanie Urdang, *And Still They Dance: Women, War, and the Struggle for Change in Mozambique*, p. 95.

21. Nira Yuval-Davis and Floya Anthias, ed., *Women-Nation-State*, (London: MacMillan, 1987), p.7, cited in Anne McClintock *Imperial Leather: Race, Gender, and Sexuality in the Colonial Conquest*, (New York and London: Routledge, 1995), p.355.
22. Stephanie Urdang, *And Still They Dance: Women, War, and the Struggle for Change in Mozambique*, cited in Amina Mama, "Sheroes and Villains: Conceptualizing Colonial and Contemporary Violence Against Women in Africa," p. 54.
23. Cynthia Enloe, *Does Khaki Become You? The Militarisation of Women's Lives*, (London: Pluto Press, 1983), p. 160.
24. Amina Mama, "Sheroes and Villains: Conceptualizing Colonial and Contemporary Violence Against Women in Africa," p. 53.
25. Cynthia Enloe, *Does Khaki Become You? The Militarization of Women's Lives*, p. 161.
26. Ibid, p. 165.
27. Amina Mama, "Sheroes and Villains: Conceptualizing Colonial and Contemporary Violence Against Women in Africa," p. 54.
28. Sita Ranchod-Nilsson, "This Too is a Way of Fighting: Rural Women's Participation in Zimbabwe's Liberation War."
29. See Tanya Lyons, "Guerilla Girls and Women in the Zimbabwean National Liberation War," in Jean Allman and Susan Geiger, eds., *Women and African Colonial History*, (Indiana University Press, in press).
30. Zimbabwe Women's Bureau, *Black Women in Zimbabwe*, (1981), p. 41.
31. Ibid.
32. Stephanie Urdang, *And Still They Dance:Women, War and the Struggle for Change in Mozambique*, p.21.
33. Interview with Joyce Mujuru, Harare, August, 1996. During the struggle Joyce Mujuru was widely known as Teurai Ropa (a fighting name meaning "spill blood").
34. *The Zimbabwe Review,* offers the reports of the Commission of the conference, (see numbers 1-8), but it does not offer any analysis of women in Zimbabwe. The review does show that the conference supported Zimbabwe's struggle for national independence, *The Zimbabwe Review,* 4:6, 1975.
35. Interview with Joyce Mujuru, Harare, August, 1996
36. See Kate McCalman, (Co-ordinator and Compiler), "We Carry a Heavy Load: Rural Women in Zimbabwe Speak Out," Report of a Survey Carried out by the Zimbabwe Women's Bureau, December 1981.
37. "Women Indispensable in Struggle," in *Zimbabwe People's Voice*, March 17, 1979.
38. "The Role of the Zimbabwe Women in the Liberation Struggle," *Zimbabwe People's Voice*, ZANU PF (UK Edition), 1979, pp. 10-12.
39. Ibid.
40. Ibid.
41. Robert Mugabe, *Our War of Liberation*, (Gweru: Mambo Press, 1983), p. 81.
42. Lenin and Mao, cited in ibid, pp. 81-2.

43. Robert Mugabe, ibid, p. 81.

44. Ho Chi Minh cited in ibid, p. 83.

45. Samora Machel cited in ibid, p. 85.

46. Robert Mugabe, ibid, p. 85.

47. ZANU Archives Women's Affairs File: *The Role of Women Before and After Liberation*, by the ZANU Department of Women's Affairs, no date supplied, but likely to be in 1977 due to ZIPA references. The ZANU Archives located on the first floor of ZANU(PF) Headquarters in Harare houses many documents from the liberation war. Some documents specifically relating to women's issues had been filed in one box titled "Women's Affairs." Other documents related to women's issues were scattered throughout the archives, but were difficult to access. Access to the archives is restricted, but I was kindly granted permission by Colonel Munemo and ZANU(PF) senior archivists.

48. Ibid.

49. Zimbabwe Women's Bureau, *Black Women in Zimbabwe*, 1981, p.41.

50. Ibid, p.14.

51. There was a good season in sight when the *Feminist Studies Centre* in Harare was established in 1995, and the *Southern African Feminist Review (SAFERE)* was produced, signaling critical debate on women's issues in Zimbabwe. However, both have since folded due to political pressure. The government closed the Feminist Studies Centre because it had not registered its name properly, objecting to the name "Feminist," and its policy that men could only come if they were invited. All things being equal, that policy went against equal opportunities legislation. The *Southern African Feminist Review* (SAFERE) had also run out of funds after four editions in 1995 and 1996.

52. Mabel Mudondo "The Emancipation of Women and Their Role Towards Liberation Struggles," in *Zimbabwe News*, 10:1, January/February, 1978, p. 24.

53. Ibid.

54. Ibid.

55. Ibid.

56. The debate continued on to discuss whether to get simple or philosophical books. See ZANU Archives Women's Affairs File: ZANU Defence Secretariat, Rally held at operational base on July 20, 1978 - Pfutskeke Base. Present at the rally were Teurai Ropa Nhongo plus thirty-six female comrades, six general staff and Field Commander E. Mhuru.

57. The ZANU Archives in Harare holds hundreds of war books, manuals, propaganda materials, magazines, exercise books used by cadres in their political education, and some records of participation. However, these documents have yet to be catalogued and remain piled two meters deep behind (mostly locked) doors, the only visitors being moths and other paper-eating bugs. I would like to thank the Archives staff for even attempting to help me sort through the top layers of the material.

58. Interview with Nyarai, Harare, September, 1996.

59. Ibid.

60. Interview with Sekai, Harare, September, 1996.
61. Ibid.
62. Interview with Teresa, Harare, September, 1996.
63. Interviews with Rudo, Harare, September, 1996.
64. Ibid.
65. Interview with Freedom Nyamubaya, Marondera, October, 1996. Nyamubaya is a published author of short stories and poems and now works for an NGO in Zimbabwe. She is an outspoken woman ex-combatant.
66. Interview with Joyce Mujuru, Harare, August, 1996.
67. "Interview with Teurai Ropa Nhongo, Minister of Youth Sport and Recreation (age twenty-five years)," in Zimbabwe Women's Bureau, *Black Women in Zimbabwe*, 1981.
68. Zimbabwe Women's Bureau, *Black Women in Zimbabwe*, 1981, p.41.
69. Ibid.
70. "Opening Address by Canaan Banana, president of Zimbabwe," *Report of the Workshop on the Role of Women in Social, Economic, and Cultural Reconstruction of Zimbabwe,* Harare, February 22 - March 4, 1982, organized by Pan-African Institute for Development East and Southern Africa, in collaboration with the Ministry of Community Development and Women's Affairs.
71. Ibid.
72. "Sex Barriers Have Stood Too Long," in *The Sunday Mail* (Harare), October 11, 1981.
73. ZANU(PF), "The Right of Women to Equality with Men," *ZANU(PF) 1980 Election Manifesto*, (Maputo: Zimbabwe Printing and Publishing House, 1980). Furthermore, Naomi Nhiwatiwa explained the concept of equal pay for equal work in her idea of "functional equality" at a conference in Mozambique where ZANU was "assess[ing] and promot[ing] the role of ZANU women in the national liberation struggle." She said that a 'working program' had been worked out. "Functional Equality is something like this: a woman decides what she wants to become and she will still get the same treatment, she will be considered equal. For example, if a woman should decide that she really enjoys getting pregnant, having babies, taking care of the house and the children, and another woman decides that she wants to be the secretary of education, or the administrator of the hospital ... they are both contributing to the development and growth of Zimbabwe." See Naomi Nhiwatiwa "Interview," with an Introduction by Carol B. Thompson, in *Women's Studies International Forum*, 5: 3-4, 1982, p. 248.
74. Joyce "Teurai Ropa" (Nhongo) Mujuru, then the Minister for Information, Posts and Telecommunications, stated that no activities have been lost by the incorporation of Women's Affairs in National Affairs. Her ministry was subsumed in 1991 by the Ministry of National Affairs and Cooperative Development. In 1997, there was still a Women's Affairs Department within this but it is largely ineffective. A report by Zimbabwe Women Lawyers pointed out that women's voices are not being heard in government and their attempts

at representation are not being taken seriously. A bill was read in parliament on March 4, 1997 making changes to the inheritance and marriage acts. None of the comments contributed by women's organizations were taken into account by the parliamentarian introducing the bill, which effectively reduces women's rights within marriage and upon the death of her husband. See *The Herald*, Monday, March 10, 1997, p.1.

75. In 1995 seventeen out of 150 parliamentarians were women; there were no women in the twenty-nine cabinet posts; two women out of thirty-one ambassadors; one woman of twenty-two mayors; two women out of twenty-one town clerks; five women out of a forty member university council: Ciru Getecha and Jesimen Chipika eds., *Zimbabwe Women's Voices*, p. 66.

76. "Be Realistic. Mrs. Nhongo Tells Women," the *Sunday Mail* (Harare), November 15, 1981, p.2.

77. ZANU Archives Women's Affairs File: "The Role of Women Before and After Liberation."

78. "The Policies and Programmes of ZANU(PF), A Proud Record of Achievement," in *Zimbabwe News*, 16:5, May/June, 1985, p. 14.

PART TWO:
A WOMAN'S PLACE IS IN THE STRUGGLE

Chapter Four

Gender in the Struggle

Women in History - The First Chimurenga

A gendered analysis of Zimbabwean history reveals what is under the skirts of the history of the nationalist struggle. Colonized by the British in the 1890s Zimbabwe was then called Rhodesia, after Cecil Rhodes who led the initial pioneer column into the region for settlement. The name *Zimbabwe* literally meaning house of stone replaced the colonial name of *Rhodesia* at independence in 1980. The history of resistance and struggle from Rhodesia to Zimbabwe has been dealt with elsewhere.[1] Yet, it is important to acknowledge, as Elizabeth Schmidt does, that *woman* as a subject has been rendered invisible by the historiographies of Rhodesia. For example, Hartmann, a Jesuit priest was told by the Shona Chief Chipanga in 1891:

> "Women are not counted." He then took a handful of dust from the ground and said, "That is the woman." Hartmann concluded that among the Shona, "Women are regarded as almost nonexistent."[2]

While Schmidt acknowledges the "exaggeration" of Hartman's conclusion, it illustrates how women were virtually nonexistent, or at least of a lower ranking than men, according to the men. Women were not considered necessary to count as members of the Ndebele elder's kraal, and, other than appearing as statistics in the Europeans' death toll (that is, white women only are mentioned), other women barely get a mention.

Ranger's research illustrates how women can be written out of a history in which they were involved. His thesis on the First *Chimurenga* against colonial domination in Rhodesia offers detailed accounts based on the written evidence surviving from that time, and also from some oral histories, where available.[3] However, as he acknowledges, "there is no literature of reminiscence from the African side as there is from the white."[4] That is, in relation to the Shona uprising, "It is a story, which has not been fully told," hence Ranger devotes quite a few pages to examining this. However, he is constrained in his examination by the predominance of European documents. Africans did not record these events on paper, and only oral histories survived, kept within families or, if recorded, by missionaries.

There is a need to read between the lines of the dominant "white" discourse even to attempt to imagine what the Africans' reminiscences might have been. As Ranger does this, however, his analyses often assume that the African is male.[5] Sylvester notes that "Ranger does not emphasize the point that women comprise approximately 70 percent of the permanent rural population in Zimbabwe."[6] This is surprising given that he discusses the peasantry and how it "gradually developed a class project to resist what it saw as state efforts to eliminate the peasant option,"[7] by alienating African people from their land. Ranger

> does not conceptualize "women peasants" at all, perhaps because he does not query the gendered content of policies that preserved industrial jobs for true "workers," understood as "men." It was the rural "woman" who maintained home fires and crops, but who, under Rhodesian law, was a minor for life - unable to negotiate credit, apply for a passport alone, or own property aside from household pots and pans.[8]

Norma Kriger also criticizes Ranger for his lack of gendered and generational analysis. Ranger's "*Peasant Consciousness*, by definition, refers to the peasants' understanding of their grievances as a class, which relate to how white farmers and the state undermine their commitment to agricultural production."[9] There is no room for concepts such as "generation, gender, or other factors internal to the peasantry or inter-African class conflicts to become important."[10]

However, if in his earlier works, Ranger does not offer gendered analyses, he does mention the names and details of important women in

Zimbabwean history, which could only benefit from further analysis.[11] In 1981, Ranger did write specifically on women in the Makoni District. While this piece of work remains unpublished it is nonetheless an important contribution to Zimbabwe's gendered history. In his introduction he states almost apologetically, that

> the research was not specifically directed towards the history of women; its intention was rather to achieve a "total" history of a Zimbabwean district under colonialism ... had I been working specifically on the history of women I should have interviewed many more female informants and sought to generate evidence particularly relevant to the experience of women.[12]

Contrary to Sylvester's claims, Ranger also acknowledges that women formed the majority of the agrarian work force in Makoni, but that men still dominated leadership of nationalist parties. Despite these gendered lacunae in Ranger's work, his *Revolt in Southern Rhodesia* remains an authoritative text on that period of Zimbabwean history.[13]

Elizabeth Schmidt criticizes the majority of histories of Zimbabwe and Rhodesia for failing to appreciate the importance of women, household dynamics, and gender relations. Schmidt argues that it is not simply that "half the story is left untold":

> Gender relations within the household are among the most fundamental social relations; they are a crucial explanatory factor in any society. Unless we understand the interrelations between women and men, we cannot fully understand the structure of a given society, its history, political and economic systems, or ideology.[14]

The importance of going over the 1896-97 uprisings through Schmidt's gendered analysis is to show how historiography and official discourse have easily excluded women from the *active* political and military arena.[15] Yet, African women were involved in military operations; the evidence of their actions remains mostly obscured by masculine versions of history. Why women were involved in the early anticolonial activities cannot be dealt with adequately here, where the aim is to contextualize the representations of women in the history of Zimbabwe in order to facilitate understanding of the women ex-combatants involved in the more recent anticolonial struggles.

Schmidt argues that white domination in Rhodesia in 1896 was severe enough, in some cases, for challenges to be made to "traditional" gender roles. Shona women's experiences were influenced by the British South Africa Company's (BSAC) occupation of Mashonaland in 1890. The raids on land, cattle, and labor once performed by the neighboring Ndebele just continued under a different name and "women and children continued to be pawns of the new situation."[16] Women were used for bargaining power either as hostages or as labor commodities by the colonists. Schmidt illustrates how some women became involved in anticolonial action when the BSAC ordered the slaughter of most of the African-owned cattle in an attempt to stamp out Rinderpest cattle disease. The killing appeared to be indiscriminate, leading to resentment and misunderstandings. This was magnified when 150 cattle at the Chishawasha mission run by the Jesuits were isolated and managed to escape the disease and hence the slaughter. Not surprisingly the mission was attacked in 1896 as it appeared unfair that they should have cattle when no one else did. In this situation women became active in ways that challenged their traditional gender roles. The *Zambesi Mission Records*, records that

> a large number of women were seen driving away the mission cattle, which had been grazing at the foot of a hill close by. The missionaries fired "a few shots" at the women, forcing them to flee. Although they left "the bulk of the herd behind," they managed to drive away about forty head of cattle.[17]

Rounding up cattle constituted a challenge to their traditional gender roles and this activity became known as a "military action" according to Schmidt because

> women's participation in this military operation was particularly significant for two reasons. First, in Shona society, men were customarily considered the warriors ... to conduct war and raid for cattle and women. Women, on the other hand, were expected to remain at the homestead.... Second ... As the symbol of male wealth and status, representative of women in the bride-wealth transaction, cattle were not to be handled by women.[18]

Therefore, women were involved in a major challenge to traditional gender roles in this "military" operation. The severity of colonial policies influenced these changes.

In the white retaliation to these actions however, women were removed from their place as actors in the discourse and became discursive pawns. The BSAC felt it necessary to destroy *kraals*, capture any remaining cattle, sheep, goats, and even some "girls."[19] In one case, four women were captured and their men were killed, but the women were unable to provide any information to the police about the uprisings.[20] Did they simply not know, or were they resisting? What can be seen from these examples is that women were being used as hostages and pawns by the missionaries and colonial officials, despite their "civilizing" objections to the Shona and Ndebele practice of hostage taking. The women and children were also captured in order to force the rebels to surrender. In order to encourage other rebels to surrender, the women and children were usually returned to their homes safely, after their husbands' surrender.[21]

Schmidt points out that while we might consider the captured women to be simply pawns or passive victims of some male-defined war, in fact, these women used strategies to defy their captors and continue the war against them. Evidence recorded in the Jesuit archives supports this case.[22] Some women who were captured did make attempts to escape, though many failed. Some women also made the very controversial move to marry members of the native contingent who were supposed to be guarding them. However, "[i]t is not clear whether the female prisoners married their captors of their own free will."[23] Some women may have assumed it was expected of them, as part of the continuation of the old practice of capturing women in war to become wives and free labor. The women may have also worked out that they could buy their freedom by marrying these men, who were in a position to ask for their freedom. Marrying the guards may have seemed like a better option than the grim fate of being a prisoner and having to work for the missionaries.[24]

However, no matter what the women's strategies in negotiating their survival, or what their desires were, they were nonetheless still "pawns in a dispute between powerful males."[25] For example, if the women were already married, the chief Native Commissioner Taberer had the power to simply send them back to their husbands, in order not to "antagonize" the chiefs and create any unnecessary "disturbances," as long as the chiefs surrendered themselves to secure this release.[26] Thus, despite normative gender roles being "shattered" in some instances during the 1896-97 uprisings in Rhodesia, "most women experienced vulnerabilities similar to those in previous armed conflicts."[27]

Women were thus clearly involved in the history of the 1896-97 uprisings. The rebellion did not come to a final close until the inspiration for resistance ended. This occurred in March 1898 with the hanging of two of the most popular and significant spirit mediums, Kaguvi and Nehanda. Their bodies were buried in secret graves to prevent the resurrection of their bones and spirits.[28] When the uprisings of 1896 and 1897 were finally crushed 450 whites had been killed and 189 injured; 372 of the dead were settlers, including women and children. The dead amounted to 10 percent of the settler population at that time. "No one knows how many Africans perished."[29] The First *Chimurenga* had failed. Or had it? As we will see below, the recent links made between the past and the present, recreates it as the beginnings of nationalist struggle, rather than a failed attempt at rebellion.

Nehanda

During the 1950s and the nationalist political stage of the Second *Chimurenga*, rhetorical links were made to the First *Chimurenga* in order to facilitate the new struggle against colonialism. Ranger wrote in 1979 that "the risings of 1896 and 1897 ... have become an essential part of the consciousness of the liberation movements."[30] Many writers of fiction in Zimbabwe since the 1970s have drawn upon the 1896-97 uprisings as inspiration for their work.[31] Of particular interest here is the representations of Nehanda, who was central to the consciousness raising efforts of nationalists.[32] Ranger has argued:

> During the Second *Chimurenga* it is well known that great use was made of Nehanda's heroic role in 1896; nationalist poems and guerilla songs were composed about her; and living mediums of Nehanda were used to legitimate the guerilla cause. By the end of the war, the idea of Nehanda as warrior ancestor spirit was very widespread in Zimbabwe's rural areas as well as in cultural nationalist circles.[33]

In Zimbabwean traditional religion and culture spirit mediums are the link between the living and the dead, and during the 1896-97 uprisings in Rhodesia they provided advice, guidance, and council to the people in relation to matters of war. For example, Nehanda[34] insisted that no one should touch anything belonging to the Europeans as this would cause defeat for the Africans. Furthermore, to give the people courage to fight against the colonizers the spirit medium said "During the rebellion the power of the spirits rendered the white bullets useless and ineffective [and thus] [n]ot many Africans were killed in the actual fighting."[35]

Nehanda was "not representative of female mediums in general,"[36] but she was the most well known female *mhondoro* (royal ancestor). Symbolizing the connections made by nationalists between the First *Chimurenga* and Second *Chimurenga* Kwanele Ona Jirira has stated that "Nehanda was a central political figure in the ... First *Chimurenga* war, and her legend became a solid basis for female combatants to struggle for inclusion in the armed struggle for the national liberation, as cadres in their own right."[37] Yet David Beach has offered the explanation that the medium of Nehanda was in fact an "ordinary woman, unjustly accused," although she could still become a national heroine.[38] An anthropological account of spirit mediums in Zimbabwe and their relationship to liberation wars and guerilla fighters has been offered at some length by David Lan in his book *Guns and Rain: Guerillas and Spirit Mediums in Zimbabwe*.[39] Lan describes the ancestral links of Nehanda and how she usually possesses female spirit mediums. Reiterating these spiritual and historical details is unnecessary here, apart from providing details of her activities in the 1896-97 uprisings, and her influence during the 1970s.

The spirit medium of Nehanda named Charwe played a leading role in the First *Chimurenga* 1896-97. Terence Ranger has documented some of the correspondence regarding Nehanda at the time of these rebellions. Native Commissioner Campbell argued in June 1896 that before the uprisings the spirit medium of Nehanda was considered "insignificant."[40] Shona belief in her and other *mhondoros* had apparently waned since the arrival of the white man. But in his report of January 1896, he wrote that

Nianda [sic] has been constantly spoken of in my hearing ever since ... 1890 by the Mashonas. At the present moment Nianda is the most powerful wizard in Mashonaland and has the power of ordering all the people who rose lately and her orders would in every case be obeyed.[41]

For the two years before the native commissioner's report the Nehanda medium had allegedly been busy "mobilising and sustaining the rising in central Mashonaland,"[42] along with other mediums. According to Ranger, the Nehanda medium was a dominating "influence" within the Mazoe area of Mashonaland, and the native commissioner feared that Nehanda "would be far more dangerous to the peace of the country than even Kagubi would be."[43] Kagubi was a *mhondoro* that usually possessed male spirit mediums. David Lan describes Nehanda as "a major leader of the 1896 rebellions ... [and] when the rebellion failed she was amongst the last of the leaders to be captured."[44] In a more feminist analysis, Christine Sylvester argued that Nehanda was actually an adviser to local rebels in 1896-97.[45] Others have also acknowledged her as a military adviser. In 1985 a magazine published in Zimbabwe detailed her alleged exploits:

Nehanda established her headquarters at Husaka in the Mazowe district. It was an impregnable mountain fortress, inaccessible except through narrow and dangerous passages and self-sufficient in water and food. The various codes to be used in the war were worked out and the targets to be attacked identified.[46]

By ascribing military language to the method and actions of a spirit medium, Nehanda was also credited with inciting violence, even if she was not directly involved:

Disciplinary codes were laid down and messages were passed by runners at night between the leaders' strongholds in an effort to coordinate the onslaught. The First Chimurenga War started in Matabeleland in March 1896 and spread to Mashonaland in June. Nehanda is said to have accompanied her forces to the actions on some occasion, but it is not known whether she actually took part in fighting. Even if she did not fight, her presence must have provided her forces with important motivation.[47]

Here, Nehanda is credited with military leadership and skills, and yet David

Martin and Phyllis Johnson's account of the Zimbabwean struggle describes her as "a frail woman."[48]

David Beach's account of the historical evidence available that supports Nehanda's actions calls into question the heroic agency of the medium herself. His research challenges the feminist and nationalist constructions of Nehanda as a military adviser and argues that she was just an ordinary woman unjustly accused of murder. She was "neither a supreme leader nor a helpless pawn." She was just "gradually caught up in a major historical event that was more or less beyond her control."[49] The following account of Nehanda might shed more details on these contradictory representations.

According to the historical records Nehanda "was directly responsible for the death of Pollard, the native commissioner of the Mazoe [sic] area at the outbreak of the rising."[50] Pollard was taken to her and she spoke to him, then she ordered [her assistant] *Wata* to kill him some way off so they could not smell the body. As Beach has pointed out, Charwe denied having ordered his death. She stated in her trial for Pollard's murder, "If I had sent him [Wata] I would own up to it. I have nothing more to say ... I did not give the order. Why should I hide it if I did?"[51] Hence, as Beach claims there is considerable doubt as to the involvement of Nehanda in Pollard's death.

When the BSAC finally got the upper hand on the uprisings Nehanda proved to be difficult to catch. Her counterpart the Kagubi medium, Gumporeshumba, surrendered on October 27, 1897. All but four of his wives had been taken hostage by the whites leaving him with little choice. Nehanda, not having any wives to worry about, was "determined not to surrender,"[52] but was eventually captured in December by Native Commissioner Kenny's police:

Nehanda was charged with the murder of Pollard, and Kagubi was charged with the murder of an African policeman. Both were found guilty and sentenced to be hanged. On the day of the hanging Kagubi resisted being converted to Christianity by Father Richartz, but was eventually persuaded to convert by the daughter of another medium, who had studied at the Chishawasha mission school where Father Richartz had been. The Kagubi medium broke down and cried when he was told the day had come to be hanged. However, the Nehanda medium "began to dance, to laugh and talk so that the warders were obliged to tie her hands and watch her continually, as she threatened to kill herself."[53] She refused conversion to Christianity, and when they took her out to the hanging platform, [h]er cries and resistance when she was taken up the ladder, the screaming and yelling on the scaffold disturbed Kagubi [who was held below] ... till the noisy opening of the trapdoor on which she stood, followed by the heavy thud of her body as it fell made an end to the interruption.[54]

The interruption was of Kagubi's conversion. He went quietly to the gallows. Even in the *BSAC Report* it was written that "Nyanda [sic] went to her death at the gallows with courage".[55] (See Plate 2)

Plate 2: "The Capture of Kagubi and the "Witch" Nyanda," from *The '96 Rebellions: The British South Africa Company Reports on the Native Disturbances in Rhodesia 1896-97*, Books of Rhodesia, Bulawayo, 1975.

Yet, as Beach has pointed out:

[A]lthough it can be argued that the "hysteria," dancing, laughing, and so forth that she displayed before, during, and after the trial, right up to her death, were due to the fact that she was a spirit medium, neither the Kaguvi nor the Choshata mediums behaved like this, and her behavior can also be seen as the reaction of an innocent woman surrounded by men who were united by a desire to see her hanged.[56]

Is Charwe still the "frail woman" Martin and Johnson describe, possessed or not possessed by a spirit? Whether she ordered the killing of Pollard or not, her actions hardly seem compatible with that of a frail woman. Beach argues that

> Charwe was obviously in favor of the Chimurenga but was no more influential than ... any of the other Mazowe Valley leaders in its initial stages, and the evidence for her playing an exceptional role after that - except in Rhodesian imagination - is not very strong. On that basis, she would not really merit the attention that she gets today.[57]

Martin and Johnson's account could be linked to the later denial (explained below) by the nationalist parties of the importance of spirit mediums in the success of the liberation war if success is only to mean appeasing the spiritual beliefs of the cadres.

Eighty years later, in 1976, a team of ZANU cadres under detention in Lusaka produced a political handbook, which recognized the power of Nehanda to inspire the recruitment of women soldiers. They stated:

> Now the wind of change is blurring in [women's] favor and there is no reason why they should not be inspired by *Mbuya Nehanda*, one of the best-known leaders of the First Chimurenga war of resistance from 1896-98. She played a major role in the organization of that war of resistance. She refused to give in to the colonialists and was finally executed by firing squad in what is now known as Salisbury Maximum Prison, in 1898, together with other prominent leaders.[58]

In 1978 Nehanda's name was invoked for revolutionary purposes that were construed as part of women's liberation movements. Teurai Ropa, the head of the Department of Women's Affairs in ZANU stated that

> [w]e, the Zimbabwean women in struggle, are the heirs of *Mbuya Nehanda*, that revolutionary heroine, who inspires every Zimbabwean woman with feelings of great patriotism. *Mbuya Nehanda* was an exemplary freedom fighter during the First Chimurenga. She fought gallantly and refused to give into the

colonialists ... Her exemplary heroism is the spirit that guides every revolutionary Zimbabwean.[59]

Teurai Ropa offers that Nehanda,

affectionately referred to as *Ambuya* (literally *grandmother*), in recognition of her social role as a religious leader, was everything that a true ZANLA-revolutionary must be [and] emulate.... Comrade Nehanda taught Zimbabweans ... that men and women are truly equal and inseparable partners in the struggle for national liberation, as well as in the postwar period of national reconstruction and development.[60]

Basing equality between men and women on the actions and representations of one woman in Zimbabwean history is truly remarkable. Nonetheless, this one woman was respected by many Zimbabweans. As the president of the ZANU revolutionary liberation party, Robert Mugabe argued in 1979 at the first Women's Seminar in Xai Xai, Mozambique, toward the end of the Second *Chimurenga*

Nehanda's importance is unquestionable.... In the early 1970s during the Second Chimurenga War one of her mediums went across the border into Mozambique, joining the ZANLA forces - at their request, which speaks for itself. Women played an important role in the Second Chimurenga and in this role they were inspired by Nehanda's example. Her example helped to overcome traditional prejudices about women's capabilities, and this enabled maximum utilization of human resources in armed struggle. That women today hold top positions in government and its various arms is a logical consequence of the efforts of the woman fighter now justly revered as Mbuya (mother) Nehanda.[61]

He continued to praise Nehanda's role:

Nehanda was obviously a distinct and exceptional character who rose to revolutionary ascendancy, not by mere display of leadership qualities such as her command, courage, bravery, and planning ability, but by principally her spiritual power as a spirit medium.[62]

Furthermore, Mugabe portrays Nehanda as a military genius and natural heroine:

> Nehanda Nyakasikana appears in our war annals of postcolonial Zimbabwe as the first war heroine and martyr. She did not lead just a battalion or a regional army but a national army in a national struggle for the overthrow of company rule and the recovery of the fatherland. She was defiant and obdurate to the end, refusing to compromise and subject herself to a process exacting her penance for a just liberation war she had proudly, valiantly, and justifiably fought but lost.[63]

During the Second *Chimurenga* the role of spirit mediums was as important as it was a hindrance to military tactics. Nonetheless, gauging from the emphasis placed on Nehanda and other mediums, it was necessary to represent her as a heroic historical figure to increase her importance in the eyes of the cadres and masses. Teurai Ropa confirmed that

> ZANLA women are proud to follow in the footsteps of Comrade Nehanda Nyakasikana who, together with her male comrades, led the armed struggle in 1896-1897. The fact that she was hanged at the end of 1897 shows conclusively that she was a mortal foe of the colonialist regime. It also shows that the colonialist enemy does not discriminate between men and women.[64]

On this platform Teurai Ropa was successfully able to argue that men and women were oppressed by both the colonial administration and Ian Smith's white minority regime, and both men and women were fighting equally to liberate Zimbabwe from it. The need to have women rallying behind the revolutionary struggle was strong, and the need to utilize the maximum amount of human resources available for the struggle was equally strong.

Janice McLaughlin, who argued that Catholic missionaries played a significant role in the struggle, described how the spirit medium of Nehanda was protected by ZANLA forces. In 1973 Rex Nhongo (now Solomon Mujuru), the commander of Nehanda Sector apparently

> gave the orders to rescue the medium of Nehanda and take her to Mozambique when it appeared that the Rhodesian authorities would

arrest her as they had arrested the medium of Chiwawa in February in 1973. This reinforced the view that ZANLA and the mediums were one.[65]

Nhongo argued that mediums were useful to instill discipline amongst the ranks, especially in relation to personal conduct between men and women, and also about where to go, when and what to eat and what to do.

However, while the spirit of Nehanda was invoked to encourage people to fight, especially women, there was some contention among the ZANU nationalists about mediums and religion, especially around the time of the Zimbabwe People's Army (ZIPA) between 1975 and 1977. McLaughlin points out that in 1976 ZIPA shifted "away from close relations with mediums" for pragmatic rather than ideological reasons because

the Rhodesians, aware of ZANLA's links with mediums, were using them to lure guerillas to their deaths. Some of the ZIPA ex-combatants claim that the Rhodesians placed false mediums in the border areas, who would call the guerillas to meetings where they were ambushed by Rhodesian forces. The ZIPA leaders reacted by banning all contact with mediums.[66]

Here we see that it was not just the medium of Nehanda that was important but other mediums too.

Nonetheless, it was under ZIPA command that the remains of the medium of Nehanda were buried during the Second *Chimurenga*. According to one ZIPA leader, the spirit medium of Nehanda was in Chifombo Camp in Zambia. When she died (she was an old woman) her remains would have had to be buried in Zimbabwe or the war would have been "in trouble." However, she was buried near the border on the Mozambican side near Lake Cabora Bassa because it was too dangerous to take her into Zimbabwe. In 1976, ZIPA was requested by other mediums to rebury her in Zimbabwe. Many of the soldiers in ZIPA at the time were from the Northeast of Zimbabwe and were "very traditional," placing much importance on appeasing their ancestors. Hence, ZIPA ordered that the reburial be allowed.

Two spirit mediums were chosen to retrieve the bones for reburial. To organize the transport, these two mediums had to be disguised as soldiers who were on a mission to collect some guns, because the

Mozambican Frelimo forces, who controlled the transport, would not have allowed spirit mediums to go through. For example, one Frelimo soldier had told the ZIPA leader that he himself had killed four mediums. Religion was not promoted by the revolutionary Marxist rhetoric. Frelimo provided the transport for these "soldiers," but the mediums could not get back into Zimbabwe, due to floods, and they became lost somewhere near Cabora Bassa Lake. Instead of crossing the border, they decided to bury her bones on an island in Mozambique.[67] The ZIPA command had given the mediums the leeway and authority to do this and so they were happy to have the chance to rebury Nehanda with the proper rituals. However, her bones have still not been returned to Zimbabwe. There were many people opposed to mediums, as McLaughlin above has suggested, and when Frelimo found out what had happened they were not at all happy about it.[68]

The spirit of Nehanda was important during the Second *Chimurenga*. Even the Rhodesians, like the BSAC before them, were aware of her power, not necessarily as a witch or spirit medium but as a symbol of the Zimbabwean nation. In 1982 the *Zimbabwe News*, the mouthpiece of the ruling party ZANU, continued to discuss Nehanda as a revolutionary leader. As part of their history in the new Zimbabwe, the magazine stated:

> What some Zimbabweans may not be aware of is the tradition of resistance on which ZANLA forces of the 1970s built the fighting strategy that led to victory. The fighting cadres drew some of their inspiration and succour from the revolutionaries of the first Chimurenga war of 1896-97, more particularly from the exemplary leadership provided by the spirit medium Mbuya Nehanda Nyakasikana ... What is even more remarkable is that Mbuya Nehanda did not fight a one-man [sic] war but mobilized the entire nation in an effort to wrench the country from white settlers. In this she was supported by a host of fighting cadres and spirit mediums ... including Sekuru Kakubi [sic].[69]

The article concluded that Nehanda and Kakubi [sic] were "cool scientific revolutionaries who had studied the situation in colonial Rhodesia, concluded that colonization negated human freedom and dignity, and that this crass contradiction ought to be removed through armed struggle."[70] Re-reading the situation from a Marxist view has misrepresented the role of spirit mediums, but it has also reinscribed Nehanda as a symbol of the nation. In 1982, *Moto* Magazine stated that Nehanda and Kaguvi remain influential figures:

> Their great-grandchildren proudly display T-shirts depicting the national heroes of the "First Chimurenga." Pop singers singing their praises can be heard on the radio; hospitals and schools have been named after them.[71]

Nehanda, embodied by the female spirit medium Charwe, is remembered as a dominant influence during the uprisings of 1896-97, especially in the Mazowe area of Mashonaland and she has become a legend. During the Second *Chimurenga,* the spirit medium of Nehanda was considered a threat by the Rhodesian forces, who saw her ability to mobilize the masses; and she was important enough to the liberation forces to protect her and appease her spirit through traditional burial ceremonies. On two separate occasions, separated by nearly one hundred years, representations of Nehanda as a symbol of resistance and courage interrupted the dominant discourse of the colonial settlers and the BSAC, who found it difficult to capture and silence her rebelliousness, and the nationalist forces who had to compromise their revolutionary ideologies to cater to the importance of Nehanda's other spirit mediums.

Thus, understanding the history of Nehanda's role in the First *Chimurenga* and the way that it has been represented, provides a link to women's roles, experiences, and representations in the Second *Chimurenga.*

Women in the Nationalist Political Stage of the Second Chimurenga
The Second Chimurenga has been divided into two stages. The nationalist political stage (1950s - 1965) and the armed struggle stage (1965-1980). Women were significant actors during the nationalist political stage of the Second *Chimurenga*, but they have been effectively written out of mainstream nationalist history.[72] Again, it is important to understand women's motivations for political action in anticolonial struggle. Such research cannot be dealt with here adequately, and more detailed research in this area is required. Memories are fading, and opportunities to record oral histories are diminishing. To uncover and extract this information is an urgent task for historians. What is important here, though, is that women

did *act,* and their experiences, histories, and voices need to be heard. Without further research, and relying upon mainstream histories, their voices will remain silent. There is limited literature that represents women involved in male dominated nationalist events. Thus the following draws on what is recorded and published in Zimbabwean historiography.

African nationalism began to develop in the 1930s but was only established in the late 1940s and 1950s with the Southern Rhodesian African National Congress (SRANC) and City Youth League (CYL).[73] In 1960 the National Democratic Party (NDP) formed, but it was soon banned after thousands of women protested in the capital Salisbury. From the remnants of the NDP, the Zimbabwe African People's Union (ZAPU) formed, but later split into two factions in 1963, creating the Zimbabwe African National Union (ZANU). In 1965, after Ian Smith's Rhodesian Front announced the Unilateral Declaration of Independence (UDI) from Britain, these two nationalist parties resorted to the armed struggle.

Lapchick and Urdang have provided a brief overview of women's involvement in the early nationalist political stage of the struggle. They cite women's support in the 1948 general strike as the key to its success. Women's commitment to the struggle, they argue, was demonstrated when some women were arrested alongside men in 1959 when the Southern Rhodesia African National Congress (SRANC) was banned. However, they provide little detail of women's actual involvement in these events.[74]

Yet Zimbabwean women were actively involved in political action against colonialism and oppression. In most narratives of women's involvement in the nationalist movement accurate details of events, places, and women's actions are missing.[75] For example, the *Zimbabwe Review* reflecting on women's involvement during the early stages of the struggle, simply reported that

> [w]hen the women took up to struggle with their men they organised themselves into branches, districts and indeed into other cells according to the party structure. There is a department of the women's affairs in The Central Committee of our party. Women have taken such active part in the struggle that the enemy has sent many to jails and concentration camps.[76]

Yet, without the specific details of women's actions, their roles became homogenized as "supportive" to the male-led and male-dominated nationalist movement. For example, Robert Mugabe has described how women were mobilized *en masse.*

> During the days of the ANC [African National Congress], NDP [National Democratic Party], and in the earlier ZAPU [Zimbabwe African People's Union] period, the struggle was mainly in political form, consisting in regular mass meeting, [sic] occasional demonstrations, strikes and boycotts. Public rallies were always a successful feature when our women attended them in large numbers, chanting slogans and nationalist songs, ululating and dancing. This gave the meetings the necessary and rousing effect which boosted morale and gave the impetus to go on with the struggle until final victory.[77]

As the "cheerleaders" to men most women involved in these political actions did not rise to the top hierarchies of power. This has been explained by the fact that Zimbabwean women "were often too bone-wearily busy supporting their families to rise to early nationalist prominence."[78] Rudo Gaidzanwa has argued that the women who did become involved in the hierarchies of the nationalist movement were the wives of the (male) nationalists.[79]

1956 Bus Boycotts

However, women's involvement in Zimbabwean nationalism cannot be described simply by noting their cheerleading roles or their positions vis-à-vis men. The following account of a nationalist action in 1956 highlights a wider gender problem. The bus boycott was called in 1956 to protest against increased bus fares. During the bus boycott sixteen women were raped at the Carter Girls Hostel in Harare by a group of protesters.[80] The apparent motivation for raping these women was because they had broken solidarity and used the buses. Robert Blake reported that these women were seen as black "prostitutes" who could afford the bus fares and had to go to their jobs by bus. These "prostitutes" were charging £1 for their services, which was more than enough to cover bus fares.[81] A mother asked, "raping my daughter, is that the bus boycott?"[82] Brian Raftopoulos has argued that this boycott importantly highlights the *gendered* problems of the nationalist movements, and the rapes, signified problematic power relations between men and women in the movement.[83]

The 1956 bus boycotts can be seen as a precursor to women's contested locations within later nationalist actions in the 1960s and 1970s.

On the first day of the bus boycott the *African Daily News* reported that it was 90 percent effective in Harare, and 75 percent effective in Highfields. The boycott was orderly, but there were apparently

> one or two buses ... [which] contained a few old women on their way to a religious meeting. They were dressed in the uniform of the Church Women's Union. One man in the crowd remarked "its a pity that these women don't know we have a boycott on."[84]

Unable to win the support of everyone, the City Youth League blamed these old women for not understanding the reasons for boycotting. However, the boycott did not remain orderly for long. Once the bus boycott was in full swing more than 200 "nationalists" were detained when "rioting" took place around dusk. Cars were stoned, and a bus waiting room was demolished:

> At about 8 p.m. the crowd left the market and started a township wide looting. The Carter Girls' Hostel was raided and a woman stabbed ... The restive and growing crowd, composed mostly of teenagers went to most parts of the township just as it pleased. In one instance at the no. 8 football field, the crowd met a young girl. She was raped. One man who wanted to rescue her was hit. Noises of yelling women, breaking glass windows and thudding doors and roofs followed the mob wherever it went.[85]

Women became defined within nationalist struggle as both the enemy and the victim. Yet, the women targeted by the CYL were independent, single women working as secretaries or domestic workers in Salisbury, who could not afford to go to their places of work by private taxis. Most working women did not have much choice but to go to work by bus: "One girl was heard saying she had enough money to pay the extra three pence; she would not obey the strike orders from poor men."[86] Such independent, single women were often considered by men to be a threat, especially to men's economic control. By raping and harassing the women, and glorifying the violence against them, the men were reasserting their power over women to punish them for stepping out of traditional gender roles, for taking valuable jobs and for not joining the boycott. The *African Daily News Bulletin* reported that some of the (male) "hooligans" who were not arrested

> are already framing phrases which they are likely to use in later days as a memento of their plunder. One such phrase in Shona, and coined to commemorate the attack on the girls hostel is known to already be in use. It is mainly used against any girl who assumes an indifferent attitude to anything the brutes do to attract attention. The literal translation of the phrase is 'Be *thankful* that you were not in the hostel when I went there.'[87]

The young male nationalists, and hence the nationalist movement, were reminding other women that they should not consider becoming independent women. They would not cater to women's needs within the nationalist struggle, and did not approve of single women coming to the urban areas. In Zimbabwe today, many independent women who move to the city centers are commonly referred to as "prostitutes." It also illustrated that the City Youth League were unable to win the respect of some women and women's organizations, and that women's concerns were not an important factor in nationalist protest.

The attitude of the nationalist leaders to the rapes is significant for a gendered analysis. Nathan Shamuyarira and Maurice Nyagumbo argued that the rapes were *justified*. Shamuyarira stated that the rapes were a "calculated revenge by strikers for the way the girls had defied their strike orders and boarded buses."[88] He said that when the Europeans had cried out that these acts were

> utter barbarism and the wanton desire of strikers and rioters to victimize these girls ... [they had] deliberately misinterpret[ed] the reasons for some of the ugly incidents which occur whenever there is a riot ... but there is always some reason like the one I have outlined behind the incident.[89]

Nyagumbo stated that while

> the leaders of the [City] Youth League were terribly embarrassed by the unruly youths who had attacked the girls at the Carter

Hostel for ignoring the call for a boycott ... [he had] no reason to feel regret for the incident. I actually believed that the girls deserved their punishment.[90]

Hence, it would seem that the raping of women was considered justified and in fact necessary for the sake of the broader nationalist struggle. It was not surprising when the *Daily News* reported:

Harari [sic] residents enjoyed their usual Friday night dance in the recreation hall last night ... fewer girls attended. This was the first dance after the riots on Monday.[91]

Many women were scared off from supporting the nationalist's protests given the violent actions of the "unruly" men. By failing to deal with the problem the CYL alienated and excluded women from the nationalist movement and failed to accommodate and respect "the varying interests and opinions of different classes of women."[92] The 1956 bus boycotts signified a wider gender problem within the nationalist movement. Women were alienated from decision making and were threatened with rape if they did not agree with the methods of the young male nationalists.[93]

1961 Women's Protests
With the formation and support of the National Democratic Party (NDP), women were able to take a leading role in nationalist action. Women were able to challenge their traditional gender stereotypes and move away from a victim location in an attempt to engage equally in nationalist action. The image of women as victims or cheerleaders of a male led nationalist movement was challenged in 1961 when thousands of women marched on Salisbury against a new racist constitution; more than 2,000 women were arrested. They were not all wives of leading male nationalists. Women in the National Democratic Party (NDP) autonomously organized the demonstration against the new constitution that allocated only fifteen out of sixty-five seats in parliament to Africans. Sally Mugabe stated

We didn't tell our husbands about our plans. Early one morning, we left our homes, and by 7 a.m. we were all assembled in the foyer of the Prime Minister's office in the city centre to protest in a peaceful manner, by means of placards, against the new Constitution. The placards read: 'Women Do Not Accept This Backward Constitution,' 'Give Us Our Land and Country,' and 'One Man [sic] One Vote.' Soon our numbers had increased to the extent of over 1,500 women. The police were in their hundreds with dogs, and appealed to us several times to leave the Premier's office. We refused. They called upon me, as leader, to keep order, and warned if I failed to do so, the dogs would be set upon us. I protested, and informed them we had no leader. The crowd responded to this with clapping, songs and slogans.[94]

According to the *Zimbabwe Review,* these demonstrations proved that women were determined "to play their role in freeing Zimbabwe."[95] Thousands of women were arrested, beaten, and put in jail: "Police dogs tore many of their dresses as well as biting them. That strengthened women[96]." Sally Mugabe said that when the police asked them to leave

"we refused to leave, they set the dogs on us," ... "Finally they gave the order - we were to be arrested. We were and we appeared in court." The women ... did not believe they were in the wrong and refused to be tried by a court they believed was not impartial. However, they were found guilty of obstruction and sentenced to £6 - or six weeks imprisonment. "We refused to pay the fine and went to prison.... It was just a big joke, I think."[97]

Sally Mugabe's husband, then a leading nationalist and later the president of Zimbabwe, said that the women in Salisbury and Bulawayo organized the large protests because the men "had failed to respond to the nationalist call for several strike actions."[98] Some men actually hindered the women's actions:

Tens of thousands of women with children on their backs surged into the Salisbury city centre at the Prime Minister's, then Edgar Whitehead's offices to register the Party's [NDP's] protest. Two thousand women were arrested and put into Salisbury prison, this only after ferocious police dogs had been set upon them and inflicted injury on many. The arrested women, when charged in court and fined, refused to pay the fines, preferring to serve their jail sentences. Alas this they were not allowed to do, for it was the men, and not the women who had brought about the collapse of the demonstration.

Men - husbands, I mean - came to prison and threatened their wives with divorce unless they agreed to the payment of fines, which the husbands had readily brought. They told them that unless that were the case they could find other wives in their place by the time they returned. Women had shown greater courage and resolve indeed far greater commitment than the cowardly men.[99]

According to Ngwabi Bhebe, there were at first only 380 women, led by Sally Mugabe, demonstrating outside the British High Commissioner's Office, because it was Britain that had approved the constitution. Later on the protest "moved to the Rhodesian Prime Minister's Office, where [the women] were arrested and charged with trespassing."[100] The next day another hundred women came to demonstrate outside the British High Commissioner's Office, and they were joined by another 400 or so women who had come by bus from Highfields. They arrested 503 women. Apparently that afternoon "an angry crowd of 200 persons attacked the Main Police Station with stones and had to be dispersed with tear gas,"[101] with the result that another eighty-five people were arrested. In Bulawayo, seventy-five women demonstrating outside the magistrates court for the same reasons were also arrested.

It is interesting to note how the events were reported in the *Rhodesian Herald*, because it shows discrepancies in data collection and relates a story that may not have happened but was something the general public were told. Sally Mugabe was identified as one of the ring leaders of the disturbances in Salisbury, although, as she had stated, there were no leaders. She was convicted in the magistrates court with eighty other African women. In "passing sentence, the Enkeldoorn Magistrate, Mr. H. Hastings, said he must recognize that Mrs. Mugabe was the leader of the group, and that consequently her blame-worthiness was much higher."[102] Between Friday, December 8 and Wednesday, December 13, 332 women had been convicted.[103] By Thursday, December 14, 600 women had been arrested and more than 200 still had to appear in court.[104]

Bhebe's figures seem to be more in line with the *Rhodesian Herald* reports, but Mugabe's figure of tens of thousands of women seems somewhat exaggerated. Sally Mugabe's 1,500 women then seems to be more realistic. According to the reports approximately 600 women were arrested in Salisbury alone and within one week 435 had been bailed out. The stalwarts who remained in gaol were either supported by their husbands or defied their attempts to bale them out. The news reports do not deal with these 'nationalist' negotiations between husbands and wives. While Mugabe has praised these women for organising and demonstrating, Naomi Nhiwatiwa has pointed out that this action by women demonstrates how Zimbabwean women were oppressed and threatened by their men, while they were fighting for the nationalist cause. Nhiwatiwa explains that at first the women refused to pay bail to the government but later their men "said that if they stayed there for a very long time they should not come back because the men had other plans."[105] Sally Mugabe explained the women's position:

> Our plan of action [while in jail] was to refuse without exception to cooperate with the authorities, and finally we were charged and brought before the court. We went on a hunger strike and refused to eat the horrible food we were given... The concept was total disobedience. We refused to do any work, and eventually the prison was filthy ... but no one was able to persuade us to digress from our promised course.[106]

Many women were released after their husbands paid their fines. The editors of Sally Mugabe's biography stated that

> the husbands of some of the women were not so loyal to the cause; like men the world over, they had resented playing housewife and proxy mother to the children, and began threatening divorce if their wives did not take the soft option and pay up to be released. Sally and several others with more committed and less selfish spouses, stayed in prison until they were freed shortly afterwards as part of a release exercise of nationalists.[107]

According to the *Rhodesian Herald,* there were about 1,000 African women in Cecil Square, protesting the new constitution, and a senior National Democratic Party official was arrested. Indeed, the *Rhodesian Herald* suggests that the women were intimidated by the NDP to join the protest, and did not do so out of their own ideological convictions. For example, one husband whose wife's name was Gladys, was worried she had been intimidated into joining, because she was not normally involved in such things.[108] In this case, the men's disapproval of the women's actions clearly portended wider gender problems in the nationalist struggle.

At midnight on December 8, 1961, Prime Minister Edgar Whitehead banned the NDP and all gatherings until January 10, 1962. Martin and Johnson have argued that the banning was ordered because the NDP refused to accept the new constitution.[109] Yet, as Ngwabi Bhebe has pointed out, since the banning coincided with the women's protests their actions were the catalyst that shifted the struggle to a more militant style. Instead of a more moderate nationalist movement emerging after the banning, as the white Rhodesians hoped, African nationalism increased, with rising levels of consciousness and more militant behavior.[110] This was despite Whitehead's belief that

> [o]n the African side a new Nationalist party will probably gradually replace the NDP. It can render the African people a great service if it repudiates the methods of the banned organisation and avoids some of its major policy errors.[111]

On December 17, 1961, ZAPU was established as a direct successor to the NDP; but it was banned only nine months later. This banning order caused some internal disunity within ZAPU, and on August 8, 1963, ZANU split off from ZAPU.[112] The women's actions in 1961 have not been accorded the recognition they deserve in Zimbabwean history, with the praise going to male nationalist leaders.

1972 Pearce Commission

More than a decade after the 1961 women's protests, women again rallied support and mobilized mass protest in favor of a campaign, the outcome of which would affect all Rhodesians. In 1972 the Pearce Commission was sent out from Britain to gauge the opinions of black Africans on the proposal of another new constitution in Rhodesia. Judith Todd was involved in the campaign to educate the Africans about their rights in relation to the commission and the constitution: what a "yes" vote would mean to them and why they should vote "no" to this new constitution.[113] Both her actions and those of her father, Sir Garfield Todd (former prime minister of Rhodesia), typed them as "world-travelers," as Christine Sylvester would argue, because they had transgressed their racial and gender identities in support of black majority rule.[114] However, as Judith Todd has stated, she had "no view of [her]self within the struggle ... It was all simply part of daily life."[115]

In her book *Right To Say No!*, Judith Todd talks about "the people" and the "majority." Men and women are never separated into gendered categories in her version. She does mention some women by name but as participants, not "women." It was their political action that was important. Judith Todd has said that she has

> as much an abhorrence of the use of gender as an instrument as I would have for any similar use of race, colour, creed or regional affinity.[116]

Judith Todd's actions in defying the government during the nationalist period show that she was committed to the fight for democracy, with no reason to consider a gendered analysis of it then or now. Her actions show that political consciousness can also transcend gender, and in a very different way, that the Rhodesian government did not discriminate between men and women when it came to determining punishments for "subversion." Both Todd and her father were detained during this period.[117]

Apart from the actions of Judith Todd which illustrate white women's ability to be more than cheerleaders or wives to a male nationalist movement, the *Zimbabwe Review* congratulates black African women for organizing themselves around the Pearce Commission:

> Women of Zimbabwe as well as their men were getting to be really organised. They have followed the same party machinery which makes it easy for them to come together any time there is a need. The Pearce Commission would have had different results had the women of Zimbabwe not completely organised to influence their menfolk. It does not mean that men would have sold-out but they would be half the force in Zimbabwe and thus more vulnerable to arrests and all forms of intimidation.[118]

Women not only rallied for support, but they were recognized as forming half of the African population. Thus they should be included among the "nationalists." By May 1972 the Pearce Commission had found the settlement terms unacceptable to the African majority. This outcome was achieved with women's support. The acknowledgment by the *Zimbabwe*

Review in 1973 that women were essential to this outcome, as a group of organized people called *women*, differs from most other accounts of the Pearce Commission, which do not mention or acknowledge the role of women per se. In times of crisis, gender analyses seem to get pushed aside in favor of generalized political accounts. However, as we have seen in the 1961 women's protests and in the 1956 bus boycotts, women were significant to the outcome, despite it being perceived as a male dominated nationalist movement. The importance of women in the nationalist movement cannot be underestimated. The challenge now is to recognize women's roles in the popular discourse about the war.

The Armed Struggle Stage

The nationalist movement moved from a political arena to armed struggle in 1965. ZAPU led the initial armed struggle stage in the 1960s, building up its armed force, the Zimbabwe People's Revolutionary Army (ZIPRA), in Zambia. From 1972 onward ZANU's armed wing, the Zimbabwe African National Liberation Army (ZANLA), dominated the struggle, and in 1975 ZIPRA and ZANLA united briefly to form the Zimbabwe People's Army (ZIPA), in order to change the course of the revolution.[119] ZANLA resurfaced as dominant in 1976 and remained so until the end of the war in 1980. Thus, after a protracted guerilla war against colonialism, white minority rule, and race-based oppression, Zimbabwe's political independence was finally negotiated at Lancaster House in late 1979.[120] In April 1980 Zimbabwe held its first democratic elections, which saw the victory of the Zimbabwe African National Union (ZANU) led by Robert Mugabe.

It was during the armed struggle that the traditional gender roles between men and women became increasingly blurred.[121] When whole communities are involved in a war, when they are submerged in the depths of turmoil and crisis, often without choice, there is seldom time for gendered distinctions to be made. Typically, liberation armies are nonstate or antistate forces, which need to be decentralized. The gendered distinction between a geographically located front and rear may not be possible, or even desirable, because of the need to have the support of the masses.[122] Zimbabwe's national liberation war provides an excellent example of a decentralized military/guerilla war, waged both from outside Rhodesian borders and from within, with the support, (whether by coercion or consent)[123] of the rural masses. Women and men in the rural areas of Zimbabwe found the liberation war to be increasingly played out in their everyday lives. Often they were faced with little choice but to support the guerillas by providing food and shelter, while risking punishment and prosecution from Rhodesian forces for doing so.

Many young Zimbabweans were either recruited to or volunteered to join ZAPU and ZANU and their armed wings. ZIPRA and ZANLA trained their recruits for guerilla warfare outside of Rhodesia, mainly in Zambia and Mozambique. Many young men and women were sent back across the borders to Rhodesia to fight, and to educate and politicize the majority of peasants living in the rural areas on the need for revolution and armed struggle. These "freedom fighters" aimed to liberate Zimbabweans from the shackles of colonialism.

Young Women's New Opportunities

Young women were thus provided with new opportunities to negotiate their traditional gender roles.[124] The young male guerillas realized the need for women's support and challenged the authority of elders by giving women new and different opportunities. Terence Ranger has described the dilemma faced by the chiefs and elders in Makoni District, when young women gained some power to choose their futures:

> There were some substantial discontinuities also which made it difficult for there to be intermediate or total collaboration between peasant elders and the young guerillas. To begin with the young guerillas *were* young and they were closer to the teenagers of Makoni District than they were to the resident elders. Men in their fifties who had hitherto dominated Makoni peasant radicalism and who were used to controlling a flock of dependent women - wives, daughters, daughters-in-law - now found that the initiative had passed to young men with guns. These young men called upon the unmarried women of Makoni to act as their cooks, informants and messengers and in these latter two roles teenage girls were able to exercise a good deal of power, for the first time in Makoni history.[125]

David Maxwell has argued that "some young girls seized the opportunity of the war to escape the drudgery of domestic chores and replace them with the attentions of 'heroic' young men with guns."[126] The enticements for women to follow the comrades left the old patriarchs unable to control the women in their communities.

Norma Kriger has argued that the generational conflicts between young men with guns and older chiefs would benefit from a gendered analysis. There were "different attitudes between male and female *youth*, a male *youth* leader empathised with *youth* and lambasted *parents* for not letting their daughters stay with them in the mountains."[127] Kriger argues that the parents "feared that their daughters would become pregnant," but the youth leader insisted that they

> had our rules not to touch women. We would have to beat the *parents* sometimes before they let their daughters live in the mountains.[128]

There were taboos placed on sex to which the guerilla fighters were supposed to adhere. As Maxwell points out, the taboos were

> popular means of associating ZANLA/ZIPA forces with both hunters and ancestors. For example, hunters never had sex the night before a hunt ... [but more] common-sense explanations ... were offered by more educated comrades who for instance, recognised that unwanted pregnancies would be detrimental to their cause.[129]

Maxwell argues that in 1976 the ZIPA guerillas respected these so-called taboos because "they were unfamiliar with the terrain and the people, and insecure in their status."[130] However, by 1978 the "guerilla rank and file," no longer organized by ZIPA, but under the control of ZANLA, were breaking these taboos regularly. Maxwell argues that "this tendency was compounded by the decrease in the length of their training in 1978 as emphasis was placed on the final 'big push' to overthrow the settler state."[131] Hence, while taboos about certain foods were maintained by guerilla fighters, having sex with women (assuming the guerilla is a male) was popular, and this "caused widespread resentment," especially among chiefs and elders within Zimbabwe.[132]

Ranger cites the young male guerillas as confronting traditional gender roles and generational politics. Maxwell and Kriger use the examples of male youths challenging parents and encouraging female youths, or unmarried women, to participate in the struggle. Yet women's actions here are seen as a direct response to male request, rather than initiated by women themselves. Nonetheless, the recruitment of women was seen as a challenge to traditional gender roles, and it had to be balanced between engaging women in the fight (sometimes with offers of socialist style women's emancipation) and appeasing local chiefs and headmen with assurances that the women would not become "too" liberated or dominant over men.

Rural Women as Agents

Sylvester has argued that within the guerilla movement's strategic necessity for women's involvement in the struggle, women momentarily became "agents" in the revolution. The majority of people in the rural areas were women farmers, and they "could form the nucleus of a peasant center of force ... and some had a brief guerilla-aligned, project-within-an-anticolonial-project."[133] Peasant women were empowered with the help of young, male guerillas who supported women's rights not to be beaten by their husbands and called for an end to male dominance in the communities. Sylvester bases her arguments on Norma Kriger's research of this phenomenon in Mutoko District during the war. Kriger argued that "married women ... saw ... the guerillas [as] potential allies,"[134] often taking the initiative in getting them to punish their unruly husbands:

> Guerilla appeals to families to be united and to men to stop beating their wives and drinking excessively originated with married women ... [whose] success in winning the support of the guerillas gave them a strong motive to continue to provide support for the guerillas.... "Comrades could come through a village at night, hear a woman crying and find her husband beating her," said a woman. From all accounts, the guerillas then punished the husbands by beating them ... women felt empowered and reported to the guerillas whenever their husbands beat them. Men were not only afraid [especially of being labelled sell-outs], but they also resented young people intervening in their private lives and constraining them from wife-beating.[135]

Soon there was a backlash from the husbands, and the guerillas had to back off. After all, the guerillas' "central platform was against racial discrimination."[136] This, Sylvester argues, led to waning support for women by the guerillas "until 'women' once again reverted to a status of controlled subjects."[137]

That is, women reverted to support roles for the guerillas "rather than [remaining] agents of change in their own right."[138] This meant that a Gramscian council-type revolution that emerged in the countryside with women at the subcenter may have been "momentarily victorious against abusive local men, [but] was thereby further diffused by appeals to support the national liberation struggle as defined and led by heroic men."[139] Sylvester's argument that a women's revolution was based on the actions of married women taking advantage of the situation is thus weakened. Generalizing these women's actions into a wider feminist political movement is unsubstantiated.

To claim that these women made a conscious attempt at revolution is inspired only by a feminist hope for the future. However, realignments of gender relations were not on the agenda in such clear-cut terms. Sylvester does argue that women's "efforts neither prevailed ... nor met total defeat,"[140] and this meant that it was only "in the shadowy margins between revolutionary victory and defeat that one finds women."[141] The gendered characteristics of Zimbabwe's revolution emerge from the shadowlands of "simultaneous revolutions," revealing male domination.[142] "[O]n both sides [white and black] women's roles were largely of a support nature as local nationalist versions of what Jean Elshtain often refers to as civic cheerleading."[143]

Thus during the First Chimurenga and the two stages of the Second Chimurenga, women played central roles in the anticolonial struggles and nationalist actions. Despite the lack of detail concerning women's actions in many historical accounts of the struggle, women do have a presence and their experiences shed light on the history and how it has been told. It is important that such a women's history is not treated as insignificant in mainstream histories. Within this gendered analysis of Zimbabwean history we have seen that women are not invisible in anticolonial struggle and nationalist action, and often their roles and presence have been important to the outcomes. Nehanda inspired many women's participation in later struggles and provided guidance to male and female guerilla fighters. From women's active involvement then in nationalist political actions during the Second Chimurenga it is important now to turn to our central theme women's roles as guerilla fighters in the war of national liberation.

Endnotes

1. There is an extensive body of literature on Zimbabwean history. See, for example, Terence Ranger, *The African Voice in Southern Rhodesia 1898-1930*, (London:, Heinemann, 1970); and David Beach, *The Shona and Zimbabwe, 900-1850: An Outline of Shona History*, (New York: Africana Publishing House, 1980).

2. A. Hartmann, S.J., "In the Early Days of Mashonaland," *Zambesi Mission Record*, 1,4, May, 1899, p.131, cited in Elizabeth Schmidt, *Peasants, Traders, Wives: Shona Women in the History of Zimbabwe, 1870-1939*, (Harare: Baobab, 1992), p.1.

3. The *First Chimerenga* has also been called an uprising, a revolt, a war, a riot, and a revolution. See Terence Ranger, *Revolt in Southern Rhodesia, 1896/97*, (London: Heinemann, 1967).

4. Ibid., p.194.

5. See ibid; and Terence Ranger, *Peasant Consciousness and Guerilla War in Zimbabwe*; and Terence Ranger, *The African Voice in Southern Rhodesia 1898-1930*.

6. Christine Sylvester, "Simultaneous Revolutions and Exits: A Semi-Skeptical Comment," in Mary Ann Tetreault, ed., *Women and Revolution in Africa, Asia and the New World*, (Columbia: University of South Carolina, 1994, p. 419).

7. Ibid; also see Terence Ranger, *Peasant Consciousness and Guerilla War*.

8. Christine Sylvester, "Simultaneous Revolutions and Exits," p. 419.

9. See Terence Ranger, *Peasant Consciousness*, pp. 15, 42, 48, 84, cited in Norma Kriger, *Zimbabwe's Guerilla War: Peasant Voices*, (Cambridge: Cambridge University Press, 1992, p. 174).

10. Norma Kriger, *Zimbabwe's Guerilla War: Peasant Voices*, p. 174.

11. For example, Tenkela Wamponga. She was the female associate of Mkwati who was the medium of Mwari. After he died, she planned to escape with the Nehanda medium to Portuguese East Africa. But she was caught, put on trial, but there was not enough evidence to convict her. The "natives" in the Chishawasha district believed "that she was the prime mover of the rebellion." (see Mhlope's Statement, November 20, 1938, WI 8/1/3. and *Zambesi Mission Record*, 3:40, April, 1908: cited in Terence Ranger, *Revolt in Southern Rhodesia*, p. 307). Julian Cobbing mentions Lobengula's wife, Mbida Mkwananzi; Lobengula's widow, Lozigeyi, who had distributed ammunition before the uprisings. See Julian Cobbing, "The Absent Priesthood: Another Look at the Rhodesian Risings of 1896-1897," in *Journal of African History*, 1:18, 1977, pp. 65-7. But these women are only briefly mentioned and there is no analysis of their roles or positions.

12. Terence Ranger, "Women in the Politics of Makoni District Zimbabwe 1890-1980," manuscript, (University of Manchester: Department of History, 1982), located in the Zimbabwe National Archives.

13. It is argued that Ranger himself has "invented" Zimbabwean history! Interview with Julian Cobbing, Adelaide, May, 1995. Also see Julian Cobbing, "The

Absent Priesthood: Another Look at the Rhodesian Risings of 1896-1897," where he offers an alternative account of the uprisings.

14. Elizabeth Schmidt, *Peasants, Traders, Wives*, p. 1.
15. Elizabeth Schmidt opens the way for a gendered perspective to shed light on this historical moment, in her chapter "Beholden to Two Patriarchs: Shona Women on the Eve of European Conquest and in the Early Years of Occupation," in ibid; also see Terence Ranger, *Revolt in Southern Rhodesia*; and Julian Cobbing, "The Absent Priesthood;" and David Beach, "'Chimurenga': The Shona Rising of 1896-97," *Journal of African History,* 20, 1979.
16. Elizabeth Schmidt, *Peasants, Traders, Wives*, p. 36.
17. "History of Zambesi Mission," in *Zambesi Mission Record*, 3, 40, April, 1908, p. 397, cited ibid, p. 39.
18. See Diana Jeater, "Women's Bridewealth in the Restructuring of Shona Society 1890-1930," (paper presented at University of London, African History Seminar, S.O.A.S., 1985), cited in ibid.
19. "About 200 goats [were] captured, fifty head of cattle and four girls of Marvagnanga." See Jesuit Archives, Box 357, Biehler to Richartz, 25 July, 1896, cited in ibid.
20. "Punishing Shishawasha," *Rhodesia Herald,* July 24, 1896: cited in Elizabeth Schmidt, *Peasants, Traders, Wives*, p. 39.
21. Elizabeth Schmidt, *Peasants, Traders, Wives*, p. 40.
22. Box 98, letter Book 1896-1924/ Father F.J. Richartz, Chishawasha, to Chief native Commissioner H.M. Taberer, Salisbury, April 29, 1897; and May 12, 1897 / Richartz to Campbell, Native Commissioner, Fort Chikwaka, Salisbury District, October 9, 1897/ and Box 99/8 Campbell to Richartz, September 24 and 27, 1897, cited in ibid.
23. Elizabeth Schmidt, *Peasants, Traders, Wives*, p. 40.
24. Ibid. Some detailed case studies of this strategy are offered by Schmidt.
25. Ibid, p. 41.
26. See Jesuit Archives, box 99/8, H.M. Taberer, C.N.C., Salisbury, to Father F.J. Rhichartz, Chishwasha, 20 September, 1897, cited in ibid.
27. Elizabeth Schmidt, *Peasants, Traders, Wives*, p. 42.
28. Robert Blake, *A History of Rhodesia*, (London: Eyre-Methuen, 1977), p.142.
29. Ibid.
30. Terence Ranger, *Revolt in Southern Rhodesia 1896-97,* p. xvii. Julian Cobbing, "The Absent Priesthood," pp.61-84. Cobbing argues that the connections between the two *Chimurenga* are "fallacious."
31. For example, Ranger recommends we read Solomon Mutswairo's "The Picture of Nehanda and Kagubi," in *Zimbabwe Prose and Poetry*, (Washington: 1974); or Stanlake Samkange's, *Year of the Uprising*, (London: 1978). But there are many other writers doing the same. For example, Ruth Gabi's "The Secret Cave," in *Zimbabwe Women Writers' 1994 Anthology*, (Harare: Zimbabwe Women Writers, 1994), which also draws on the spirit of Nehanda to guide a young woman through her own personal liberation in the 1990s. See also Alex Pongweni, *Songs that Won the Liberation War*, (Harare: College Press, 1992).

Also see "Chimurenga - A People's War," in *Zimbabwe News,* 9,3, March/April 1977, pp. 9-15, cited in Terence Ranger, *Revolt in Southern Rhodesia,* p. xviii.

32. A discussion of precolonial, colonial, and patriarchal institutions and the position of women would illustrate how women's positions, roles, and perceptions have changed and were redefined especially under the impact of Christianity and colonial land policies. However, these questions and issues have been raised adequately by other Zimbabweanist scholars such as May and Weinrich and need not be repeated here. See Weinrich, A.K.H., *Women and Racial Discrimination in Rhodesia,* (Paris: UNESCO, 1979); and Jean May, *Zimbabwean Women in Customary and Colonial Law,* (Gweru: Mambo Press, 1983).

33. Terence Ranger, ed., *Violence and Memory: Zimbabwe, 1896 - 1996,* (The Britain-Zimbabwe Society's Research Day Newsletter, June 8, 1996, electronic edition).

34. The Nehanda referred to here is Charwe, the female spirit medium.

35. Terence Ranger, *Revolt in Southern Rhodesia,* p. 210. Julian Cobbing however, contradicts this unquestioned belief in the myth espoused by the *mhondoros,* by pointing out that the Ndebele warriors had three generations of experience with guns and military techniques. They would not have rushed in to an attack believing the white man's bullets would not have killed them. Julian Cobbing, "The Absent Priesthood," pp. 76-77: Also see Ruth Gabi, "The Secret Cave," in Norma Kitson, ed., *Zimbabwe Women Writers Anthology 1994,* (Harare: Zimbabwe Women Writers, 1994).

36. Elizabeth Schmidt, *Peasants, Traders, Wives,* pp. 91, 192.

37. Kwanele Ona Jirira, "Our Struggle Ourselves: Shaping Feminist Theory in our Context: The Zimbabwe Scenario," in *Southern African Feminist Review,* 1:1, 1995, p. 77.

38. David Beach, "An Innocent Woman, Unjustly Accused? Charwe, Medium of the Nehanda *Mhondoro* Spirit, and the 1896-97 Shona Rising in Zimbabwe," (University of Zimbabwe: Department of History Seminar Paper, no. 98, 1995).

39. David Lan, *Guns and Rain: Guerillas and Spirit Mediums in Zimbabwe,* (London: James Currey, 1985). This is one of the main books about the role of mediums in the liberation wars and adequately details their importance, thus there is no need to go into the roles of all of the spirit mediums here.

40. From N. C. Campbell's Report, January, 1896, N1/1/9; N.C. Salisbury, to C.N.C., March 3, 1893, N1/1/9; cited in Terence Ranger, *Revolt in Southern Rhodesia,* p. 209.

41. Ibid.

42. Terence Ranger, *Revolt in Southern Rhodesia,* p.209.

43. Ibid, p. 216.

44. David Lan, *Guns and Rain,* p. 6.

45. Christine Sylvester, "African and Western Feminisms: World-Traveling the Tendencies and Possibilities," *Signs,* Summer, 1995, p. 943.

46. "Ambuya Nehanda: Fighter for Justice," in *Social Change and Development,* special supplement, "Religion for Liberation," no. 21, September-November,

1985, pp. 3-4.
47. Ibid.
48. David Martin and Phyllis Johnson, *The Struggle for Zimbabwe: The Chimurenga War,* (London: Faber and Faber, 1981), p. 49.
49. David Beach, "An Innocent Woman, Unjustly Accused? Charwe, Medium of the Nehanda *Mhondoro* Spirit, and the 1896-97 Shona Rising in Zimbabwe."
50. Terence Ranger, *Revolt in Southern Rhodesia,* p. 209.
51. S.2953, Queen v. Nianda *et al.,* 2 March 1898; S.401/252, Preliminary examination of Nianda, January 12, 1898: cited by David Beach, "An Innocent Woman, Unjustly Accused? Charwe, Medium of the Nehanda *Mhondoro* Spirit, and the 1896-97 Shona Rising in Zimbabwe," p. 12.
52. Terence Ranger, *Revolt in Southern Rhodesia,* pp. 307-8.
53. Ibid, p. 309.
54. From Father Richartz of Chishawasha Mission, "The End of Kagubi," *Zambesi Mission Record,* 1:2, November 1898; cited in Terence Ranger, *Revolt in Southern Rhodesia,* p. 309. Ranger also argues that Nehanda defied death. The first two attempts to hang her failed. See ibid, p. 394.
55. The British South Africa Company, *The '96 Rebellions, the British South Africa Company Reports on the Native Disturbances in Rhodesia 1896-97,* facing page 127, caption under a photograph of the "captured Kagubi and Nehanda."
56. David Beach, "An Innocent Woman, Unjustly Accused? Charwe, Medium of the Nehanda *Mhondoro* Spirit, and the 1896-97 Shona Rising in Zimbabwe," p. 18. Beach's research of the period of Nehanda's actions and death need not be repeated here.
57. Ibid, pp. 26-27.
58. *The Zimbabwe Revolution: A Political Education Handbook,* "produced by a team of ZANU cadres during their detention (Kamwala, Lusaka Remand Prison), [written before April 1976], one year after the imprisonment of all ZANU leaders and cadres stationed in Zambia after the Chitepo Assassination in accordance with Vorster's Detente initiative." This manuscript was smuggled out of prison and made available to the freedom fighters, (located in ZANU Archives).
59. "Comrade Teurai Ropa: Women Have Total Involvement in Struggle," *Zimbabwe News,* 10:2, May-June, 1978, p. 30.
60. Ibid, p. 65.
61. Robert Mugabe "The Role and History of the Zimbabwean Women in the National Struggle," opening speech, first ZANU Women's Seminar, Xai Xai, in Naomi Nhiwatiwa, *Women's Liberation in the Zimbabwean Revolution: Materials from the ZANU Women's Seminar, Maputo, Mozambique,* (San Francisco, California: John Brown Book Club, Prairie Fire Organising Committee, May 1979).
62. Robert Mugabe, *Our War of Liberation: Speeches, Articles, Interviews, 1976-1979,* (Gweru: Mambo Press, 1983), p. 73.
63. Robert Mugabe, "The Role and History of the Zimbabwean Women in the

National Struggle."

64. Nehanda and Kaguvi were both hanged, not shot by firing squad as the ZANU cadres above stated. See ZANU Archives Women's Affairs File: Zimbabwe African National Union Women's Affairs (League): unsigned document by Teurai Ropa (Secretary for Women's Affairs) member of National Executive of Central Committee of ZANU, p. 2. The article was written sometime before the first ZANU Women's Seminar.

65. Interview with Solomon Mujuru in Janice McLaughlin, *On the Frontline: Catholic Missions in Zimbabwe's Liberation War*, (Harare: Baobab Books, 1996), pp. 241-42.

66. Janice McLaughlin *On the Frontline: Catholic Missions in Zimbabwe's Liberation War*, p. 243.

67. The whereabouts of the Nehanda medium's remains are still officially unknown.

68. Interview with Dzino, Harare, December 30, 1996.

69. "The Trial of Mbuya Nehanda and other Chimurenga Revolutionaries," *Zimbabwe News*, 13:1, 1982, p. 14.

70. Ibid.

71. *Moto*, 1:2, June 1982.

72. See David Martin and Phyllis Johnson, *The Struggle for Zimbabwe: The Chimurenga War*: Also see Julie Frederikse, *None But Ourselves: Masses vs. Media in the Making of Zimbabwe*, (Harare: Anvil Press, 1982). Both of these mainstream historical accounts of the war do mention women, however, the first only mentions a few women (e.g. Nehanda and Susan Rutanhire) and offers no detail of gendered issues, and, while the latter does give anecdotal evidence from women actors, it does not offer any political analysis of women's participation throughout the 100 years of anticolonial action.

73. See Brian Raftopoulos and Ian Phimister, eds., *Keep On Knocking: A History of the Labor Movement in Zimbabwe, 1900-97*, Zimbabwe Congress of Trade Unions, (Harare: Baobab Books, 1997).

74. Richard Lapchick and Stephanie Urdang, *Oppression and Resistance: The Struggle of Women in Southern Africa.* For an overview of women's involvement in Zimbabwean history see Ruth Weiss, *The Women of Zimbabwe*, (Harare: Nehanda Publishers, 1986): Also see Brian Raftopoulos and Ian Phimister, *Keep On Knocking: A History of the Labor Movement in Zimbabwe, 1900-97*, (Harare: Zimbabwe Congress of Trade Unions; Baobab, 1997).

75. See Rudo Gaidzanwa, "Bourgeois Theories of Gender and Feminism," in Ruth Meena, ed., *Gender in Southern Africa: Conceptual and Theoretical Issues*, (Harare: Sapes Books, 1992), pp.107-13.

76. Ibid.

77. Robert Mugabe, "The Role and History of the Zimbabwean Women in the National Struggle," p.12.

78. Christine Sylvester, "Simultaneous Revolutions and Exits: A Semi-Skeptical Comment," p. 418.

79. Rudo Gaidzanwa, "Bourgeois Theories of Gender and Feminism," p.108.

80. "A Number of Girls at Carter Girls' Hostel were Raped, and One Criminally

Assaulted 5 times," the *African Daily News Bulletin*, (special edition of the *African Weekly*) Tuesday, September 18, 1956.

81. Robert Blake, *A History of Rhodesia*.

82. *The African Daily News Bulletin*, Tuesday, September 18, 1956.

83. Brian Raftopoulos, "Gender, Nationalist Politics and the Fight for the City: Harare 1940-1950s," in *Southern African Feminist Review (SAFERE)*, 1:2, September/October, 1995, pp. 30-43.

84. The *African Daily News Bulletin*, (special edition of the *African Weekly*), Monday, September 17, 1956.

85. The *African Daily News Bulletin*, (special edition of the *African Weekly*), Tuesday, September 18, 1956.

86. Nathan Shamuyarira, *Crisis in Rhodesia*, (London: Andre Deutsch, Trinity Press, 1963), p. 43.

87. "Aftermath of Riot - Danger Signs," The *African Daily News Bulletin*, (special edition of *the African Weekly*) Thursday, September 20, 1956.

88. Nathan Shamuyarira, *Crisis in Rhodesia*, p. 43; also see Brian Raftopoulos, "Gender, Nationalist Politics and the Fight for the City: Harare, 1940-1950s," pp. 41-42.

89. Nathan Shamuyarira, *Crisis in Rhodesia*, p. 43.

90. Maurice Nyagumbo, *With the People*, (London: Graham Publishers, 1980), p.105; also cited in Brian Raftopoulos, "Gender, Nationalist Politics and the Fight for the City: Harare 1940-1950s," pp.41-42.

91. "Fewer Girls," The *African Daily News Bulletin*, (Special Edition of the African Weekly) Saturday, September 22, 1956.

92. Brian Raftopoulos, "Gender, Nationalist Politics and the Fight for the City: Harare, 1940-1950s," p. 4.

93. See Brian Raftopoulos and Ian Phimister, *Keep On Knocking: A History of the Labor Movement in Zimbabwe, 1900-97*.

94. Sally Mugabe in Sarah Kachingwe, et al, eds., *Sally Mugabe: A Woman With a Mission*, (Harare: Department of Information and Publicity, ZANU(PF), 1994), p. 17.

95. *The Zimbabwe Review*, The Official Organ of ZAPU, October 20, 1973, p. 6.

96. Ibid.

97. "A Long Wait for Victory of Zimbabwe," The *Herald*, March 7, 1980.

98. Robert Mugabe, "The Role and History of the Zimbabwean Women in the National Struggle," p. 13.

99. Ibid.

100. Ngwabi Bhebe, "The Nationalist Struggle, 1957-1962," in Canaan Banana, ed., *Turmoil and Tenacity: Zimbabwe, 1896-1990*, (Harare: College Press, 1989), p. 102.

101. Ibid.

102. "City Disturbances: 80 Women Fined," The *Rhodesian Herald*, Tuesday, December 12, 1961. They were fined Rhodesian £6 (or six weeks in jail) for contravening the Police Offences Act by trespassing in Compensation House on Wednesday, December 6, 1961. Another twenty-eight women were found

guilty of this offence on Monday, December 11, and were fined Rhodesian £3 (or three weeks in jail).

103. The *Rhodesian Herald*, Wednesday, December 13, 1961. Another fifty-one women were fined Rhodesian £10 for obstructing the pavements of Baker Avenue in Salisbury on Thursday, December 7. On Tuesday, December 12, another 214 African women appeared at the magistrates court: 197 were fined Rhodesian £3, seventeen were fined Rhodesian £10 and only three admitted the offence. Few women elected to pay the fines. Groups of forty women appeared at each session, many carrying babies, which disrupted the proceedings.

104. The Report noted that 250 had now paid their fines and been released and 185 women were allowed bail during the week. See the *Rhodesian Herald*, Thursday, December 14, 1961. By Friday, December 15, twenty-six women were still remanded in custody until December 20. See the *Rhodesian Herald*, Friday, December 15, 1961.

105. Naomi Nhiwatiwa, *Women's Liberation in the Zimbabwean Revolution: Materials from the ZANU women's Seminar*, p. 28.

106. Sally Mugabe in Sarah Kachingwe, et al, eds., *Sally Mugabe: A Woman With a Mission*, p. 18.

107. Ibid, p. 19.

108. The *Rhodesian Herald*, Saturday, December 9, 1961.

109. David Martin and Phyllis Johnson, *The Struggle for Zimbabwe: The Chimurenga War*, p. 68.

110. Ngwabi Bhebe, "The Nationalist Struggle, 1957-1962," p. 102.

111. The *Rhodesian Herald*, Monday, December 11, 1961.

112. Terence Ranger, *Peasant Consciousness and Guerilla War in Zimbabwe: A Comparative Study*, p.ix.

113. Judith Todd, *The Right to Say No! Rhodesia, 1972*, (Zimbabwe: Longman 1987). First published in 1972. Banned in Rhodesia, December 6, 1972.

114. Christine Sylvester, "African and Western Feminisms: World Traveling the Tendencies and Possibilities."

115. Correspondence from Judith Todd, September 28, 1996.

116. Ibid.

117. See Judith Todd, *An Act of Treason: Rhodesia 1965*, (Zimbabwe: Longman, 1982). First published 1966.

118. The *Zimbabwe Review* (ZAPU), October 20, 1973, p. 6.

119. David Moore, "The Zimbabwe People's Army: Strategic Innovation or More of the Same?" in Terence Ranger and Ngwabi Bhebe, eds., *Soldiers in Zimbabwe's Liberation War*, vol. 1, (Harare: University of Zimbabwe Publications, 1995), pp. 73-86.

120. The Lancaster House Conference commenced on September 10, 1979. An agreement was signed on December 21, 1979. The delegation headed by Robert Mugabe (ZANU) and Joshua Nkomo (ZAPU) consisted of twenty-one men and one woman, a Miss E. Siziba. Bishop Muzorewa's delegation had twenty-two men, and the United Kingdom delegation had twenty-one men and one

woman, a Mrs. A. J. Phillips.

121. Miriam Cooke and Angela Woollacott, *Gendering War Talk*, "Introduction," (New Jersey: Princeton University Press, 1993), p.ix.

122. Cynthia Enloe, *Does Khaki Become You?: The Militarisation of Women's Lives*, (London: Pluto Press, 1983), p. 160; also see Miriam Cooke, "Wo-man Retelling the War Myth," in Miriam Cooke and Angela Woollacott, *Gendering War Talk*, p. 200.

123. See David Moore, "Democracy, Violence, and Identity in the Zimbabwean War of National Liberation: Reflections from the Realms of Dissent," in *Canadian Journal of African Studies*, 29:3, 1995.

124 Terence Ranger, *Peasant Consciousness and Guerilla War in Zimbabwe*, pp.206-7. On April 28, 1966, ZANLA forces engaged with Rhodesian forces in the "battle of Sinoia" (Chinoyi). This day is now celebrated in Zimbabwe as Chimurenga Day, the start of the armed struggle.

125. Ibid.

126. David Maxwell, "Local Politics and the War of Liberation in North-East Zimbabwe," *Journal of Southern African Studies*, 19:3, September 1993, p. 375; also see Mike Kesby, "Arenas for Control, Terrains of Gender Contestation: Guerilla Struggle and Counter-Insurgency Warfare in Zimbabwe, 1972-1980," in *Journal of Southern African Studies*, 22:4, December 1996, pp. 561-84.

127. Italics in original. Norma Kriger, *Zimbabwe's Guerilla War: Peasant Voices*, p. 181.

128. Ibid.

129. David Maxwell, "Local Politics and the War of Liberation in North-East Zimbabwe," p. 373; David Lan, *Guns and Rain*, pp.160-66; also see Amy Kaler, "Gender and Fertility in a Post-Colonial Moment: The Prohibition of Depo-Provera in Zimbabwe 1981," paper presented at *Gender and Colonialism in Southern Africa*, (International Conference, University of Western Cape, South Africa, January 1997).

130. David Maxwell, "Local Politics and the War of Liberation in North-East Zimbabwe," p. 379.

131. Ibid.

132. Ibid.

133. Christine Sylvester, "Simultaneous Revolutions: The Zimbabwean Case," p. 472; Sita Ranchod-Nilsson, "This Too Is a Way of Fighting: Rural Women's Participation in Zimbabwe's Liberation War:" also see Christine Sylvester, "Simultaneous Revolutions and Exits: A Semi-Skeptical Comment," p. 418.

134. Norma Kriger, *Zimbabwe's Guerilla War: Peasant Voices*, p. 194.

135. Ibid, pp.194-95.

136. Ibid, p.194. Kriger does not mention what this "backlash" actually involved.

137. Christine Sylvester, "Simultaneous Revolutions and Exits: A Semi-Skeptical Comment," p. 420; and see Christine Sylvester, "Simultaneous Revolutions: The Zimbabwean Case," p. 472.

138. Christine Sylvester, "Simultaneous Revolutions and Exits: A Semi-Skeptical Comment," p. 420; she quotes Meggi Zingani from Irene Staunton, ed., *Mothers*

of the Revolution, p. 126.

139. Christine Sylvester, "Simultaneous Revolutions and Exits: A Semi-Skeptical Comment," p. 421.

140. Ibid, p. 418.

141. Ibid.

142. Christine Sylvester, "Simultaneous Revolutions: The Zimbabwean Case."

143. See Jean Elshtain, *Women and War*, 1987, cited by Christine Sylvester, "Simultaneous Revolutions and Exits: A Semi-Skeptical Comment," p.418.

Chapter Five

Women in the Second *Chimurenga*

Zimbabwean women have been playing a major role too in the fight
for their country's freedom. They have joined their men in large
numbers and assumed active roles at various levels of their national
organisation. They are found in military, political and socio-economic
wings of their national organisation, ZAPU - Patriotic Front.... They
contribute as equals of their menfolk. They have shown in many
difficult situations that their determination to liberate their motherland
is second to none. As more of them get political education more will
get more deeply committed than ever before. Zimbabwe needs
everybody's service. Zimbabwe shall and must be free. Our girls
are playing a big part in this patriotic struggle.
- Thokozile Ushe in *Zimbabwe Review*, 1977

This statement made by Ushe for ZAPU in the *Zimbabwe Review*
attempts to rally the patriotism of women to join the struggle
for liberation. Here, ZAPU's rhetoric differs little from ZANU's in
its promotion of women being equal to men in the struggle. It claims that
women have joined in large numbers and hopes all will achieve the level of
political education to become truly committed to the struggle. However,
even though recruits were being trained as early as 1963 for guerilla warfare,
with some women being sent from Rhodesia to be educated in other
countries, it was not until 1972 that the first women were recruited into the
liberation armies as part of an essential guerilla strategy. Women's access
to the armies of ZAPU and ZANU was varied, and their reasons for
joining differed. In contrast to much of the rhetoric about women's
involvement in the war detailed above, some women who volunteered to

join the armed struggle did not stop to think about being women in the struggle, but simply joined up because of widespread oppression and perhaps out of patriotic duty. Following are excerpts from the interviews with some women ex-combatants who told their stories about why they joined up.

Joining Up

Sekai, who became a security officer within ZANU, said that she "decided to join the struggle because [she] wanted to liberate Zimbabwe."[1] Women joined as Zimbabweans to free the country from white minority rule. One woman ex-combatant stated that she

> wanted to liberate the country because the British colonised us, and there were some jobs only whites could get. I was eighteen years old when I joined. I had not heard about UDI [Unilateral Declaration of Independence - declared by Ian Smith in 1965] as I was too young. We wanted to liberate Zimbabwe. If you are a boy you can come to liberate Zimbabwe. If you are a girl you can come to liberate Zimbabwe.[2]

Rudo began her involvement in the armed struggle as a *chimbwido* in the rural areas of Rhodesia. The following is her story of joining up:

> I met the comrades first in 1972 [inside Rhodesia] ... I used to bring information from very far distances, where I knew that they are there. Later on ... I went to training. [When] I was finished my training I was pregnant. I trained at Chimbichimbi. In my case I didn't manage to come back [to Zimbabwe during the war]. Military training is not only jumping and the like. You have some lessons ... it makes you stronger. Sometimes you happen to discover yourself. You discover what you are, and what you are really made of.... Military training is something else. It is unique, it's quite different.... You feel different; the only difference is that you know what you are. I was in ZANLA and became a teacher in the camps ... I was teaching kids how to read and write. I was doing that up until 1980 and did not teach political education at all. Although it was a refugee camp it was no different to the other camps. Myself, I can use a gun; nearly everyone, most of them were trained. At Mafudzi [another camp] we were not excluded from the struggle; we were part of the struggle.[3]

Nhamo joined the nationalist forces in 1974 at sixteen years of age, after completing school at the level of form three. One of her girlfriends from the Mt. Darwin area had heard that some people were being educated by the nationalist forces in their camps across the borders in Zambia, Mozambique, and overseas. Nhamo's girlfriend suggested to her that they should both go to join the nationalist freedom fighters to receive this education. At first they went to Botswana where they were recruited to go to Zambia, and later they stayed in ZAPU's Nampundu Camp.[4]

Not Volunteers
Not all were voluntary recruits. Some young girls and boys were press ganged or "abducted" from their schools and forced to join the fighters. In January 1977, ZIPRA guerillas took the children from Manama Mission School and marched them to Botswana at gunpoint. They were later airlifted to Zambia. Teresa remembered how the Rhodesians had sent the children's parents to Botswana to collect them. However,

> only form one students turned back, a few of them, hardly twenty. The rest of the school, which was more than 500 students, had been convinced that by joining the liberation struggle, you'd be freeing yourself of a lot of conflict and a lot of colonialism within the country. So it is time you people stood in support of the liberation struggle. So, there was enough political knowledge which was given to us at that stage, so we gave the same back when we saw our parents. Then we decided to stay in Botswana. After our parents had gone back to Rhodesia, we then went to Zambia.[5]

Initial Roles
Although some women were already incorporated into the nationalist armed forces in 1972, before 1973 there is very little evidence to suggest that women were being recruited to train to fight.[6] At first women who joined up were mainly used to carry supplies and weapons to the front. This was dangerous but necessary and women were often confronted with ambushes and attacks from Rhodesian soldiers. In 1973 more women than before were demanding to be trained in order to protect themselves. Nhamo for example stated that

> our job was mainly to carry weapons to the border.... In 1975-76 I

became a teacher; and in early 1976 I was sent to Mozambique ... to ... [a] camp near the border. There were less than fifty women there and only a few men, mainly commanders. It was dangerous to be so close to the border, as there was always the threat of attack.[7]

It was not until 1976, however, that Nhamo was trained in guerilla warfare. She recollected:

I was trained for three months in Tembwe. I trained in all the war tactics.... We went to Mafudzi camp for refugees and I was promoted to the level of general staff and became a teacher, and also I was Mafudzi Camp Commander because of my position. That camp was holding almost 5,000 people including the masses and the refugees. *Vatoto* [Swahili - "young children"] there were about 2,000, about 2,300 masses - our parents, our mothers, and fathers. At that camp they didn't want trained people. Only sixteen people there were trained, and we went there disguised, because we wanted to teach people, because we didn't want our Zimbabweans to just stay and do nothing. We were not teaching political education but academic.[8]

According to Maxey, "The first women fighters to be heard of were a women's detachment in Centenary District in the northeast of Zimbabwe in August 1973."[9] Ruvimbo confirmed this view when she pointed out that because women had been used to carry war materials they could not go back to being civilians uninvolved in the guerilla war. She stated that

[o]nce the women were in the bush they couldn't return because they had been exposed. So it happened that in 1973, the first women were trained in exactly the same way as men.[10]

Three Key Women in the Struggle
1. Teurai Ropa
After finishing form two in 1973 Joyce Teurai Ropa Nhongo[11] left school to join the freedom fighters in Zambia and then Mozambique. She understood that the oppression of Africans could be challenged. Remembering her experiences she told me that after she had joined she was rapidly promoted:

I was just lucky to be one of the few who were chosen as leaders at that time. I was one of the few women who got trained to either do the commissariat work, the political training, or the military training. ... When selections for women representatives in the central committee or politburo were being carried out I was the only one to be chosen to be the politburo member. And when Mrs. [Sally] Mugabe came to join us, she then became the second one.[12]

She trained in light infantry for three months, using AK-47s and submachine guns. She also became a medical assistant and trained for six months. At age eighteen, she was promoted to the general staff and given political instruction. By 1975 she had become the political instructor at two successive military bases. At age twenty-one she became camp commander at Chimoio military and refugee camp in Mozambique, where she met her husband (Rex Nhongo, one of the party leaders). She then became military commander of the ZANLA women's detachment. In 1976 she was appointed director of politics in Chibawawa refugee camp. In 1977 in Mozambique, at the age of twenty-two years, Teurai Ropa became the youngest member of the central committee and was on the national executive. She was then appointed Secretary of Women's Affairs.

As a politically active woman Teurai Ropa became a prime target for Rhodesian security forces, which wanted to capture her. However, they were unsuccessful. In 1978, when the camp she was in was attacked by Rhodesian soldiers, Teurai Ropa fought on for two days, despite being in a late stage of pregnancy, before giving birth to a girl. Her daughter, Priscilla Rungano, was sent away to Zambia one month later, and Teurai Ropa continued to fight until liberation was won in 1980.[13]

During and after the war Teurai Ropa glowed in the international spotlight as a heroine of the liberation war. In 1981 *The Herald* reported that

Mrs Nhongo [Teurai Ropa] fought for what she believed in. With a gun in hand she rose through the military ranks to the position of Commander when she was little more than a girl. Her political talents were recognised and she became a member of the party's national executive and central committee.[14]

Teurai Ropa typified the heroic symbol of African woman warrior, with baby in one hand and gun in the other. However, when I interviewed her she admitted that she had never fought in combat inside Zimbabwe, since her role was to coordinate ZANU's Department of Women's Affairs in Mozambique. She stated:

> The operations that I carried out whilst I was still in the country are the only ones. The moment I went out I couldn't come back because the responsibilities out there were much more demanding than the responsibility of coming to fight an enemy. Because you know to plan to look for weapons, to really get people to train, to look for medicines, first in order to look after the sick. I think the rear job was more important than the front job.[15]

2. Naomi Nhiwatiwa

While I did not interview Naomi Nhiwatiwa for this study, there have been quite a few published interviews with her on the topic of women in the struggle. She was a spokesperson for ZANU and often promoted women's emancipation. In many cases her achievements were heralded as synonymous with those of other women in the struggle. However, she gained her position through an overseas education and political action, rather than by military or guerilla training. *The Herald* reported that

> Dr. Nhiwatiwa's self-confidence stems, perhaps, more from her academic achievements capped by the role she was chosen to play by Mr. Mugabe's fledging government. She left this country in the 1960s with a yen for education and she did not waver from the course she had set herself until 1979 when, armed with her doctorate in communications, she was ready to return home. During this lengthy period spent in the United States, Dr Nhiwatiwa was politically active. Her return coincided with the birth of Zimbabwe and her appointment as Deputy Minister of Posts and Telecommunications.[16]

3. Fay Chung

Fay Chung, a Chinese Zimbabwean, fought at the "rear" of the war. Her involvement in the struggle is significant for a woman, and a non-black Zimbabwean. During the struggle she taught ZANU teachers from schools for Zimbabwean refugees in Mozambique. She "joined ZANU in 1973 when she was a lecturer at the University of Zambia."[17] She organized theater pieces to educate people about the struggle. In 1974 she "spent ... twelve months getting food and clothing for the comrades in Zambia as well as refuting the enemy propaganda, which tried to discredit ZANU, the liberation struggle and the comrades."[18] When soon after an attempt was made on her life, she knew that she had become a serious threat to the colonial regime. After traveling to Tanzania and London she returned to Mozambique to establish a revolutionary education system.[19] Like Teurai Ropa after independence, Chung received a ministerial post. She became Chief Education Officer in the Ministry of Education.

Teurai Ropa, Naomi Nhiwatiwa, and Fay Chung were all considered to be successful women in the liberation struggle. All achieved government positions at independence. Their international and "world-traveling" experiences must be considered and weighed appropriately when comparing their experiences of war to the experiences of other women in the struggle - the women who have remained silent.

Other Women in the Struggle

By 1974 it became obvious that Zimbabwean women were entering the frontlines of the war. A court report from the trial of a ZANLA (male) guerilla fighter held in Salisbury during May 1974 "confirmed that there had been four women in the accused's party."[20] However, from this report it is unclear if the women were carrying weapons or if they were trained to fight. In my interviews with women ex-combatants few had experienced intensive guerilla military training upon arrival in the training camps, and few had been specifically sent to battle. Sekai explained how she was deployed and acted on the frontlines:

> I was in Teresera camp in Mozambique, Tete province. We were told to carry ammunition between the Zambezi and the front, en-route to the training camp. There were more than 100 women. I Spent six months in the camps before being trained, then we were trained for six months in (ZANLA) Chifombo camp in Zambia. We would meet the guerillas at the Zambezi to give them ammunition. There was a two-man boat/ferry which carried these goods from Zambia to Zimbabwe. In the training we were taught the use of weapons and to be physically fit. But there was too

many people and not enough food so we would share.[21]

Evidence of women's frontline activity is scarce, and in most cases it seems that women's main task was to ferry ammunition to the front. But as we saw earlier, to do so effectively required them to have some military training. Later, women's experiences of fighting will be discussed in more detail, but here it suffices to demonstrate the reasons why other women joined up and their initial experiences of war.

Freedom Nyamubaya

Some women did not join simply to liberate Zimbabwe, but to use the nationalist struggle as a means to facilitate their own agency as women or for personal reasons. Freedom Nyamubaya[22] admitted that one of the reasons she left to join the war was because she did not like the fact that her headmaster had not given her a scholarship. She said that she had wanted to get a gun and kill him. So, in 1975 Freedom Nyamubaya left Rhodesia with ten boys and was the only female at the time to arrive in Tete, Mozambique. Nyamubaya trained at ZIPA's Wampoa College until it was renamed Chitepo College after the demise of ZIPA. It was only after the political education she received that she gained an appreciation for the armed struggle and understood the different participation of all the actors at different levels in the war, for example, the role of the masses and the roles of the nationalist leaders.

Maria

Maria, who joined the struggle in 1975, did not give any particular reasons for wanting to join. She described how she was politically educated in ZIPA, then was deployed to educate "the masses" inside Zimbabwe on the need for revolutionary warfare. Her experience of joining up also highlights the difficulties with language and ethnicity within the political parties. As Vaughan has pointed out there were internal conflicts between ZAPU and ZANU based on ethnicity:

> The rivalry between ZANU and ZAPU had never been purely political. ZANU ... appealed to Shona ethnicity as a tactical necessity in building ties with the local population [east and northeast Zimbabwe]. On the other hand, ZAPU garnered the loyalties of

the Ndebele, not least because that was the ethnic origins of [ZAPU's leader] Joshua Nkomo.[23]

Maria felt these ethnic tensions during her training. She stated:

> I am from Bulawayo and I didn't know about ZAPU or ZANU. I went to Beira, [then to] Tete [in Mozambique] for training as a recruit, but I couldn't speak Shona, only Ndebele. So this made it difficult. I would cry when trying to talk to the other women. Gradually I learnt Shona because no one spoke Ndebele. This was in 1975 with other women we were training. Sometimes we were mischievous when training. We would run and hide then come back before the others. I was a political commissar in Tete and taught others about the struggle. In the evenings we would make slogans. I trained at Wampoa College, [ZIPA's] institute of political science ... So many women were equal like men. After the training we would go to the front to teach the masses.[24]

Without any particular reason or any particular political affiliation at the time, Maria was strikingly naive in her recruitment. When she described her involvement with ZIPA's Wampoa College to express the equalizing of the sexes through political education, Maria was censured by other women ex-combatants present at the interview. They suggested that what she had to say was unimportant, although it may have offered more clues to women's status within nationalism. What it also suggested was that it was better not to speak of ethnic rivalries between Shona and Ndebele.

Margaret Dongo

Compared with Maria, Margaret Dongo had a clearer idea why she joined up. She explained in detail about some of the important ideological reasons she had for joining up. Her father was politically active in the nationalist movement and was often arrested by the Rhodesian regime, but, as she states, she was also influenced by another girl who had received some political education from the guerilla fighters. After she had decided to join the nationalist army of ZANLA she walked across the border to Mozambique with her friend. Dongo described the training camps after she arrived:

> When I got to the camps, I was asked who I was, to surrender

what little, whatever I had, and choose a name for myself, a pseudonym. They said, "That's the end of calling you Margaret Ntetwa. You should find yourself a pseudonym you'll remember and that you'll call yourself." I said to myself, my name is "Tichaona Muhondo," meaning "we will see what will happen..".. The short cut was Ticha! From there, I am cutting the story short. I am not talking about the experience I got in those days. It was very nasty. What I expected to see was that now that I have come to the camp, I'm going to see shelter where I will sleep; I'm going to a bath, and here's a piece of soap. The first thing when we were released from the security camp/security holding, where you actually undergo interrogation and investigation before you go [and join in] with [the] other people, we went to bath. It was after some days before I had bathed. I had my school clothes, and when I got there I saw the veterans, the women veterans who were there.... You know I was still a recruit, and they said, "Well, you get these leaves and [*she pounds the table*] hit them, when you hit them ... you wash your body, and you can wash your pants and everything. You dry your clothes and put them on and go." And before I put on my trousers, they came up to me and said, "By the way, you are fresh, and coming from home, let's also get us to put on fresh clothes from home! One thing you must remember here, you are now a comrade." And a comrade will share everything: my pants and dresses went. There I was just like a refugee. Ah, it was terrible. And then I went to the barracks - shelter - thinking I would have somewhere nice to sleep, only to find someone say, "well there is your grass. You can thatch your bed there if you want to sleep on the bed. If you want to sleep on the floor, then there are these fleas which feed on human blood. Then they'll eat you. So you get this grass to make your mattress ... and you can make your bed." I started to cry. They said, "You are crying?" And I was lucky because there was somebody crying just next to me. And that person asked, and I said, "Oh, my god!" The veterans were already sleeping. And I said, "Okay, that's part of the struggle!" Then I had to say to myself, I had to learn to live with it. Nobody forced me to come. I think I had to adjust, and I did adjust, and in less than two weeks I was already part and parcel, with the hardships, and witnessing, you know, the situation that we had there. We could stay for two weeks without enough food, feeding on water or skimmed milk. Probably the time when you are too hungry a consignment of food comes up and you are told it is poisoned.[25]

Dongo's description illustrates the hardships in the training camps, not just for women, and the difficulties for new recruits thrust into the middle of a guerilla war. It is noteworthy that Dongo could provide such a detailed description of camp life. Margaret Dongo was the first female and independent member of Parliament (for Harare South) in Zimbabwe. She is an outspoken ex-combatant and helped establish the Zimbabwe National Liberation War Veteran's Association (ZNLWVA). Compared with the anonymous women ex-combatants cited above, Dongo did not fear reprisals for what she said because she wanted the world to know what it was like being a "guerilla girl," fighting for the liberation of one's country and then being then marginalized after the war.[26]

However, simply hearing some women explain why they joined up and their experiences of war and training as they remembered it does not give a complete account of the experiences of "guerilla girls" in the rest of the struggle and the war. Thus it is important to discuss the war as it encroached upon women's lives at both the rear and the front. Distinctions between front and rear were blurred during the struggle. This became apparent when refugee and training camps outside of Rhodesia were the focus of military attacks. The fighting then becomes located at the rear where women were serving in non military roles.

The Fighting

Three surprise attacks on guerilla training facilities outside of Rhodesia are discussed below to highlight the roles, experiences, and vulnerabilities of women guerilla fighters during the war.

Monica

When the Rhodesian Forces attacked ZANU's Nyadzonia Camp in Mozambique on August 9, 1976, thousands of refugees, mainly women and children, were killed. Monica's experience after arriving at Nyadzonia as a refugee highlights the brutality of the war:

> ... I had not seen a gun; I had not seen anything. All I had come to was to join the struggle.... As we were sitting on the ground ... cars came, and everybody else who was there were going to the cars, especially those who had been there for a longer time than us because to them cars signified training ... and I sat there with my other three colleagues, because we thought we have just arrived and our chances

of going training had maybe not come ... I asked, "How did the Rhodesians get through to the camp in the cars?" I don't know how .... and the next thing we are sitting there, and well pah pah pah! [gestures gun fire].[27]

The Rhodesian soldiers were using Mozambican uniforms, cars, and weapons to infiltrate the nationalists' camps. Some of the white soldiers had painted their faces black:

[A]fter gathering together part of the camp population and shouting slogans they opened fire indiscriminately with light weapons but also anti-tank and anti-aircraft guns.[28]

Monica had not been trained in military skills and so decided to run. She was shocked by the sound of gunfire. She explains the confusion during the attack:

As you are running you would actually feel the bullets "whoosh," and you'd see the other guy in front of you falling, you'd see the whole head coming off, and actually when that was happening. I'll tell you these people were refugee people who didn't know anything about the war. You know some of them would even stop the bullets with their hands, because they just thought, "What is this?" You hear this "zoom!"[29]

According to a captured Selous Scout[30] member, the Rhodesians attacked the unarmed refugees because

[i]t would be easier if we went in and wiped them out while they were unarmed and before they were trained rather than waiting for the possibility of them being trained and sent back armed into Rhodesia.[31]

In Monica's case, although she was eventually trained for guerilla warfare, she was never sent to the front. The Rhodesians' preventative measures, however, was not the only reason why Monica and other women guerilla fighters did not make it back into Rhodesia with arms. Monica talked about the tough guerilla training and where she ended up:

There were no clothes for training; we just had to go without clothes. I mean now, down the line you wouldn't be able to see the scars of training ... especially for us without good clothes, especially crawling. [We were wearing] anything we could get, and most of the clothes were donated to us by sympathizers.... You are crawling on the ground on stones and everything because it is in the forest ... there are [no] training fields ... When you fall, you can just fall on a stone or anything.... but you wouldn't give up. There was no choice like that ... this feeling that I want to train to be a soldier and go back and fight. The training is extremely tough. It was not training for fun, it was training to go and face the enemy.... despite the fact that we didn't have enough ammunition or armies like the enemy. I was appointed to [guard a camp]. As much as I wanted to go to the front, since I had come to fight the enemy, they always wanted people who would look after the camps. We were given our rifles to go and guard the women in this camp, Osibisa. All our camps had guards.[32]

For all her training and desire to go back and fight, Monica instead became responsible for guarding other women at Osibisa Camp, mainly pregnant women and mothers. She wanted to face the enemy like any guerilla soldier at the time and resented being kept in the camps.

Margaret Dongo
Starting on November 23, 1977, for three days, the Rhodesians forces attacked Chimoio Camp in Mozambique, which catered for both civilian and military personnel. Over one thousand people were killed. "The dead included hospital patients and almost a hundred schoolchildren, and some of the mass graves contained only women."[33] Margaret Dongo was in Chimoio and survived the attack:

I was one those who witnessed the Chimoio attack and the Tembwe attack, which was terrible. I survived because a friend of mine, [who] was shot, and in fact, where she was shot, there was this blood spilled over and I also fell asleep because of the gun powder and so forth. And when they were coming - they were kicking, "This is dead," and this and that, and this is how people would survive. When they find you they just take your gun and get it away from you and so forth. And immediately after that I was taken to Tembwe Base. And it was unfortunate that during the struggle we used to be very secretive, and when we got there we were told not to tell anyone that there was a surprise attack. And that's where we were coming from: we are coming from a war.[34]

The frontline of the war had reached the rear. This news was to be kept quiet somehow to reduce fear and panic. For Dongo, however, the experience of one attack helped her survive the next:

And when I go to there, I was supposed to proceed to the camp. And I want to say this time I want to believe that my ancestors played a role, and it was during this time that someone came and said, "No, Margaret has to go to the border because we need a consignment of whatever, treatments, and medicines, and so forth because there was another attack." And the truck that I was supposed to have used to go to the camp was attacked by the same people who had attacked us in Chimoio, and thousands and thousands of people died. Some lost their hands, some died, and that's where I lost a number of friends of mine. And so I survived. I survived more than three or four months of attacks. After that I went back to the military camp especially for women, and I was in transit. I was supposed to go to West Germany to specialize in certain things.[35]

Shupikai
Shupikai also experienced the Chimoio attack and survived to tell her story:

I was in Chimoio when it was attacked by the Rhodesians. I had just got the guns out for the day's training and sent a girlfriend to get more from the gunhold, and the spotter plane flew over. The first thing I did was lie on the ground, still, to see what was happening and when the bombs started dropping, I just ran ... for maybe twenty kilometers. Then I hid in the grass as paratroopers started dropping from the sky. At one point I was surrounded by these soldiers, and somehow I managed to avoid them. At one point I lay down and just fell asleep, only to be awoken by the footsteps of a comrade. I thought this was the end of me, and prayed to God that I was dead, so my parents wouldn't be harassed and tortured back home. The comrade turned out to be a "brother" so together we escaped. I then went to another training camp.[36]

Ruvimbo Mejeni

Another woman who survived the attack on Chimoio was Ruvimbo Mejeni. During the liberation war she went to Mozambique to join ZANU and married Edgar Tekere, who was associated with Robert Mugabe. At first she spent her time boiling lice ridden blankets, then lived and taught at Chimoio refugee camp until the 1977 attack. Ruvimbo Mejeni said,

> After the bombing I spent three days in a pit latrine. I didn't think that I would live. I wanted to leave a sign for other people, so I wrote my name and the date on a charcoal map of Zimbabwe, and threw it out of the toilet, hoping that some day someone would pick it up.[37]

Someone eventually found her. Ruvimbo Mejeni was not considered heroic enough to be buried at the National Heroes Acre in Harare. [38]

In Dongo's, Shupikai's and Mujeni's accounts of their experience of the fighting, it is interesting to observe that they survived through passive action - running away and hiding, or falling asleep from shock, gun powder, and stress. When women joined the struggle, like their male counterparts, they expected to be trained in the camps and then sent back to fight inside Rhodesia. However, the "joy" of going home to fight[39] was shattered by the Rhodesian air attacks on their camps. Women, men and children attempted to run to safety, but thousands were killed.[40] For those who survived, it is their experiences of war that need to be heard, and their pain that needs to be healed.

ZAPU Women in Zambia

While ZANU women were suffering daily hardships or death in Mozambican camps, in 1977 ZAPU established Victory Camp for women cadres in Zambia. ZAPU's approach to training women guerilla fighters was different from ZANU's because it insisted on separating the women from the men in women's training camps. It is important to distinguish between ZAPU's and ZANU's treatment of women guerilla fighters, before we describe the Rhodesian forces' attacks on Mkushi Camp in Zambia. In the Nyadzonia and Chimoio attacks, women were part of the collateral damage to the nationalist forces. In Zambia women became the actual targets.

Rufaro

Rufaro was committed to the struggle, even though she was "abducted" from her school by guerillas seeking recruits:

> I was born in Bulawayo. I went to the Bostwana/Zimbabwe border and crossed the river with over 200 children from the school. The guerillas took us, and Rhodesian soldiers followed us but didn't fire. Then after that they said all our group must go to Zambia for training. We were taken by plane. When we reached Zambia we were taken to Victory Camp. This camp was used by the MPLA [Movement for the Popular Liberation of Angola] freedom fighters. We found other children from the Manama Mission, who were captured by the same guerillas who captured us. There we stayed for some months doing military activities. We were training how to use guns, but this was not enough for us, because we left the country thinking of being trained as soldiers. Then we used to cry for that, saying, "Why are you discriminating us from men. Men are training in camps, we, just keep us here in V.C. [Victory Camp]. So why should you keep us in here? Please we want to train as soldiers."[41]

Rufaro, like many of the young students, was educated by the guerilla fighters about the political reasons for war and decided to stay on in Zambia to fight, despite the Rhodesian government program for parents to bring their children back from Botswana and Zambia.

Teresa

Teresa, who was also in Victory Camp, elaborated:

> So we were given military training as well. Victory camp was purely meant for refugees, initially. But the Manama students, when they started residing in that camp, were all given training. That is, political training as well as military training. It was not as intensive as what came or followed later in Solwezi and Mkushi and other military camps. I had "O" levels, so I became a medical doctor in the camps. The girls were moved from that place [where they first arrived] to open a new camp that was purely going to be for ladies. A camp which was formerly used by NATO people [sic] from Angola. So we went and started using that camp. It was Victoria Camp; for us it was Victory Camp because of the victory now coming to

Zimbabwe, through the enforcement by the children and women from the society in Zimbabwe; which meant all the society, parts, or structures were represented now in the liberation struggle. At that stage we continued to be convinced that we had taken a proper decision in coming to join the liberation struggle, by the politicians, rather than the commissars. In V.C. there were initially about 200 of us from Manama, but each evening we would get a truck, if not three trucks, so that the number we would get would be about 100. Then that is how they started training militarily.[42]

Thus, ZAPU placed the women into separate camps, but still trained them militarily.

Ruth
Nonetheless, ZAPU's focus seemed to be more on education than bush fighting to prepare them for the new Zimbabwe.[43] Ruth stated that ZIPRA treated its women differently compared to ZANLA, because it did not send as many women across the border into Rhodesia to fight or to be subjected to attacks on the frontlines. She said that

in Zambia ... it was very very, rare for women to come in and operate.... [They] were mainly used for political spreading, ... as commissariats as well as instructors for military training. They were very good. They mainly did not want to send female combatants to the front to come and fight. They usually sent men. That is why in Zambia the females were more protected. They were more advantaged than the females in Mozambique.[44]

Thus, while ZAPU appeared to treat women differently from ZANU, the outcome was similar for both groups, although ZAPU women appear to have been better educated. This education, however, did not protect them from the violence of war. This is demonstrated by the Rhodesian air and ground attack on Mkushi Camp in Zambia.

Mkushi Camp
ZAPU's Mkushi Camp located 150 kilometers north of Lusaka in Zambia, a refugee and training camp for women, was attacked and bombed by the Rhodesian forces on October 17, 1978.

Rhodesia's daring and devastating self-defence raids against terrorist camps deep inside Zambia [Freedom, ZAPU's main military camp and alleged terrorist training headquarters, Mkushi Camp] represented the biggest operation yet mounted by security forces in the six-year war. Three major terrorist complexes and nine satellite camps were bombed, large quantities of arms, explosives and equipment seized and destroyed, more than 1,500 terrorists - including trained, uniformed and armed women - were killed, and many other injured.[45]

The report continued to describe the carnage:

Corpses, large quantities of communist small-arms and literature, camping equipment and boots by the hundred lay strewn among the bomb craters and smouldering mud-and-thatch barracks ... "We were shown a large quantity of communist rifles, both Russian and Chinese, landmines, grenades and rocket launchers." At a newly erected barracks seven corpses were seen lying on the veranda. They and other bodies all over the camp - were invariably young men and women, scarcely out of their teens.[46]

"Women" became central to the war propaganda of both the Rhodesians and Nationalists, who used images of women to create tensions in a masculine discourse. Women were represented as victims of a male "terrorist" campaign. The attack on Mkushi Camp was different from the previous attacks on Nyadzonia and Chimoio Camps because it was a deliberate attack against women guerilla recruits. Joshua Nkomo, the leader of ZAPU, stated that

the Rhodesians heard that there were women terrorists and wanted to capture them, so the commander ordered that they [the women] retreat to Tembwe camp. They didn't want to kill but capture.[47]

Ken Flower, an ex-Rhodesian intelligence officer, reported that the Mkushi bombings resulted in massive deaths and injuries, but they were not intended as an attack on women:

1,600 "trained terrorists" and other members of ZIPRA were killed and the Lusaka hospitals were inundated with wounded.... A proportion of those killed in the Mkushi area were women under military training who gave a fair account of themselves but whose sex could not have been identified through aerial reconnaissance or the more remote intelligence on which we had to rely. Over thirty civilians and ZIPRA "dissidents" being held in underground bunkers were released. Thousands of weapons were destroyed on the ground and tons of war material blasted from the air.[48]

Flower's comments justify the attack on women in that they "gave a fair account of themselves" - fighting back like soldiers (and not like women).

Nevertheless, Nkomo reported that there were only refugees in Freedom Camp, denying the existence of any trained women guerillas. He said the attack on Mkushi Camp was a "cowardly attack on a camp of unarmed young women." There were only twenty-seven men and 1,606 women there who were training to be "civil servants for a future Zimbabwe."[49] Evidence had shown that "Zipra [sic] had been trained more for use as a conventional army in the post-independence era than for guerilla warfare,"[50] hence the focus on education rather than bush war.

Despite Flower's claim that the Rhodesians were not aware there were mainly women in the camp, Nkomo stated that:

> [t]he Rhodesian intelligence service was remarkably well informed, and their forces were capable of precise actions, such as the raid on my home in Lusaka, which they carried out in trucks painted in the colours of the Zambian army... This makes me think that some of their worst atrocities were deliberate, not accidental.[51]

Nkomo accused the Western media (for example, *Focus on Rhodesia*) of labeling it a guerilla camp, and of confusing forty-eight rifles "only for defence," with thousands of Russian AK-47s. ZAPU's account of the attack was more far more graphic than the Rhodesians' or Western media's accounts, highlighting the specific target of "women guerillas." The *Zimbabwe People's Voice* described how three or four jet bombers and eight helicopters attacked,

> while the girls were having breakfast - a late morning breakfast around 11:00 hours. Smith's fascist forces rampaged through the camp. They seized a girl, [Jane Gumbo, the head of the camp] one of the instructors. They coerced her at gun point into calling her students to parade by whistle. Not many girls came out of hiding. Only a few, about eighty to ninety responded to the whistle. It has

to be remembered that these girls are not trained militarily. After they were lined up, eight to ten white men stood with their guns. The girl instructor was given a gun and ordered to shoot her students. She refused and was shot. The white soldiers then opened fire and all the girls were shot.[52]

Nkomo wrote that "the white soldiers who seem to have been mercenaries rather than Rhodesians, massacred ninety-one girls: the black troops under their command helped large numbers of girls to escape, and came close to mutinying against their orders."[53] It was a situation of white men killing black women. When Mkushi Camp was specifically attacked by Rhodesian forces in 1978, ZAPU's confidence was shattered. While the nationalists claimed that the women killed in Mkushi had been unarmed refugees, they still could not protect them. The fact that Rhodesians appear to have targeted a women's camp demonstrates their desire to destroy the nationalists by undermining their ability to protect their women.

However, despite the nationalists' attempts to vilify the Rhodesians for attacking unarmed women, some women ex-combatants who survived the attack admitted that they were trained in military tactics. Teresa claimed that ZIPRA was specifically training at least one thousand women for active urban guerilla warfare, but the war ended before they were deployed.[54] Tsitsi spoke of her experience in Mkushi Camp in Zambia as being dominated by military training:

> In Mkushi life was not all that different [for men and women], because we were the first group of women to train there. So we had more advantages than men. In our camp there were a few men. These were instructors and old men who used to cook food for us. We trained heavily ... we were very much anxious to do so.[55]

Rufaro was also trained at Mkushi Camp and was there when it was attacked. Her story also contradicts the reports from the nationalists and the Rhodesians, and highlights the superior artillery power of the Rhodesians, whether the women were trained or not. She said that

> [when] they decided to open a new camp ... for women [in Zambia] I was in the first group. It was called Mkushi. We went there, we

were more than a thousand ... But I was one of the first women ex-combatants trained there ... for guerilla warfare. We trained how to use explosives, machine guns, AK rifles ... and even how to mine a field.... Men were instructors. When Mkushi was bombed by air in 1978 some of us fought back, but it was too late, the camp was encircled. And to fight somebody using helicopters, and you using small guns, is very difficult. And we did not know whether the enemy was going to attack women. That was being coward. This was to provoke the situation. Even now when I sleep, I dream of some of the comrades who died there. After the bombing we were transferred to A-. Some of us went to hospitals, some to B-., some to C-. I went to the hospital and after that I went to D-. I was injured. I was shot in the shoulder. So after there I stayed in Victory Camp.... I was fifteen years old.[56]

For this ZIPRA ex-combatant the Rhodesian bombing of the women's training camp was horrific and shocking: "We did not know whether the enemy was going to attack women." While the Rhodesians may not have been discriminating between women and men terrorists, they were using the propaganda that women were being trained as "murderers" to justify their actions. The impact of the bombing of women's camps on ZAPU and ZIPRA was severe. Nkomo emphasized that the women were civilians, and it was not a military installation. Yet the ZIPRA women ex-combatants confirm that it was used for military training.

However, does this justify the Rhodesians attacking it with such severity? Is it the case that the attacks were more to prove the women could not be protected by their men? It has been suggested by Martin Meredith that the Rhodesian raids inside Zambia were simply to boost the morale of the white population in Rhodesia, which had suffered a severe blow since the shooting down of the Air Rhodesia Viscount by ZIPRA forces on September 4th, (and to pre-empt a ZIPRA rainy season offensive).[57] It was not only that the plane crashed, but the survivors were tracked down and massacred. One passenger, a young white woman was raped before being killed. For ZAPU the attacks on Mkushi women's camp seemed more like revenge than a case of mistaken identity as Flower suggests.

The Rhodesians and the nationalist parties established particular representations of women, either as civilians or guerillas. The particular "femaleness" of women in ZAPU's training camps was exploited by ZAPU and ZIPRA to show how cowardly the Rhodesians were to attack a camp full of "innocent" women, gaining international sympathy for their cause. The Rhodesians also exploited a particular understanding of women by highlighting how depraved and desperate the nationalists must have been to use women in their army. Each side was using constructions of gender as an instrument to promote their own political agenda within the field of representations. Whether at Nyadzonia, Chimoio, or Mkushi, women's survival, suffering or death, not only illustrates the brutality of war and unnecessary levels of violence, but highlights the blurred boundaries between front and rear during wars of liberation.

White Rhodesian Women's Roles
In this gendered analysis of war we must also consider the violence against white women during the war, and the role that they played in the war. It also serves as a comparison of the roles of women in war on opposing sides, to illustrate the continuities and departures between black and white women's experiences of war in Rhodesia. A study of Zimbabwean women's heroism in times of war cannot ignore the role of white Rhodesian women at the front, middle, and rear, and that some of them stayed on in independent Zimbabwe.

White women were needed to support the Rhodesian government and the white minority state. As one Rhodesian advertisement suggested, white Rhodesian women were also important within national security debates:

"Be a Dumb Blonde - Think About National Security-Don't Talk About It"
"Think About National Security"

"For His Sake Keep Quiet"[58]

As the above advertisement suggests, white women were in a position to know what was going on in the war, possibly through conversations with their husbands, but were told to keep quiet. This representation of white women locates them only as wives or girlfriends of male actors. The only connection they have to war is information overheard; their only action is perceived to be gossiping. Here white women were imagined as "dumb blondes," which contrasts significantly with the roles of black women as

128

chimbwidos, entrusted with messages and information for the guerillas. Yet, far from being passive bystanders, many white women actively rallied behind the Rhodesian government and their men, as this advertisement urged them to do:.

> *You know ... our country is going through fairly difficult times right now ... We need more girls to step forward though, someone like you!... The Velvet Gloves of the BSAP.*[59]

While black Zimbabwean women were symbolizing the nation as mothers and challenging the usual distinctions between front and rear in their support of the guerilla war, white Rhodesian women were found at the rear, on the "home front" supporting the Rhodesian war effort in their roles as mothers, wives, and "dumb blondes." Yet they challenged these gendered and patronizing roles when it was necessary, for example, to defend themselves on their farms from guerilla attacks. The following section will focus on these activities at the so-called rear of military action, which as mentioned before often became the front.

In the Rhodesian press and nationalist propaganda white Rhodesian women embodied the "natural" woman's place at the rear while the men "protected" them by going to the front. Yet, the stereotype of women at the rear being protected by men, is challenged by white women wielding guns on the home front to protect themselves from attacks while their men were off at the *real* front. For example, the BSAP magazine *Outpost* highlighted the important role of the "pistol-packing Mamas" in its Feminine Folios: "For the third year in succession Mrs Jill McCracken of the Borrowdale Field reserve has proved herself to be the top 'pistol-packing Mama' among Salisbury's women field reservists ... [in their] annual shoot-out on the range."[60] White women proved themselves to be very capable of fighting, like men, when required for national service.

In 1975, while thousands of African women were joining the nationalists to fight against colonialism, white women were also recruited to support Rhodesian military operations. Incorporating women in a predominantly male domain - of war - causes much disruption to the discourse and action of war. Thus much effort also goes into minimizing the challenges to traditional gender roles. For example, Mrs. Pay Cooper, the public relations officer of the Business and Professional Women's Club, stated in June 1978

Women can be useful and if we have to make an all-out effort now, our contribution is necessary. But I hope single women or those with older children will join first. Those with young children should make sure their families are well cared for before they join.... What we need now very badly is a strong, united sense of Rhodesian loyalty and nationality. For that reason I hope that women of all races will be considered for these services. I know that African women police constables play a very valuable part in the Women's Police Service. Now women are joining with men to help our country and I think there should be no racial distinction.[61]

Women "of all races" were necessary for the Rhodesian war effort. This initial request for their services however did not require mothers to disrupt their child-rearing roles.

White Rhodesian women, like black Zimbabwean women, were not homogenous in their thoughts and actions. Some women supported the black nationalist movement, like Judith Todd, while other women supported Ian Smith's white racist Rhodesia. One woman in the police reserves pointed out, "We were working with the government of the day,"[62] which is not to say she was in total agreement with Smith's Rhodesia. David Caute reports the attitudes of a group of white women about their role and feelings of being at the rear in Rhodesia. He writes that Trish Pennington "in her drugged lethargy" wanted to get out of Rhodesia, "nostalgic about the old days when you could picnic anywhere." She could not cope with the war.

One lady loses no time in explaining [to a dinner party] that she bought her Sten gun from the District Commissioner for $(R)90 but that a magazine of thirty rounds cost $(R)3 and the Salisbury gunsmiths are now charging extortionate prices, "but that's your Jew everywhere, isn't it?"[63]

Boasting about her gun, this woman was prepared to face the front at the rear: she was not adverse to using her gun to protect her country. White Rhodesian women were located on the (home) front both in rhetoric and reality. Women were promoted in the media as tough and capable, yet feminine: Headlines read, "What the Fashionable Woman Will Be Wearing This Year. You Have Always Been Proud of Our Boys - Now You Can Join Them."[64] "Blue Birds Are a Hit with the Air Force."[65] and "The

Lethal Lovelies - Policewomen Can Take Care of Themselves."[66] *Focus on Rhodesia* reported:

> Typical of frontier folk throughout the world, Rhodesian women have shown great pluck and endurance in the face of terrorism and the economic problems posed by sanctions. They can face drought, fear, armed attacks on their homes, the ever present risk of being blown up by a terrorist landmine - and emerge as practical and charming as ever.[67]

Nonetheless, despite women's contributions to the army, air force and police,[68] white women were also reminded of their important "female" role of emotional support for the real soldiers - the men.

> An important contribution that Rhodesian women can make to the national effort is to maintain the morale of their menfolk.... Colonel Hopkins said morale was one of the principles of war and military textbooks said "success in war depends more on morale than on physical qualities."[69]

Women were needed as understanding and patient females for the sake of the returning male soldiers. The following romanticized narrative quoted by David Caute locates women happily at the rear in their roles as mother, wife, and "woman," there to please the man who comes back from the front for the recuperative feminine touch.

> The sight of soldiers always stirs the female heart ... This is an emotion as old as history. But when the local *recce.stick* - rugged, hairy, weary, hungry - pitches up at the farm back/front door ... I get positively weepy. It's one of the nicest sights in the world. Besides wanting to burst into tears of pure pleasure and patriotism, I also wish (a) that I'd cooked roast or T-Bones with chip-potatoes instead of stupid macaroni cheese, (b) that I'd had time to put on my best dress and lipstick, (c) that I'd remembered to put the beer on ice, and (d) that I could write poetry. Recce.sticks always make me want to burst into verse.[70]

Some white women, however, did become involved in more active duties. For example, one twenty-seven year-old woman, Mrs. Beryl Sheehan, an "attractive mother,"[71] who was the only woman in the Women's Services Corp Dog Troop, had been on several operational tours detecting landmines with her Labrador bitch. When asked what it was like in the operational area for a [white] woman, she said:

> Being two females Bracken [the dog] and I, going out among all the males was a bit difficult at first. But when we found what we had been trained to find for the first time we all celebrated together. I was treated the same as the men and I asked no favours. I carried what I had to carry plus dog's rations - and we found mines.[72]

Women also became police officers. In 1977 there were sixteen African women constables and forty-two European women police officers.

> The maintenance of law and order is one of Rhodesia's top priorities and her women are playing an integral part in keeping it. Their roles range from full-time service in the Rhodesian Womens Service - the Army and the Air Force - to civilians running canteens and restaurants.[73]

The ZAPU nationalist forces in Zambia described the Rhodesian inclusion of women in its security and defense ranks as "ludicrous." They claimed that the Rhodesians had been forced to form a "mummies army." The *Zimbabwe People's Voice* stated that "women are now becoming an integral part of Rhodesian Defence Force."[74] Since 1975 women were involved in clerical work but

> the situation has of recent times changed and the women are now going into the field to do the jobs previously reserved for men. The women in the Rhodesian Women's Service (RWS) and those in the Women Police Auxiliary Service (WPAS) actually go to the battlefield to help with casualties. The women toting machine pistols go to the operational areas in bizarre looking mine protected vehicles.[75]

According to this source there were 170 full-time RWS while the WPAS had only part-timers, mainly farmer's wives who operated the Agri-Alert radio service. The photo accompanying the article showed women being taught how to use 9 mm commando guns by a member of parliament, Mr. Andrew Holland. They were all white women. The point of the nationalists' article was to illustrate to the world the desperation of the Rhodesian forces. Even white women had to "fight." However, in an interview with one ex-service woman, seventeen years after independence, she remembered how proud and enthusiastic she was to volunteer her services in the war effort. Jill was the women's section leader in the Police Field Reserves. She said that all of the women were volunteers, while for the men it was compulsory. However,

> the majority of women in Salisbury didn't know what was going on. We were out in the bush. The war started terrorising the farmers. For people in the city it did not really affect them, only an inconvenience.[76]

Jill described how women supported the war effort:

> The big thing that women did, when the men were confined to barracks, was, every night a woman would cook for them and take it up. We'd ask women who were not in the Police Reserves to do their duty.[77]

Jill's job required her to organize all of the women. Through the Agri-Alert radio system he would "call all the people around a wide area - if they didn't answer our chaps would go out and see what's wrong." She said:

> Our role was purely security, law and order, working with the government of the day. We were not fighting a war, but protecting ourselves, our families and our workers. For my own protection and [that] of my family and workers I carried a pistol. I slept with it under my pillow. If I went out at night I'd wear camouflage.[78]

While Jill's role was important, most Rhodesian women were concentrated in domestic activities including cooking for the Hartley Forces' canteen to feed the boys on their way to or from the front. One hundred women cooked in their homes and at the canteen: "The women provide the men with a 'real home from home' at the Forces Residential Centre and Canteen

133

close to the city centre."[79] The white women's gendered roles here can be compared with the African "mothers of the revolution" who fed and clothed the guerilla fighters. The only difference here is race and ideology. Gendered distinctions were almost universal.

Located both at the front and the rear, white women transgressed these boundaries by going "international" and appealing to other countries not to support the "terrorists." A group called "Women for Rhodesia" was formed in order to "tell the world the truth [and] unite the Nation."[80] Their main strategy was collating newspaper articles about terrorist atrocities from the local press and sending these out to Australia and England, with an accompanying phonogram pleading with the rest of the international community to help stop the terrorists. They were playing at international relations and deploying "women" as symbols in the struggle to win the ideological war. One phonogram sent from Salisbury sometime in 1978 said:

PEOPLE OF [Australia/England, etc]. ARE YOU PREPARED TO WATCH ANOTHER CIVILISATION GO DOWN UNDER THE RUSSIAN HAMMER? BY YOUR INDIFFERENCE YOU CONDONE TORTURE MUTILATION AND HIDEOUS MURDER STOP THE RAPE OF *LITTLE GIRLS* STOP THE SLAUGHTER OF HELPLESS MISSIONARIES AND THEIR FAMILIES STOP CAN YOU ACCEPT AN *AFRICAN WOMAN* FORCED TO DECAPITATE HER HUSBAND IN FRONT OF HER CHILDREN? AN 18 MONTH OLD *BABY GIRL* USED AS A FOOTBALL AND BAYONETED TO DEATH? [my emphasis][81]

This appeal to the international community by women was their contribution to the events of the war. Analyzing the women's use of propaganda highlights the way gender is perceived and utilized in war. *Women for Rhodesia* attempted to "illustrate how helpless and defenseless men, women and children of all races are being tortured, mutilated, and murdered by Communist-trained terrorists that the world calls 'freedom fighters.'"[82] Their appeals to the international community to help stop the war (by not supporting the terrorists), relied upon the emotive image of women as victims. For example, the newspaper articles they included in their press releases highlighted the vulnerability of women to black male nationalists:

a black woman being forced to decapitate her husband's head with an axe by guerilla fighters; another involved the murder of a baby by a group of twenty terrorists. It was reported that a black domestic worker and nanny for a white family was subjected to a guerilla attack when the war front came to her home/workplace. She was forced to protect her charge, six and a half month old baby Natasha Glenny, by strapping the baby to her back and pretending it was albino. When the group of twenty 'terrorists' discovered it was a white baby, the nursemaid was beaten badly, and Natasha was stabbed several times in the back.[83] It was suggested the nanny should get a bravery medal, but she could not be identified because of potential reprisals from the guerillas) and so her status dissolved in the turmoil of war.[84] While these cases show that war is very cruel and that women suffer at the hands of men, to reinforce stereotypes of women as victims is to undermine the agency that black and white women experienced during the war. It contributes to the discourse of war that women have no control over it and hence are not central or important to it.

Yet during the war,[85] one Rhodesian minister urged women to play an active role in ending the war by using their influence as "women." Mr. Gibson Magaramombe, the co-minister of education spoke to a group of women at the National Council of Women in Rhodesia annual conference, stating that:

> he believed there was no one who had suffered more during the war than the women of this country ... Rhodesian women should help to end the terrorist war by using their influence to persuade black leaders both inside and outside the country to agree to a round table conference.[86]

Magaramombe stated that women should be involved in politics and wanted also to see African women MPs because they had "not been involved in party politics" and therefore could be impartial. However, the national president of the NCW, Mrs. Leila Creewel, summed up by saying that she believed that "women have a special duty to prevent humanity from accepting such terrors as the norm. Women have a particular role to play in maintaining the human touch."[87] It has been demonstrated, however, that both black and white women were involved in the fighting and in the process challenged such stereotypes of women as being essentially nurturers, rather than being able soldiers on an equal footing with men.

White women played a significant role in the war, although they did not fight as soldiers alongside men to the same extent that black Zimbabwean women did. The voices of white women are somewhat silenced given the outcome of the war: many indeed left the country. In Jill's own words: "I shouldn't really be talking about this."[88] The victory of majority rule has silenced the experiences of white Rhodesian women in the war. Further investigation of their experiences could contribute to a greater understanding and overall historical analysis of the incorporation of women in war in Africa. For the present purposes, however, it has been sufficient to outline the role of white women as represented in the media, propaganda, and the discourse of war.

Juxtaposing this analysis with the voices of black Zimbabwean women telling their stories of their involvement in the struggle has been important to highlight a women's history of the liberation war. Privileging their voices over the drone of previous historical accounts allows the women to be heard in the discourse of war - to represent themselves. In particular for the black Zimbabwean women silenced by the oppressions of colonialism, to listen to their voices representing themselves enables them to no longer be subaltern. Surrounding the attempts to center women's location in the war effort, their voices have been supported by published accounts of women's roles. However, these have often been hidden by their location in the history of "women's issues" rather than that of the war or national struggle. By bringing women's issues into the war, their voices will be heard.

Endnotes

1. Interview with Sekai, Harare, September, 1996.
2. Interview with Nyarai, Harare, September, 1996.
3. Interview with Rudo, Harare, September, 1996. Interestingly Rudo admits she was pregnant by the end of training.
4. Interview with Nhamo, Harare, September, 1996.
5. Interview with Teresa, Harare, September, 1996.
6. See Elaine Windrich, *The Rhodesian Problem: A Documentary Record 1923 - 1973*, (London and Boston: Routledge and Kegan Paul, 1975), pp. 285-90. She cites "Document 55. The Zimbabwe African People's Union (ZAPU) statement to the UN/OAU Conference on Southern Africa, Oslo, April 9-14, 1973 taken from *Southern Africa, The UN/OAU Conference*, O. Stokke and C. Widstrand eds., Scandinavian Institute of African Studies, Oslo, 1973. In this document

there is only one reference to women involved in the war, in that ZAPU requested "material needs, shelter, blankets, large quantities of all types of clothing - male and female - to meet the needs of freedom fighters as well as for welfare purposes."

7. Interview with Nhamo, Harare, September 1996.
8. Ibid.
9. K. Maxey, *The Fight For Zimbabwe*, (London: Rex Collings, 1975), p. 153, cited in Leda Stott, *Women and the Armed Struggle for Independence in Zimbabwe, 1964-1979,* p. 28.
10. Ruvimbo, quoted in Ruth Weiss, *The Women of Zimbabwe*, (Harare: Nehanda Publishers, 1986), p. 72.
11. During the struggle new recruits were asked to take on new names so that their families would not be persecuted by the Rhodesians if they were caught. Teurai Ropa meaning "spill blood" was the name taken on by Joyce Mujuru. She became the most publicized woman guerilla fighter when she was promoted to head the ZANU Department of Women's Affairs in Mozambique in 1978. After independence she became the youngest and first female minister in the first democratically elected government in Zimbabwe. She married a ZANLA commander, Rex Nhongo during the war. Joyce Mujuru was the Minister for Information, Posts and Telecommunications in 1996 when I interviewed her. In 1998 she became the Minister for Water Development and Rural Resources. In the text I refer to her as Teurai Ropa to avoid confusion.
12. Interview with Joyce Mujuru, Harare, October 1996.
13. Tanya Lyons, on "Joyce Mujuru" in *Military Women Worldwide: A Biographical Dictionary*, (Greenwood Press, forthcoming).
14. "Confidence the Key to Women's Future Hopes," The *Herald*, March 6, 1981.
15. Interview with Joyce Mujuru, Harare, October, 1996.
16. "Confidence the Key to Women's Future Hopes," The *Herald*, March 6th, 1981.
17. See "Fay Chung: Educator for Change," in *Moto*, August 1982, pp.41-42.
18. Ibid.
19. Ibid.
20. Leda Stott, *Women and the Armed Struggle for Independence in Zimbabwe, 1964-1979,* p. 28.
21. Interview with Sekai, Harare, September, 1996.
22. Freedom Nyamubaya is a published author and outspoken woman ex-combatant in Zimbabwe. Interview with Freedom Nyamubaya, October, Marondera, 1996.
23. Richard Vaughan and Ian Murphy, *Zimbabwe: Africa's Paradise*, (London: CBC, 1994), p.24.
24. Interview with Maria, Harare, September, 1996.
25. Interview with Margaret Dongo, Harare, March, 1997. Dongo had already been interviewed extensively by researchers, and thus only agreed to be interviewed for this research because it was in conjunction with an interview by Joyce Makwenda on behalf of the *Women in Culture in Southern Africa* group. See Zimbabwe Women Writers, eds., *Women of Resilience: The Voices*

of Women Ex-Combatants, (Harare: Zimbabwe Women Writers, 2000).

26. It has been suggested that Dongo was influenced by the teachings at Wampoa College during the war, and was thus able to articulate women's rights and the need for democracy in Zimbabwe. Interview with Dzino, Harare, August, 1996.

27. Interview with Monica, Harare, August, 1996.

28. David Martin and Phyllis Johnson, *The Struggle for Zimbabwe: The Chimurenga War*, p. 24.

29. Interview with Monica, Harare, August, 1996.

30. The Selous Scouts were a Rhodesian special army unit formed in November 1973 notorious for impersonating guerilla fighters and committing atrocities against missionaries and refugees. See Janice McLaughlin, *On The Frontline: Catholic Missions in Zimbabwe's Liberation War*, p. 152.

31. Copy of Prince Sadruddin Aga Khan's message circulated to all diplomatic missions in Maputo on August 25, 1976, cited in David Martin and Phyllis Johnson, *The Struggle for Zimbabwe: The Chimurenga War*, p. 241.

32. Interview with Monica, Harare, August, 1996.

33. David Martin and Phyllis Johnson, *The Struggle for Zimbabwe: The Chimurenga War*, p. 288.

34. Interview with Margaret Dongo, Harare, March, 1997.

35. Interview with Margaret Dongo, Harare, March, 1997.

36. Interview with Shupikai, Harare, September, 1996.

37. Ruvimbo Mujeni in Kathy Bond-Stewart, *Independence Is Not for Only One Sex*, (Harare: Zimbabwe Publishing House, 1987), p. 25.

38. Ruvimbo Mujeni took a while to readjust to society after that experience, and in 1979 the party sent her to Tanzania to "study the experiences of other women in independent countries." Ibid. She divorced Tekere after the war and died in mid-July 1996. Her death receives only small mention in the local *Sunday Mail* (Harare), July 14, 1996, p. 5.

39. See Gremerina Zembbiti, in *Moto*, 94, November, 1990, pp. 4-5.

40. An estimated 40,000 perished during the liberation war. See *Africa Confidential*, August 19, 1987, cited in Norma Kriger, *Zimbabwe's Guerilla War: Peasant Voices*, p. 4.

41. Interview with Rufaro, Harare, September, 1996.

42. Interview with Teresa, Harare, September, 1996.

43. See Jeremy Brickhill, "Daring to Storm the Heavens: The Military Strategy of ZAPU, 1976-79," in Ngwabi Bhebe and Terence Ranger, *Soldiers in Zimbabwe's Liberation War*.

44. Interview with Ruth, Harare, September, 1996.

45. "Massive Raids Were Enormously Successful," in *Focus on Rhodesia*, 3:7, 1978.

46. Ibid.

47. Interview with Nhamo, Harare, September, 1996.

48. Ken Flower, *Serving Secretly: An Intelligence Chief on Record, Rhodesia into Zimbabwe, 1964-1981*, (London: John Murray, 1987), p. 214.

49. Joshua Nkomo, *Nkomo: The Story of My Life*, (London: Methuen, 1984), p.

169.

50. Martin Meredith, *The Past Is Another Country: Rhodesia - 1890-1979*, (London: Andre Deustch, 1979), p. 351.

51. Joshua Nkomo, *Nkomo: The Story of My Life*, p. 169.

52. "Massacre of Defenceless Girls at Mkushi," *Zimbabwe People's Voice*, October 28, 1978, (National Archives of Zimbabwe microfilm collection).

53. Joshua Nkomo, *Nkomo: The Story of My Life*, p. 169.

54. Interview with Teresa, Harare, September, 1996. ZIPRA's Zero Hour Plan that signalled a shift in ZAPU's military strategy from guerilla to conventional warfare was threatened to be implemented right up until the end of the Lancaster House Talks. The pressure to settle at the negotiating table was greater however. See Jeremy Brickhill, "Daring to Storm the Heavens," pp. 61-65.

55. Interview with Tsitsi, Harare, October, 1996.

56. Interview with Rufaro, Harare, September, 1996.

57. See Martin Meredith, *The Past Is Another Country*, pp. 349-50.

58. Rhodesian Advertisements from the war period on Display at the National Archives of Zimbabwe.

59. Advertisement for the British South Africa Police Force, The *Sunday News* (Bulawayo), June 25, 1978, p. 18.

60. "Feminine Folios - Jill's Hat Trick," in *Outpost*, Magazine of the BSAP, February, 1975.

61. "Big Welcome for Women's Forces Plan," The *Sunday Mail*, June 29, 1975.

62. Interview with Jill, ex-section leader, Borrowdale Police Reserves, Harare, March, 1998.

63. David Caute, *Under the Skin; the Death of White Rhodesia*, (London: Allen Lane, 1983), p. 36.

64. The *Sunday Mail*, June 29, 1975, p. 3.

65. The *Sunday Mail*, December 7, 1975.

66. The *Sunday Mail*, September 25, 1977.

67. "Progress By the Feminine Task Force," in *Focus on Rhodesia*, 2:2, 1977.

68. See for example, "Women to serve in Army and Air Force," The *Herald*, Saturday June 28, 1975: and "Women Anxious to Join the Forces," The *Herald*, July 2, 1975.

69. "Women Urged to Help Men's Morale," The *Herald*, Monday August 23, 1976.

70. My emphasis: recce.stick was the name used to describe a group of people usually men, who went out on reconnaissance missions. David Caute, *Under the Skin: The Death of White Rhodesia*, p. 53.

71. "Sergeant Beryl and the Dogs with a Nose for Danger," in *Sunday News* (Bulawayo), April 23, 1978, p. 7.

72. Ibid. The article emphasised that the dog was also female, a "bitch."

73. "Petticoat Power Backs Men in the Bush," *Focus on Rhodesia*, 2:6, 1977.

74. "Rhodesia Forms Mummies Army," *Zimbabwe People's Voice*, September 29, 1979.

75. Ibid.

76. Interview with Jill, Harare, March 1998.
77. Ibid.
78. Ibid.
79. "Food to Feed the Fighters, " *Focus on Rhodesia*, 2:4, 1979.
80. Women for Rhodesia, *Extracts From the Rhodesia Herald and Sunday Mail*, 1978 (National Archives of Zimbabwe).
81. Ibid.
82. Ibid.
83. Ibid. A *Rhodesian Herald* report stated, "Bravery Award Recommended for Nursemaid," but her identity had to remain anonymous.
84. Ibid.
85. This was during the time of the internal settlement, signed in March 1978 by Muzorewa, Sithole, and Ian Smith. It created a transitional government until elections were held in April 1979. Muzorewa became the first African prime minister in the new Zimbabwe-Rhodesia. See Norma Kriger, *Zimbabwe's Guerilla War: Peasant Voices*, p. 87.
86. "Minister Urges Women: Help End the War," in *Sunday News* (Bulawayo), August 20, 1978, p. 7.
87. Ibid.
88. Interview with Jill, Harare, March, 1998.

Chapter Six

Mothers of the Revolution

The presence of the young mothers was an indication that the war for the liberation of Zimbabwe was coming to an end. "If these mothers failed to liberate their country then these children born into the turmoil would not fail." - The *Zimbabwe Review*, June 5, 1978

"Women Are Breast Feeding the Revolution"
- Headline, The *Zimbabwe Review*.[1]

When the *Zimbabwe Review* announced that "women are breast feeding the revolution," women's roles in the struggle were simplified and their actions were located within the realms of "natural" women's roles. Yet, the presence of young women in the guerilla training camps was interpreted to signify an end to the struggle, because the women as new mothers in the war had a responsibility to end it for the sake of their children. As "mothers of the revolution" women are conflated into one patriotic representation of mother. If considered only in their roles as mothers of the revolution, it is difficult for women to gain the political recognition for any heroic actions or suffering they may have endured during the war. It was considered to be a natural role - a natural duty that deserves no reward. Women as mothers have also been slighted in recognition of the political significance they held during the war - without the mothers the guerillas would not have had the necessary support in the rural areas. The appreciation that some "mothers" expected from society after the war was rarely fulfilled. Thus, it is necessary to turn our historical discussion to the roles and experiences of mothers in the struggle.

Fiction Speaks Louder Than Words

The mothers of the revolution are the women who remained inside Rhodesia and supported the struggle from their homes by providing food and shelter to the guerilla fighters, often at risk from attack by Rhodesian security forces, and often under threat by the guerilla fighters. A collection of thirty personal stories in Irene Staunton's book *Mothers of the Revolution*, documents the conditions under which women in Zimbabwe's rural areas operated; the prices they had to pay; and the sacrifices they made for the liberation of Zimbabwe.[2] For these women the war was played out in their homes and villages. Unlike the young women who crossed the borders to be trained as guerilla fighters, these women often had no choice - either they had to support the guerillas, face being labeled a "sell-out" by the guerillas and villagers, or cooperate with the Rhodesian soldiers or face being arrested, beaten, and raped. Ruth Weiss stated that:

> The Rhodesian forces combed the countryside and bullied the villagers, all of whom they suspected of "running with the terrs" [terrorists]: As the majority of the rural population was, in any case, composed of women, it was the women who sheltered and fed the *vakomana* [young male guerillas]. Women carried ammunition under their everyday loads and used their children as messengers for the fighters. Their suffering was terrible. Their huts were raided, their men were taken away, they were beaten, raped, and massacred.[3]

Meggi Zingani spoke of police harassment because her son had disappeared to join the guerillas:

> [T]he police again drove up to our home and told us that our son was a terrorist... that my son had crossed into Mozambique. I said that as he had not told me, I could not know if this were true. From that time I was considered as a "terrorist mother" and I was in trouble. Often, when the police officers passed by, they would say, "Hello, *mai vatororo*," meaning, "Hello, terrorist mother."[4]

Meggi Zingani stated that in recognition of women's roles, and in order to gain their support

> the comrades often said *"Pamberi nana mai"* [forward with

142

women/mothers]. Mothers were cooperative, they prepared good, clean food for the comrades. The men were not as careful as the women.[5]

The guerilla fighters had to gain and maintain the support of the people living in the rural areas for the success of the guerilla war. The people in the villages, mainly women, fed, clothed, and protected the guerilla fighters from Rhodesian soldiers. Ruvimbo pointed out that this happened because, "A woman always feels motherly towards any young boy," and the *vakomana* in turn trusted the women in the villages to look after them.[6]

During wars, women as mothers performing motherly duties like cooking and bearing children (for the nation) are given more political significance. One mother, Rhoda Khumalo argued that:

> The comrades would have not been able to shoot a gun if they hadn't been fed. We cooked for them, washed their clothes and even protected them, because it was we who gave them information about the security forces. Women worked hard.[7]

Women as mothers were (re)producing the next generation of soldiers, and looking after the soldiers already fighting. Women were then important to the war effort, but still as "mothers."[8] Another mother, Maudy Muzenda argued that:

> I do not think the war would have been won without the women. Women played a very important role in the struggle. It was a very big role that they played. Now women have to liberate themselves. We should not accept our husbands as our superiors. We are equal and we should be seen to be equal because we all did a great job during the struggle.[9]

Muzenda's comments point to the lack of recognition "mothers" received after the war for their war roles - if they want equality they must liberate themselves. However, rather than politicizing their roles as mothers these women have remained unrecognized for the military significance of their contributions. The significance of women as *natural* mothers despite their war efforts, has repercussions for women after independence in the struggle for equality. For example, as Margaret Viki states, women have been forgotten, their roles ignored:

> Sometimes while we were busy cooking [for the freedom fighters],
> the soldiers would come and we had to run away and hide, leaving
> the pot burning. But now we, the women, the *'povo'* [the people]
> as we are called, have been forgotten. The freedom fighters have
> forgotten us and how much we helped them. The fact is we fought
> a war. Carrying hot pots of food up the mountains is no joke. I do
> not think that the men would have managed if the women had not
> been there to do all this. I think they would have ended up being
> killed by the freedom fighters after they had refused to cook and
> carry food for them. The men were around but they used to tell the
> women to "hurry, before the soldiers come and beat you up!"[10]

Instead of being acknowledged for their military significance the mothers
are expected to be satisfied with a feeling of being grateful and proud of
their sons and daughters. Lisa Teya points out how proud she was to be a
mother in the struggle:

> I was really very grateful for the role my own son had played in
> liberating our country. I ululated and ululated and my joy was
> boundless. When I saw the comrades returning triumphantly, both
> men and women in their combat gear, I wished I'd been young
> enough to have gone to war.[11]

Those women that did not *go to war*, but who endured the repercussions
of the war in their villages, the mothers, did not have their stories
incorporated into the official discourse about the war. However, they are
present in some postcolonial Zimbabwean literature, which has enabled
the experiences of women as mothers to be aired publicly. These are
representations, but as fiction they can speak louder than the words of
Zimbabwean women who were mothers in the struggle, because it is
Zimbabwean literature and it can confront some of the unresolved issues
of the liberation war. Mothers emerge in this literature as victims and
sometimes as heroes.

Lisa Teya's role as the grateful and proud mother above is only
overshadowed by those mothers whose children did not return from the
war. Alexander Kanengoni describes a mother's loss and pain in his novel

Echoing Silences. As an old woman is looking for her son at the demobilization point. She says to Munashe (the main character in Kanengoni's novel), a male guerilla:

> "There is no need to be afraid, my son ... We have become accustomed to death. Tell me, is he still alive?"
> "I don't even know him, Mother. We were so many out there. Thousands of others are still in the camps in Mozambique. He is alive."
> "Then whose children were they that we saw dying in battle and those we were told were massacred at Nyadzonia and Chimoio?" Munashe shook his head. He felt helpless before her pain.
> "Take these sweet potatoes and roasted groundnuts and eat them. You are the son that I shall never see." And she walked away as the others had done before her.[12]

For these mothers there is nothing to show for their "war efforts" but an unrecognized pain, which is (un)suitably healed by the knowledge that their children died for an independent Zimbabwe. Women as mothers were expected to sacrifice their children for the nation, yet, despite this the women remain only as the mothers, while the men are remembered as the nationalists.[13]

The representation of women as mothers in the revolution, as symbols of the nation, at once gives them the proud role of mother of sons who fought and died in the war, but at the same time, it denies them any recourse or compensation for those sons or daughters lost or killed in the war, or for any actions or sacrifices the mothers may have made to protect other mothers' sons or daughters.[14]

Furthermore, as mothers symbolized the nation in nationalist rhetoric, their roles are romanticized and glorified, denying many of the horrors of the war that some mothers faced. For example, Kanengoni has written about the fate of one woman in the rural areas of Rhodesia during the war. She was a mother, but her "crime" was being the wife of the chief lieutenant responsible for a revolt within the nationalist party. Her punishment was death. Munashe was ordered and forced to kill her - to kill a mother of the revolution:

> "Someone help me, please!" Munashe cried, looking down at the

hoe with the broken handle at his feet ... and the female combatant shouted:

"He is wasting time, *chef.*"

And somehow that incensed the security officer who grabbed the hoe and shoved it into Munashe's hands howling that if he did not go ahead and finish off the woman and her baby that would leave him no choice but to shoot him ... He knew that the woman was looking at him through her swollen eyes. He also knew that the base commander was behind him, his head averted.... Then Munashe tightened his grip around the broken hoe handle ... and tears and sweat rolled down his face.... He could also hear, above the noise of the crying baby, her faint, agonized breathing and he saw that she was shaking....

"I can't do it!" a scream broke from Munashe.

"Can he not use the gun?" the base commander implored.

"Shut up!"[15]

Munashe did not know what the "revolt"[16] had been about, and he did not understand why he had to kill this woman. He hoped that she would not ask him to forgive her:

Then he looked at the haggard figure of the woman and it lost its shape and its edges got torn and the baby on her back became a protrusion of her hunched back and then he swung the hoe, and he heard the blade swishing furiously through the air ... The woman fell down with the first vicious blow and the sound of Munashe's jarred and violent cry mingled with that of the dying baby as the hoe fell again and again and again until Munashe was splattered all over with dark brown blood.[17]

Munashe "wished that someone had killed him because he could not live with such a memory ... Nightmare and war became interchangeable."[18] The murder of this woman with a baby on her back reveals not only the absurdity of war, but the paranoia, politics, and power struggles within the nationalist liberation forces. The struggle was not a homogenous revolutionary attack against Rhodesia, but here women symbolize the nation, and Munashe has destroyed one of its potential manifestations. Kanengoni's novel, while a fictionalized account of the struggle, exposes these truths that have been avoided in the discourse about the war. "It helps the nation to revise its romantic notion of the struggle and in the process appreciate the post-war stress disorder that continues to afflict so many former freedom fighters."[19] The intersection of Munashe's nightmare of having to kill the woman, and the death of the woman who would otherwise have remained the unacknowledged wife or mother of the revolution, symbolizes the tragic but necessary challenge to the constructions and representations of mothers in the struggle.

Alexander Kanengoni continues the horrific themes of coercion and violence within the guerilla movement in his short story, *Things We'd Rather Not Talk About*. His character of the mother is left to pick up the pieces after the war. During the war her husband is accused of being a "sell-out" by the guerilla fighters operating in her area. Her son Paul is forced to kill his father with an axe in front of the whole village. The horrific description of this brutal act does not need to be repeated here, as it pales in comparison to the nightmare of being involved. After the war Paul's nightmares follow him - the comrades now want him to kill his mother. He seeks refuge in a city shop hoping to elude his nightmares, but they follow him in. He takes up an axe to protect himself against these ghosts from the past and is finally arrested by the police. Kanengoni writes:

> Back at home in Mhondoro, when Paul's mother discovered that her son had forgotten his bottle of medicine and knew that even if the last bus to Harare had not gone she did not have the money to use it, she remembered to put on her torn black tennis shoes and began the long walk to Harare, more than sixty kilometres away, whispering to herself, pleading with God and all those gone, especially her husband, to help keep her only child safe and alive as the other one had not returned from the guerilla war that had freed the country.[20]

Paul's mother must pick up the pieces shattered by the war - she must protect her remaining son from the "freedom fighters." Her task is neither glorious, nor heroic, but she is expected to be grateful for political independence. Kanengoni's 'mother,' like many mothers after the war, did not benefit from the fruits of independence. Two of her sons were taken in the war, yet she cannot even afford the bus fare to town. In Kanengoni's fiction, the mothers of the revolution are silenced by the efforts to destroy them. The mothers cannot be glorified in such brutal contexts of war. Located between the violence of both sides the mothers bear the brunt of the war. Some mothers' had to choose between Rhodesian violence and Zimbabwean nationalist violence in order to fulfill their roles as mothers. These choices are rarely discussed in the discourse of war.

Yet, Chenjerai Hove has written about these choices in his fictional account of the mother who meets her fate at the hands of the Rhodesians while she searches for her lost son in the war. Hove's main character Marita, is based on a real woman, a laborer he met at a plantation. He creates this character in order to explore the depths of power and powerlessness of women. Hove has stated about the mother, that "she's powerless, you know, in terms of gender, you know politically, physically, you know but in the strength that I discovered, she's a powerhouse of moral strength and that to me was an adventure that was worth taking."[21] In exploring Marita's gendered powerlessness Preben Kaarsholm has pointed out, "while searching for her son, Marita is captured by the Rhodesians, tortured and sexually molested and eventually killed."[22]

> Marita, how they brought you back torn like a piece of cloth. How they brought you back bleeding through the ears. It is difficult to kill a human being, Marita ... They had burnt you with burning things all over the body, even the places that cannot be mentioned. They had done things to you, things which people cannot do even to their rabid dogs which they do not want to come back. Bad things Marita. Did you not say some of them must have tried to make you their wife? ... They kept you naked all of the time, bringing even the village boys to come and see all they wanted to see. Then they put a lot of hard things through you where you say children come from. Hard things which made you weak for many days.[23]

Marita's only crime was being a mother of the revolution. Hove has attempted to speak for marginalized women/mothers, but in doing so, his mixed images are typical blends of heroism and pity.[24] As in Kanengoni's characters, the mother in Hove's story will never be pitied nor will she become a hero of the war. Her brutal fate at the hands of the Rhodesians silenced her voice and her claim for acknowledgment.

Yvonne Vera has represented the reality and struggles to be a mother in Zimbabwe both during and after the war, in her novel *Without a Name*.[25] Yvonne Vera's character Mazvita carries the burden of woman as mother during the war. Vera's book is significantly different from Kanengoni's *Effortless Tears* and Hove's *Bones* in that it tells the story of a woman from her own point of view. It does not attempt to glorify women's roles in the war nor does it essentialize women as "mothers." Rather it describes the complex relationships that being a mother involves. Mazvita becomes an unwilling mother due to the events of the war, but she resists, and her challenge highlights the differences between an essentialized identity seen from a masculinist discourse and the personal perspective of a woman.

Mazvita is escaping the violence in the rural areas at the height of the armed struggle in 1977. When her village is burnt down she is raped by soldiers when trying to escape. She travels to the city where she only has her name, Mazvita. She cannot face the horror of her war experiences. She cannot even tell her partner, but must face the pain alone:

Mazvita carried a strong desire to free herself from the burden of fear, from the skies licked with blue and burning with flame. She had not told Nyenyedzi everything. She had not told him about what that man who pulled her down had whispered to her, how she ran though the mist with torn clothes, with his whispering carried in her ears, how the sky behind her exploded as the village beyond the river burnt, and she shouted loud because her arms reached forward, but not forward enough to rescue the people, to put out the flame, and she cried and ran with her two legs missing, buried.[26]

She ran with the slipperiness between her thighs, except she was not aware that her legs were still hers ... Mazvita had lost her seasons of motherhood. She did not question this dryness of her body but welcomed it as a beginning ... The unknown bird had silenced her when she needed to tell of her own suffering, to tell not to someone else - certainly not to the man - but to hear her own suffering uttered, acknowledged, within that unalterable encounter.[27]

Mazvita's rape and forced pregnancy conceives not a child but the horror of war for women. Alone in the city Mazvita is unable to find herself. She is the mother of the child of war, a heavy burden of pain strapped to her back:

She leaned forward and felt the apron grow loose over her shoulders.

It cut her shoulders, the apron. It pierced the place where her arm swung forward, backward. Her arm swung forward ever so loosely, like wet bark hanging on the side of a trunk, freshly peeled. She was surprised that she could still manipulate her arm, bring it forward, pull that last bit of strength from it to the knot forming on the apron. How was she to undo that knot but to lie down, and die. She had lost her freedom. Death was another kind of freedom, and she longed for it. Her death, that is.[28]

The mother is supposed to protect her child, but through Mazvita's pain, we learn of the tragedy of 'motherhood' in independent Zimbabwe:

Her rejection was sudden and fierce and total. She stood with the baby balanced on one arm. She took a black tie from a rack in a corner of the room and dropped it over the child's neck. It rested over the child in a huge loop, which, on another occasion, would have made her laugh. She did not pause. She claimed her dream and her freedom. She was winged and passionate. She drew the bottom end of the tie across the baby's neck. She pulled at the cloth while the baby remained blinded and trusting. She strained hard and confidently though this pulling choked her and blinded her and broke her back.[29]

Tragically Mazvita kills her baby to be free of the burden and horror of war. "She was responsible for some horrible and irreversible truth concerning her actions."[30] As a "mother" she took what action was necessary to free herself from the war. Vera's story differs from the others as it shows that to be a mother in war is not heroic. Women do not always fight as "mothers" to protect their children against a common enemy. As a mother, her pain is expressed in the few choices the political situation has left her with. The mothers of the revolution had few choices.

Thus, we have seen while women were breastfeeding the revolution in nationalist rhetoric, as mothers of the revolution their roles and experiences were not particularly glorious. For the women who remained inside Rhodesia and supported the war from their villages, the violence and suffering that they endured has not been officially recognized. It was expected of them as mothers - that is all. For the mothers to speak out about their lives during the struggle, has depended upon their being interviewed for collections on women in the war, such as Staunton's

Mothers of the Revolution, and for their stories to be included in fictional accounts of the war. Alexander Kanegoni, Chenjerai Hove, and Yvonne Vera are three major examples of Zimbabwean authors dealing with the dirty details of war in order to facilitate the voices of women as mothers being heard in the discourse of war. This overview of mothers in the struggle also points to the differences in mothers, that is, in the opening quote above, it was the appearance of young mothers in the training camps that suggested an end to the struggle, because the women guerilla fighters, giving birth away from their homes would want to win the war quickly so they could bring up their children in peace. If they failed, it would be up to their children. As mothers they would either fight for or reproduce for the nation. However, most considerations of women as mothers in the struggle have focussed instead on the women who remained inside Rhodesia as mothers. Their role as mothers was unproblematic. However, for the young women who crossed the Rhodesian borders to join the guerilla training camps in other countries, when they became mothers, they actually became a problem for the struggle. It is their experiences that we turn to next.

Endnotes

1. Cited by Amy Kaler, "Maternal Identity and War in *Mothers of the Revolution*" in *National Women's Studies Association Journal,* 9:1, Spring, 1997.
2. Irene Staunton, ed., *Mothers of the Revolution,* (Harare: Baobab Books, 1992).
3. Ruth Weiss, *The Women of Zimbabwe,* p. 72.
4. Meggi Zingani, quoted in Irene Staunton, ed., *Mothers of the Revolution,* pp. 123-4.
5. Ibid, p. 130.
6. Ruvimbo, in Ruth Weiss, *The Women of Zimbabwe,* p. 80.
7. Rhoda Khumalo, quoted in Irene Staunton ed.,*Mothers of the Revolution,* pp. 71-2. Also see pp. 78, 156, 181, 306, for examples of women stating that the war could not have been won without them, and hence women deserve to be equal with men.
8. See Amy Kaler, "Maternal Identity and War in Mothers of the Revolution."
9. Maudy Muzenda, quoted in Irene Staunton ed., *Mothers of the Revolution,* p. 66.
10. Margaret Viki, quoted in Irene Staunton, ed., *Mothers of the Revolution,* p. 156.
11. Lisa Teya, quoted in Irene Staunton, ed., *Mothers of the Revolution,* pp. 102-3.
12. Alexander Kanengoni, *Echoing Silences,* Baobab Books, Harare, 1997, p.44.

13. See Amy Kaler, "Maternal Identity and War in *Mothers of the Revolution*."

14. Petronella Maramba, *Tracer Study on Women Ex-Combatants*, recommends that the wives and parents of deceased ex-combatants should be included in all programs aimed to benefit in particular women ex-combatants. This has not happened yet.

15. Alexander Kanengoni, *Echoing Silences*, (Harare: Baobab Books, 1997), p. 20.

16. Ibid. Kanengoni is referring to the Nhari/Badza Rebellion within ZANLA in 1974. See Ngwabi Bhebe and Terence Ranger, *Soldiers in Zimbabwe's Liberation War*, pp. 9, 17, 33, 75-6.

17. Alexander Kanengoni, *Echoing Silences*, p. 21.

18. Ibid.

19. Davison Maruziva, "Brutalities of the War as Seen by a Former Combatant," The *Herald,* Monday, December 29, 1997, p. 8.

20. Alexander Kanengoni, *Effortless Tears*, (Harare: Baobab Books, 1993), pp. 63-4.

21. Chenjerai Hove, interview with David Moore, Harare, July 1991.

22. Preben Kaarsholm, "Coming to Terms with Violence: Literature and the Development of a Public Sphere in Zimbabwe," Seminar Paper, (Institute of Development Studies, University of Zimbabwe, January 1993), p. 15.

23. Chenjerai Hove, *Bones*, p.68f: cited in Preben Kaarsholm "Coming to Terms with Violence: Literature and the Development of a Public Sphere in Zimbabwe," p. 15.

24. Chenjerai Hove, interview with David Moore, Harare, July 1991.

25. Yvonne Vera, *Without a Name*, (Harare: Baobab, 1994).

26. Ibid, p. 25.

27. Ibid, pp. 29-30.

28. Ibid, p. 44.

29. Ibid, pp. 95-6.

30. Ibid, p. 97.

PART THREE:
THE PROBLEMS WITH WOMEN IN WAR

Chapter Seven

The Problem with Women in War

In the early days of the struggle, there were women in the ZANLA forces but they were custom bound. They did the cooking, they carried arms over the border so that the men could fight ... By 1977 we had a crisis on our hands ... We had 10,000 women trained exactly like men, but we could not face the reality that they too could fight. - Edson Zvobgo, 1980

The Problem - from Pfutskeke to Xai Xai

By 1976 thousands[1] of young women had joined up with the liberation armies of ZAPU and ZANU. The traditionally male-led nationalist movement now had to cater for increasing numbers of women who had military training, and many more who wanted training in order to fight the Rhodesians. However, the inclusion of women in the training camps resulted in disruptions to traditional gender roles and subsequently a "woman problem" emerged, especially within ZANU. In an interview with Christine Qunta, Teurai Ropa explained that the Women's Department in ZANU was established because of some of the particular problems facing women that could not be dealt with as general party matters. However, she did not mention what those "problems with women" were.[2] This chapter will discuss these "problems."

The relations between men and women became a moral, political and military problem in the late 1970s for the ZANU high command in Mozambique. In July 1978, at Pfutskeke Base, the ZANU Defence

Secretariat held a rally where the "problems of women" were discussed. Comrade Catherine, who was among thirty-six other women cadres at the rally, emphasised that women needed discipline to be good ZANLA cadres. Her criticisms laid blame on women for general problems within the party related to gossiping, jealousy, liberalism, and "groupism." Catherine stated,

> When you see Maggie misbehaving criticize her, and when you see another regardless of rank don't be liberal. Liberalism is a good factor for disunity. Gossiping is totally discouraged. Why speaking behind her back, does she bite or has no consciousness which makes you fear her. Constructive criticisms are accepted. If you criticise someone with the aim of destroying her she will not understand anything. Instead she will be more confused. We are protracting the war ourselves by not uniting because when we come to another stage obstacles will block the way and those obstacles come from within us. This must cease, alright. Another destroyer is jealousy. We are now connecting personal differences with the revolution. Groupism is another factor. In order to do your duties well solve all petty problems by consulting others but in a way that doesn't affect the Party.[3]

It was argued that without discipline the women were blocking the revolution with their petty divisions within the ranks. Gossiping and jealousy are easily seen as negative feminine qualities and problems that negatively affect the party. However, Catherine's concerns with liberalism and groupism may also reflect wider problems within the party, which emerged after the demise of the Zimbabwe People's Army (ZIPA). Nonetheless, Teurai Ropa pointed out that the main problem was that the young women were undisciplined and misbehaving and this was "bad for the revolution." She asked the women:

> What kind of families were you brought up in? Were you ever taught discipline? ... I don't indulge in other people's love affairs. That is out with me. I am not saying you should misbehave because of this statement. At this stage we are [at], the revolution demands our transformation.[4]

Here, Teurai Ropa seems to be giving approval to the affairs developing in the training camps, but is asking the women not to gossip about them so as to cause divisions in the party. Teurai Ropa is obviously disappointed in the women's behavior, and sets about distinguishing herself from them. In her speech she complains:

> We have heard the duties of all officers here. It is left to them to come and repeat what they always hammer to you. They don't even get time to plan the war. You heard the Mirage [fighter jet] over us. If you are not trained will it be merciful to you? We have failed to find the method of talking to you. OK we leave you. Do as you wish, next time we will be using another tactic ... We have a chance to learn things out here, but we waste it. In Zimbabwe I won't be where you will be.[5]

By this stage of the war, Teurai Ropa may have realized that she would become a leader in the new Zimbabwe, while the other women remained "gossiping." Nonetheless, Teurai Ropa's complaints about women's behavior during the struggle also suggest a level of frustration in being unable to control the young women and men recruited for national liberation.

> We must be women with high political consciousness so that when you go to the front carrying material you can teach the masses. Men have their outstanding role - what of us. Some of you may even fail to go and teach the refugees at Doeroi [refugee camp]. You can't even think of going to learn from other women in Pungwe III [refugee camp] etc.[6]

Teurai Ropa says here that women will not be able to fight equally with men unless they begin to take their political and military training seriously. The subsequent report from the Pfutskeke Base Rally (only available from the ZANU War Archives) illustrates that there was a problem with women's alleged behavior. Very little attention is given to the fact that it probably was not just women to blame, but men's activities were also involved. These problems stemmed from the incorporation of women into a guerilla army, and included: a) challenges and changes to traditional gender dynamics; b) restructuring of a traditionally male environment to cater for thousands of young women; and c) dissension between women themselves.

What is interesting in light of women's involvement in the armed struggle is that these "problems" were obscured by representations that *glorified* women's roles in the war. The veneer of equality between men and women guerilla fighters was being polished on the international stage. Gendered problems among the rank and file were hidden by the discourse of war that promoted the image of a functional, cohesive, and united nationalist front. Women were central to this discourse, being glorified in their war roles and portrayed as equally involved with men.

As we saw Lapchick and Urdang's research on the role of women in the struggle started a trend among some feminist authors in the 1980s, whose research adopted assumptions made by leading Zimbabwean nationalist women that Zimbabwean women in general played an equal role in the liberation war, particularly at the front.[7] Thus, on the international scene, the women who had joined the war to liberate Zimbabwe were represented as either liberated women or fighting for equality with men, as well as fighting for a democratic Zimbabwe. As the Secretary for ZANU's Department of Women's Affairs, Teurai Ropa stated:

> Today's women are not only mere bedroom women to produce children as the concept used to be, they are in the vanguard liberation struggle in Zimbabwe. This oppressive and exploitative system has affected women to the same degree as it has affected men.[8]

> Gone are the days when all women did was to sew, knit, cook, commiserate with and mourn for their fallen soldiers. Now they too participate in the fighting, they too face the music.[9]

Norma Kriger claims that these assumptions about women's roles in the struggle were based on "glorifications" made by women such as Sally Mugabe and Naomi Nhiwatiwa.[10] Lapchick and Urdang's influential research on the role of Zimbabwean women in the struggle also mainly cites the experiences of women like Sally Mugabe, Ana Tekere, Teurai Ropa, and Jane Ngwenya.[11] The position of these women in the struggle was much higher than most women's, and they were more likely to have had a Western education. Their voices should be considered with some caution as representative of the majority of women. Nonetheless, their voices are the ones that have been heard in the discourse of war and the ones consulted about women's experiences. Feminist analyses cannot overlook them or refuse to listen.

Glorifications

The most obvious way that ZANU glorified the role of women can be demonstrated by questioning the numbers of women involved as guerilla fighters, and in what roles they performed. In 1985, the Ministry of Community Development and Women's Affairs "estimated that [by 1978] there were 250,000 women actively involved in the liberation struggle."[12] Yet Norma Kriger has identified "a misleading picture of the extent to which women participated as fighters in the guerilla army."[13] She suggests that at various times during the war ZANU advocates like Sally Mugabe and Naomi Nhiwatiwa created this picture apparently "by conflating women who were full-time fighters with those who did some military training in the camps, but were primarily engaged in agricultural work, education, or other tasks."[14] Figures such as 250,000 women confuse women's military and supportive roles, which are then conflated to inflate the overall numbers of active women guerilla fighters.

In 1979, Naomi Nhiwatiwa stated ZANLA could boast that one-third of its forces were women.[15] Sally Mugabe suggested that about 20,000 women inside the country and 2,000 women outside the country were fighting.[16] Julia Zvobgo, however, "put the number of trained female fighters in Zimbabwe at between 1,500 to 2,000."[17] This significant drop in numbers occurs when we distinguish between trained women guerillas, women refugees and other women performing supportive tasks in the training camps. According to a survey conducted in 1981 at the ZIPRA demobilization points,

> By the end of the war ZIPRA had over 20,000 soldiers in its ranks, the bulk of whom had been recruited and trained between 1976 and 1978. Ten percent of ZIPRA soldiers were women, and they were largely incorporated into one unit, the ZIPRA Women's Brigade. This was a conventionally trained infantry brigade, complete with its own engineers, communications, and other support services and female commanders.[18]

These estimates are supported by other claims that there were about 2000

ZIPRA women. However, as one women ex-combatant pointed out, by the end of the war

> the raids took their toll so that when peace came and we were brought here [to Sierra Assembly Demobilization Point, at Insukamini, 30 kms northwest of Gweru], in March last year, there were only a little over 1,000 of us left; now there are only 713 girls in here.[19]

Teurai Ropa has acknowledged that no records were salvaged from the war:

> I don't think there were any records kept of numbers of women. During that time there were many raids. Even though records were kept, but time and time again they kept on being stolen by the regime, or burnt out. So, to tell you the truth we are just going by statistics [guessing].... As early as 1974-75 the numbers were small. Say 1,000, I wouldn't dispute. Towards 1978-79, the numbers were tremendous, 20,000-36,000. The camps were crowded with children and [adults]. This was not all women. It was inclusive. There were actually more men than women. And towards the end we had more school pupils, although they were not more than [adults] who were to be assigned for fighting in the front.[20]

Just going by these problematic statistics, difficulties have arisen when calculating the extent of women's participation, particularly in relation to post independence claims for compensation by the women ex-combatants. Nira Yuval-Davis argues that the estimates of women may depend on

> classification of what is a civil and what is a military task ... apparent changes in the number of women in the military could be just a side effect of a bureaucratic or ideological redefinition of the boundaries of the armed forces. Another example is statistics based on veteran registration.[21]

Although there is not an official breakdown between ZIPRA and ZANLA ex-combatants, the Zimbabwe National Liberation War Veterans Association (ZNLWVA) has acknowledged that twenty percent of its war veterans are women.[22] This percentage could be inflated if ZANLA recruited the same number of women as ZIPRA, or it could be deflated if it does not include many of the women involved in the struggle as teachers, nurses, mothers, and *chimbwidos*, which could bring the number up to as high as thirty percent. Allowing for only twenty percent of war veterans to be women may actually exclude many women who are illiterate or isolated in rural communities and who are unable or unaware of how to register as a war veteran. There are no complete statistics to show how many women ex-combatants (both ZANLA and ZIPRA) were demobilized after 1980, which hinders accurate representation of women ex-combatants, and indeed the number of women guerilla fighters at any one point during the struggle. [23]

Robert Mugabe claimed that all ZANLA cadres carried three weapons: a gun to fight the enemy with and defend the masses; politics to give direction and purpose to the struggle; and the hoe for production. It is not clear however, whether women were sent to the front for the specific purpose of fighting with those guns.[24] The main histories of the liberation war reveal "relatively few written reports ... [which] contain accounts of women actually shooting at the enemy."[25] The stories and accounts of nationalist attacks on Rhodesian targets are dominated by men behind the triggers.[26] Here it is not necessary to repeat these male centered stories, but instead to highlight the contradictions and conundrum in the representations of women who do shoot. At the same time that women's frontline roles have been glorified, their experiences on the frontline have been silenced.

At a Workshop in 1982 on the "Role of Women in Social, Economic and Cultural Reconstruction in Zimbabwe" it was stated that "the Zimbabwe African women fully participated in the liberation war both at the front-line and at the rear."[27] Teurai Ropa Nhongo, the Minister for Community Development and Women's Affairs gave the keynote address.

> Even during the armed struggle, women were at first given non-combatant duties such as carrying arms and food. It was only to be realised later that women could fight boldly, if not more courageously, side by side with their male comrades. Many girls and women were put in the frontline. As a result a division of women in the war command was created to specialise on the needs and problems of women combatants both outside and inside the country.[28]

Not surprisingly, feminist writers like Gisela Geisler conclude that in

Zimbabwe "[f]rom 1972 onwards women joined the armed struggle, first as carriers of military equipment and later as front-line fighters."[29] This kind of statement supposes that women were indeed on the frontline of the guerilla war, "shooting just like men," and assumes that such claims are not in doubt.

It is noteworthy that Moorcraft and McLaughlin argued that the propaganda from ZANU overstated the military role of women. For example a ZANU poster depicting women in the struggle represented women in combat poses rather than actually in combat. The five photos on the poster depicted various roles of women:

1. In Combat - (a woman holding a rocket grenade launcher)
2. Information - (two women sitting in the grass, both wearing trousers one has a gun resting between her legs, pointing up! The other holds two grenades).
3. Taking care of the sick - (a woman gives an injection to another).
4. Building the people's army - (a woman and two men cleaning guns).
5. Secretariat - (five people, two of them women sitting in the grass discussing some papers).[30]

Moorcraft and McLaughlin argued that "[a]lthough propaganda like this [ZANU poster] exaggerated the combat role of women in the guerilla forces, there were considerable numbers of females who saw action."[31] Yet there remains some doubt that women fought with guns, because women's military actions have had little recognition. However, just because there are few records of women being sent to the front to fight did not mean that women were not involved in combat. As seen in the cases of Nyadzonia, Chimoio and Mkushi Camps most experiences of attacks occurred while the women were in training camps outside of Rhodesia. However for the purposes here it is necessary to narrow the focus to women guerilla fighters in the frontlines.

The Frontlines

The controversy surrounding the Zimbabwean film *Flame*, which will be discussed in detail below, illustrates the dilemma in representing women who shoot. In the film female guerilla fighters are depicted carrying guns and shooting at the enemy. In one scene the heroine Comrade Flame, resents the (male) orders not to fire on a Rhodesian truck because there are too many soldiers, outnumbering the small group of guerillas. These Rhodesian soldiers had attacked a nearby village and killed one man for allegedly helping the guerillas. When Flame spots a jeep following the truck with only two soldiers in it, she runs down from the rocky escarpment and standing directly in front of them, fires a rocket propelled grenade into their jeep which then explodes. She is disciplined for disobeying orders, but is later acknowledged by her colleagues for being heroic. This particular scene in the film showing a woman *shooting at the enemy* offended the ZNLWVA, who subsequently attempted to ban the film. The ZNLWVA argued that this representation of women shooting at the enemy was a "gross misrepresentation of the war efforts by depicting women in actual combat when their role was [*only*] to carry war equipment and ammunition as well as assist in other crucial duties."[32] According to John Gwitira, the Executive Director of the ZNLWVA, women were mainly used to carry weapons and supplies to the front and were not deployed specifically to frontline attacks as a group or groups of people called *women*.[33]

Whether or not the scene in *Flame* was based completely on a true story of a woman's experience is for the purposes of this discussion, irrelevant. It is the contestation of representations of women shooting at the enemy which is significant. For example, one woman ex-combatant involved with the ZNLWVA insisted that women did not fight at all, and stated that women only ever came to the liberated zones inside Zimbabwe and never engaged with the enemy.[34] Yet, other women ex-combatants have mentioned that they did fight "just like their men" in battles on the frontlines. For example, Freedom Nyamubaya[35] stayed inside Rhodesia after crossing the border from Mozambique. She carried out various ambushes and surprise attacks between 1977 and 1979, and commanded some operations.

When Comrade Zvisinei reported on an attack that she was involved in, she said, "When they heard that ZANLA combatants, including female guerillas, had reinforced to clear them off the area, they swaggered and boasted that they would never abandon the camp. 'Women were no force against us,' they bragged."[36] Comrade Zvisinei's testimony also supports the case that women were indeed involved in frontline military actions. She stated:

I took part in several rocket and mortar ambushes on enemy convoys along Buhera-Birchenough Bridge road. One major battle I took part in recently was our attack on Mathias Camp in Buhera District. It was an isolated garrison which housed auxiliaries and their white racist commanders who, ... On the 23rd September, 1979 we attacked Mathias Camp at nine in the evening. Our artillery and infantry forces overran the camp in a pitched forty-five minute battle. We killed thirty-seven enemy troops, captured six of them and the few that survived fled and never came back. Four trucks were destroyed and blew up the armoury during the battle. All houses were destroyed.[37]

Another women combatant, Rudo Hondo, promoted to ZANLA general staff in 1977, was given the command of female guerillas in Manica Province. She was

one of the very first women officers in the battlefield. But being a female commander did not confine her duties to those of her gender - many battles were fought with men, including under her command, and victories achieved.[38]

In February 1978, when she was in command of 30 fighters in the Jiri area, they were attacked by helicopters, paratroopers and infantry. According to the *People's Voice*, the Rhodesians had heard of Hondo's "unique military prowess," and intended to kill or capture her. After a "fierce battle" she was captured by the Rhodesians. She described this situation as follows:

It was a kind of battle I had never experienced ... We returned fire as much as we could ... My colleagues were all dead with the exception of another woman fighter ... I thought of killing myself with the revolver I had ... [as] it is better to kill oneself than to be captured alive by the enemy.[39]

Before Hondo was able to kill herself, she was injured in the chest while under attack from a helicopter.

She emptied the whole magazine on the helicopter and saw it burst into flames emitting thick black smoke before she collapsed as strength escaped her.[40]

Under interrogation Hondo refused to talk, although she did mislead the Rhodesians about her identity. Eventually she managed to escape just before the elections in 1980 and independence.

Based on Hondo's experience, Naomi Nhiwatiwa was able to claim that women *were* involved in frontline activities:

> I don't know if anybody read [of] the incident ... a group of five women that were being chased by helicopters. It is said that these women were darting in and out as though they were playing a hide and seek game. That eventually they came out, they surfaced in the open, and the helicopters that were chasing them sprayed bullets and dismembered most of the women guerillas, disintegrated their bodies, that one of them escaped, and one was going to be forced to be punished or killed. Indeed the situation happened, but I want you to know that while they were saying that - that these women with their rifles were no match to the helicopters - the super-helicopters were sent by the US ... [and they] were maiming and disintegrating the bodies of women guerillas that were trying to fight to defend their own country.[41]

Neither male nor female guerillas could compete against these odds, yet Nhiwatiwa glorifies women's roles fighting back.

> You probably have read of Chimoio when Ian Smith sent a fleet of bombers to kill the refugees at Chimoio and hundreds of the Zimbabweans were killed. It was the women's brigade that shot down Ian Smith's planes. You probably have read about the oil tanks being exploded near Salisbury very recently, it was a brigade that was being led by women that blew up the oil tanks near Salisbury. So even though the Zimbabwean woman has suffered double oppression we see her persistence and her courage to liberate her country.[42]

In the case of the Rhodesian attacks on Chimoio Camp, there is little evidence to support the view that the women's brigade was an organized military entity, which independently shot down the Rhodesian planes. Some individual women may have had access to the anti-aircraft weapons, but again the evidence remains only in the representations. In the case of the oil tanks in Salisbury being attacked, contrary to Nhiwatiwa's claims that women *were* involved actively in frontline activities, Teurai Ropa stated that it was not the assignment of women to go and blow up the Salisbury petrol supplies. She explained that Nhiwatiwa had made the claim because it was a big event in the war that stands out in the international arena: "The terrorist sabotage, the most daring and boldest incident of urban guerilla warfare in the war, was a 'serious' blow to Rhodesia's economy."[43] Teurai Ropa stated that even though it was not women who blew up the petrol supplies in Salisbury, the idea was hatched in her hut, at a ZANU base in Mozambique. She said that her husband Rex Nhongo, Air Marshall [sic] Shiri, Josiah Tongogara and Shebagawa were all in her hut planning strategic bombings. Initially, Thornhill Airforce Base in Gweru was nominated as a target, along with various bridges. Teurai Ropa asked, "What do these planes run on?" and suggested that they attack the petrol supplies. She said, "Let's send someone to go and light it." No women however, were sent on this attack to Salisbury.[44]

Nevertheless, there are some examples where women did blow up targets inside Rhodesia. Teurai Ropa herself was involved in a battle at Dotito, near Mt. Darwin, on the February 17, 1974. She described her military actions in *Moto*:

> Because I had no other alternative, I just pointed my gun at [the helicopter], and fired. I thought I had missed. I saw smoke coming from it, and thought it was just the exhaust. A few moments later I heard the *boom*! The helicopter crashed.... That is how I survived that battle ... the battle that many people have come to identify me with.[45]

Also, for example, it was reported that Ignatiana Shongedza from Mrewa, under instructions from "terrorists," took a bomb by bus to Salisbury and planted it at Chancellor House. The blast smashed 200 windows. In her defense her father stated:

> I am convinced she deliberately defied the terrorists' orders and

put it somewhere where it wouldn't do much damage - like the toilet block behind Chancellor House.[46]

Shongedza was allegedly able to leave Rhodesia after this with the help of the All Souls Roman Catholic Church. This case is exceptional because the woman involved was not necessarily a trained woman guerilla fighter, but a *chimbwido*, either acting voluntarily or under pressure from male guerillas. The report of this case stands out in the discourse of war because it focuses on the "terrorist" acts of a female, yet attempts to deny her any agency in her strategic attack.

Other histories of women's involvement in the struggle have suggested that by 1978 ZANLA women were being deployed to the front, especially as

the political commissars, medics, logistics, security, intelligence, teaching etc. It was at this time that women detachments were put in the Manica Province and Tete for actual combat duties led by their women commanders and proved to be successful in their operations.[47]

Contradicting the ZNLWVA's view, this recent report on women's history and involvement in the struggle assumes women had combat duties during the struggle. Even Teurai Ropa stated that "on the military side, women were going into combat at the front in large numbers. The climax was the shelling of Umtali under women commanders in 1978."[48] ZANU alleged that ZANLA women had bombed Umtali in 1978, when 450 ZANLA guerillas, including the first women combatants under their own command, crossed the border of Mozambique near Umtali (Mutare). However, in 1996 Teurai Ropa (Joyce Mujuru) later claimed that it was not women but men who attacked Umtali in 1978. She said there were only a few women actually in the front, and they were mainly found in the liberated zones inside Zimbabwe. In an interview Teurai Ropa explained to me that it was expedient to promote the idea to Western solidarity groups that women were involved in the major strikes against Rhodesia, rather than try to explain the importance of women's supportive roles to men's actions.[49] In April and June of 1978 when she had been abroad promoting ZANLA women she realized that:

there [was] a recognition for women and hence we [we]re being given cars. So we have gathered here [at the Pfutskeke Base Rally] to share ideas [among women].[50]

The outcome of the rally was not widely publicized as this would have dampened the revolutionary image of Zimbabwean women fighting equally with men and challenging their traditional gender roles.

The promotion of women's emancipation in the nationalist struggle resulted in extra funding and support from international sources. Nonetheless, in 1979 when the first ZANU Women's Seminar was organized at Xai Xai in Mozambique, "shared ideas" among women in the struggle were put on the international agenda. The seminar was the first opportunity for western educated Zimbabwean women activists and nationalists to share their ideas about Western feminism and women's liberation. Teurai Ropa stated that

we had Zimbabwean women delegates who came from all over the world to the First ZANU Women's Seminar in Xai Xai. Those who were in the United States, Britain, Australia, at home, in Botswana, everywhere; those whom we managed to send messages to; those who managed to come, came. It was well represented. So there was a mixture of understanding. Those who had Westernized understanding of liberation spoke about how they saw how the whole thing should be. You see all that was incorporated. There really wasn't much difference to what we were already practicing. During the war. We were even much ahead of them because to really see a woman holding a gun, going to face with the enemy when she is pregnant as well, is something else. You see those were other things that they learnt from us.[51]

She uses the images of pregnant women with guns and babies to argue that African women were more advanced in their women's liberation than their Western feminist counterparts. These statements reveal that there was some kind of global feminist necessity in promoting the activities of women guerilla fighters. The images of women fighting with guns represents an "equal citizen" of the nation. Here it suffices to say that the representations of women guerilla fighters that emanated from the Xai Xai conference are at the peak of the glorifications and misconceptions that ZANU constructed.[52] These representations, in particular the glorified accounts of women by Nhiwatiwa and Teurai Ropa solidified the view from a Western feminist perspective that it was an intended part of the revolution that women would be emancipated based on their frontline action in war, fighting side by side with men. Hence the postindependence obsession with women's lack of gains towards gender equality based on their equal roles in war. However, by questioning the assumptions we have seen that many of the representations are glorifications.

The Other View

Apart from the few examples outlined above, most of the women I interviewed for this research had not been in frontline combat, and if they had, they did not want to talk about it. Neither did they want to admit that their roles may not have been quite so "heroic."[53] Despite ZANU's glorification that women were actively fighting like men, some ZANU women emphasized that women mainly carried weapons and ammunition across the borders - an inglorious but necessary task. For example, Maria stated that

> one of the important roles that was played by female excombatants was in the transportation of ammunition between Mozambique and Zimbabwe. Because in our culture here, women carry a heap load on the head, on the shoulders, even on the back. Whereas the men here culturally would only use their hands to carry.[54]

Maria highlights the traditional gender roles of men and women, which appear to have determined women's roles in the struggle. In these roles however, women were confronted with situations that required military action. Monica said that she was "involved in more than four battles, [but] women were doing most of the carrying of weapons etc."[55] Nyarai said that she "was involved in many attacks near the border. We were carrying the materials, and the commander said, 'There is the enemy in our front, you can defend yourselves, fire fire!"[56] However, Nhamo argued that "women did not go to fight battles; they only ever went into the liberated zones to stay in villages."[57]

This suggests that women's supportive roles were diverse and there is no clear answer to the question: "Did women fight like men?" Rudo said, for example, that the camp she was in was not a training camp but a dispatchment [sic] camp. People would come and carry materials. I carried material, but because of the war in Mozambique, we carried material to the Zambezi and leave [sic] it there. Other people would take it from there. I don't know what happened to it all. We carried the stuff on our heads, backs ... but at that time we were very strong, and the spirit of fighting was in us. At first we were carrying material to the Zambezi, which was in the war again because I had to have my own gun, and then I went for training.[58]

There is no doubt that women were "fighting" and supporting the nationalist struggle. Margaret Dongo highlighted the military importance of women carrying supplies to the front, and the difficulties of carrying weapons of war:

After my military training I was trained as a medical assistant ... Part of my duties were, in actual fact, to make sure we keep supplies and also make sure that every section that goes in the forefront has enough medical and first aid kits, material, and so forth. And I went to the extent of the border ... there was a time when it was very difficult for women to come in during the early 1970s. And what our role as women was, we were the carriers of ammunition. It was more heavier than actually instituting the war itself - shooting. Because what we call a cache, that's a cane of bullets, the weight of a cane of bullets you can't even lift it for 10 kilometers or only 500 metres or so. But we would carry a cane of bullets, then medical supplies, your gun to protect you and everything else. I participated up to there, supplies to the border and so forth.[59]

Women were on the frontlines of the war, since there were no definite boundaries between front and rear.

Rhodesian Propaganda

Far from associating "women with guns" as being liberated and free women, the women ex-combatants I interviewed associated such roles as being either "murderers or victims."[60] Comrade Zvisinei outlined how this problem for women guerilla fighters was based on Rhodesian propaganda:

When we female combatants got into these areas [in Zimbabwe] for the first time, we found our people very apprehensive. It was their first time to see female combatants going into battle side by side with their male combatants. For a long time the enemy spread the baseless lies that all female cadres, who had left the country because of oppression and exploitation, had perished in Mozambique during the terrorist regime's barbaric actions of attacking refugee camps in the People's Republic [of Mozambique]. Also that all the girls who went to join the armed struggle waged by ZANU were mere concubines for the male fighters. Now our people were seeing us physically in flesh and blood, carrying guns to destroy the enemy and leading discussions on why it is necessary to wage a long and arduous armed struggle until final people's victory. They were thrilled to see us taking part in combat and routing out enemy forces who [we]re all men. Soon everybody realized that *we women have the right to fight*.[61]

Here, the contrasting images of the women guerilla fighter are juxtaposed. On one hand, the nationalists constructed her as the archetyped heroine - a shining example to the Zimbabwean population. On the other hand, the Rhodesians painted an image of female fighters as murderers and prostitutes. Both of these images are extreme, but there is some relationship between them.

One reason why women are not easily remembered as shooting at the enemy during the war is what we will call the "colonial hangover,"[62] a postcolonial legacy, which has continued derogatory labeling of women guerilla fighters. These images can be amply seen, for example, in the *African Times,* where it was reported that the nationalists were teaching women how to murder.

Murder, arson, terrorism, and intimidation are the daily lessons of these women ... during the day. At other times, as these papers show, they are being led into a life of debauchery and prostitution and it would seem, from the complaint of one camp commander, T.M. Bethune, that the terrorist High Command is unable to stop it. These papers show that the terrorists have not yet learned that it is impossible to teach people evil things, such as murder and arson and expect them to be good in other ways. Such people will find it difficult to drop their evil ways after a political settlement, no matter who governs the country.[63] (See Plate 3)

Plate 3: "They Are Teaching Our Women How to Murder," *The African Times*, February 15, 1978.

Details and stories like these resulted in the perception that women guerilla fighters were the concubines of male fighters, and were being trained to murder. Gaidzanwa has argued that the settler regime used the purported evidence of women guerillas as "concubines" to create resistance to the nationalists and their socialist cause.[64] Without being represented as traditional gendered "women," neither could they be the "heroic freedom fighters." The newspaper report was based on nationalist documents captured by the Rhodesian Security Forces, which nationalists claim were faked in order to discredit the struggle. For example, the documents supported claims made in *Focus on Rhodesia* in 1978 that women in Chimoio Camp were being trained to kill and maim with Communist weapons. Further, it was claimed that

> those [women] in Chimoio were providing casual sex for any of the terrorists who fancied them. They had been learning to slaughter their own people in the name of freedom. Now they are dead - killed in the raid on their training camp by Rhodesian Security Forces. And today they are being replaced by other women who will live the same miserable lives.[65]

Women were being discouraged from seeking liberation through black nationalism. The *African Times* published a captured photograph, which depicted about thirty women guerillas lining up for rifle practice. The caption read:

> This picture, captured by Rhodesian Security Forces when they raided ZANLA terrorist base camp at Chimoio in Mozambique, recently, shows women being trained to handle weapons in the camp. This makes a nonsense of claims in the United Nations that women killed in the raid were civilian refugees. They were terrorists and part of the terrorist organisation.[66]

The contestation of these claims can be explained by firstly examining the *Focus on Rhodesia* report, and then turning to the nationalists' response. *Focus on Rhodesia* stated that the terrorists had tried to use the Rhodesian's attack on Chimoio to get sympathy from the United Nations by showing a film that "had a commentary alleging brutality and violence against women and children and 'unarmed, defenceless, civilians.'"[67] The Rhodesians claimed at the time that

> Chimoio was not a civilian village. It was a terrorist training base for men and women of Robert Mugabe's banned ZANU organisation. And the women were not 'unarmed' and 'defenceless.' They were armed, uniformed, killers-in-training - and documents and photographs brought back to Rhodesia by troops in the raid prove it. Among the photographs found at Chimoio was one of ZANU terrorist commander Josiah Tongogara teaching two women to use AK assault rifles. Others showed women with SAR rifles; two women, one with a rocket launcher and the other with an AK, beside radio equipment ... One of the captured documents, headed ZANU, ZANLA Headquarters, Chimoio, gave the names of eighty women assigned "on a mission to Manica Province." Another listed 114 names, many of them women, and three of them commanders, with the type of weapon and its number issued to each of them.[68]

The emphasis placed on women's possession of arms here cannot go unnoticed in a gendered analysis of war. What is important is the association of women carrying arms with women as prostitutes. The newspaper article continued to outline this connection using evidence allegedly captured from nationalist sources. The newspaper claimed that "[a]nother document from

Chimoio is part of the ZANU report of the Department of Administration to the first session of the enlarged Central Committee, Maputo, and deals with the "place and role of female comrades in the revolution."[69] Part of this report read as follows:

> The party still badly needs to revolutionise its attitude to female comrades and urgently supervise the development and practice of a new attitude. In the main, the great bulk of our female comrades are still regarded as good for nothing more than casual sex and beautiful company for male comrades. They quickly become unwanted burdens of the revolution when they become pregnant. There is an overwhelming reluctance to invite and challenge female comrades to the more significant tasks of the revolution. Male comrades still think it humiliating to salute their senior ranking female comrades. Our female comrades are also to blame. Many are still just "women" in the old traditional sense. They still don't think that it is anathema for them to take up the challenge of the revolution on an equal footing with male comrades. Many have ambitions to live to the peak of a loose moral life through the revolution. The party badly needs to define with much greater exactness what role the women of Zimbabwe must play along the path of the revolution. A signed report by T.M. Bethune, the Chimoio camp commander, mentions "trained comrades engaged in corrupt debauchery, consequently the untrained comrades, both male and female had to follow their corrupt examples. This involved drunkenness to the extent of alcoholism; indulgence in opium smoking; practice of sexual intercourse to the extent of prostitution"... [there is mention of] "punishment meted out to offenders and the hope that 'discipline will grow into perfection.'"[70]

The authenticity of these captured documents was denied by ZANU, yet the problems outlined have some merit, as we will see below. The *Zimbabwe News* reported that the negatives of the photos in question were sent to a West German magazine months before the attack on Chimoio and that the poor quality of the Rhodesian's captured photograph suggests it was probably wired from Germany or elsewhere, and not captured at Chimoio.[71] However, it is noteworthy that the *Zimbabwe News* had already published the same photograph of women guerillas training in the previous year's issue.[72] While the question of the authenticity of the photographs and captured documents is important, it cannot be completely substantiated here. What is significant is that these contested representations contributed to the "colonial hangover," which affected the lives and experiences of women guerilla fighters.

One of the consequences of this "colonial hangover," and a major problem for women ex-combatants, was the pigeon-holing of all women in the liberation war as one homogenous group of anonymous women. References to women in the struggle came to mean *all* Zimbabwean women, whether they were in the struggle as guerilla fighters or not. Such a view obscured differences between women in different political parties and military wings, at different times during the war - the political stage and the armed struggle stage - and different locations - Mozambique and Zambia.[73] These references have meant, as Sylvester has argued, that "the stories of most of [the women].... have blended together over time to constitute a group of anonymous ones."[74] This blending process has been a result of the history of women's involvement in the liberation war being predominantly expressed and represented by ZANU and its women. Women who were in ZAPU, or indeed ZIPA, have been less visible and audible compared to the victorious party. "Women" have been conflated into a group of anonymous (ZANU) women, and this becomes problematic for women ex-combatants after liberation in Zimbabwe because they are all then easily associated with the "colonial hangover" as representations of murderers and prostitutes.[75]

The Differences

By just hearing about ZANU women's experiences in the Mozambican training camps, we do not get a picture of what it was like for ZAPU women who trained mainly in Zambia. For example, ZAPU's approach to training women guerilla fighters was different from ZANU's because they separated the women from the men into specific women's training camps, the Victory and Mkushi Camps, and trained them in military tactics and other skills. ZAPU's armed wing, ZIPRA, was specifically training at least one thousand women for active urban guerilla warfare; but the war ended before they were deployed.[76] Rufaro remembered that

[o]n our side there is no women who operated outside [of Zambia]. But we were near that point. If the Smith government did not accept

175

peace, we were coming in here to fight in the urban areas. We were prepared to come and fight. We wanted to fight the war at the front. We were training for urban guerilla warfare. No, we didn't get the chance to fight like men. Our leaders went to Lancaster House talks, then the Smith government accepted the peace talks, so then there was no chance of coming here to show them that we can also fight like them.[77]

Although ZAPU ex-combatants discussed how well they were trained for urban guerilla warfare, Jane Ngwenya, the National Secretary for ZAPU's Women's Affairs, argued that women were fighting, but differently from men in ZAPU:

So we are fighting side by side with our men; we are not left behind. While our men are holding guns and deployed outside to fight, women are fighting in another wing of the struggle, because they try to help themselves through self-help schemes. They have trained themselves, they are prepared for a new Zimbabwe.[78]

She admits that "a few women have trained to go and fight; but they don't train in the refugee camps or even in Zambia."[79] ZAPU's women were also being trained as civil servants. Ngwenya promoted and encouraged women to participate in more traditional female roles, especially looking after the children:

We have got a lot of programs for them - knitting, sewing and some of them are political commissars who continue to educate themselves about the political situation at home. Those women are doing fantastic work.[80]

Ngwenya's emphasis on the domestic capabilities of women, rather than their combat abilities, situates ZAPU women within the traditional female roles of women in war - as camp followers and cheerleaders, rather than revolutionaries or active nationalists. ZAPU's perspective on women's roles was conservative. ZAPU's president, Joshua Nkomo, wrote in his autobiography that the young women who had joined the struggle created a "special problem":

We could not possibly find a place for them all. It was not the girls' fault, but the presence of young women in a camp of young male soldiers caused tremendous trouble. I remembered the story of King David, who lusted after his officer's wife, and sent the man into a dangerous spot to get killed: and we had to be careful not to have our young men rushed off to bring back Smith's beard on a charger for their girlfriends.[81]

However, Nkomo also said:

Fortunately we had splendid women to face the challenge of organising the girls. Mai Nyamurowa and Thenjiwe Lesabe did a wonderful job - backed by generous help from international organisations - in setting up Victory Camp school outside Lusaka for many of our young girls, where they got a better education than they would have done at home. Some we did train to use weapons and employed as camp guards, but they were a tiny minority.[82]

"Special problems" did emerge, however, as described earlier in the case of Mkushi Camp, when many of the ZAPU women training to be guerilla fighters were massacred. Nkomo tried to emphasize women's civilian roles for a number of reasons: First, to attempt to disassociate trained women fighters from refugee camps; second, to condemn Rhodesian attacks on so-called un-armed women's camps; and third, to illustrate the brutality of the Rhodesian regime.

Nonetheless, when ZAPU revealed that there were some problems with the commitment of some women in ZAPU, they also revealed the necessity of having committed women in the struggle. ZAPU berated the women for ignoring the potential of Zimbabwe's liberation and in turn their own liberation.

Among girls who join the Zimbabwean struggle quite a number is [sic] sent abroad for various studies. After completing their academic assignments they are all expected to return to the party and continue with the struggle alongside with other comrades. Some years ago, a few of these girls did not return.... They were attracted by bright possibilities of earning large sums of money abroad and buying themselves clothing. These girls betrayed the struggle and their fighting people. These days however, Zimbabwean girls ... feel that it is their duty to remain and fight side by side with their brothers and fathers as equals. They take part in teaching, radio broadcasting and in other fields to alert the world about the atrocities and crimes of the Rhodesian regime. Women's organisations have helped a lot of female students to understand how the struggle needs them. Those who deserted might have thought that their services were not needed. This could have been a result of traditional thinking. Nowadays girls are not inhibited by such feelings.[83]

ZAPU's account of its women fighters was markedly different from ZANU's. ZANU did not admit to a declining retention rate, and they were not adverse to promoting the image that their women were actively involved in military actions. The differences between ZAPU and ZANU women were remarkable, in both rhetoric and reality. That these differences and problems have become unclear due to the conflation of women in the struggle suggests that other differences in experiences, opportunities, and roles of women have also been obscured.[84]

The Zimbabwe People's Army
When the Zimbabwe People's Army (ZIPA) formed in 1975 as the combined forces of ZANLA and ZIPRA, a more radical ideology of revolution and women's emancipation emerged. However, this has also been suppressed by ZANU's dominant perspective on the war. What is not discussed is how the leaders of the *vashandi* (workers)[85] held a radical perspective on the position of women, which followed from their Marxist and socialist ideologies. Indeed it was through the formation of ZIPA that real possibilities for women's liberation emerged. ZIPA's ideas differed substantially from the old guard, and they wanted to change the course of the revolution.[86]

Moore has alluded to ZIPA's different treatment of women compared to ZANU's, although substantial research has yet to be done. He argues that ZIPA was critical of the "commandist approach" to guerilla warfare that ZANLA commander Tongogara displayed, especially in his treatment of women "both in the training camps and in 'the bush.'" Moore suggests that ZIPA's intentions were more liberationist for women.[87] In particular, the leaders were concerned to expose how the military command of ZANLA had been using and exploiting women. Suggesting that ZANU had only promoted women based on their relationships with senior men,

ZIPA did not tolerate the promotion of women in the ranks simply because they happened to be the girlfriends of the commanders. An immediate task of ZIPA was, for example, to demote Teurai Ropa because at the time she had no training to suit her position.[88]

Nonetheless, some of the leaders of ZIPA expressed a great degree of respect for their female comrades, which included notions of liberating them.[89] ZIPA enforced a one third quota of women at its political education college Wampoa, in Mozambique, despite there being less than one third women in the refugee camps.[90] One woman ex-combatant said that "the women who went to Wampoa college were more educated [than other women] on ideas like women's emancipation."[91] Some women remember the numbers of women in the college as being different. For example, Shupikai stated that "[a]t Wampoa college there were maybe five hundred people/students and comrades there, and half were women."[92] Freedom Nyamubaya stated that "at Wampoa there were no more than twenty women."[93] Most women were too young to be in the hierarchy of the movement (they were mostly teenagers). But according to some of their leaders, most were active and participated in debates over revolutionary ideology. The women and men were taught radical socialist political education which focussed on the need for struggle against colonialism and imperialism.[94] Revolutionary ideas for women's emancipation also emerged during the formation of ZIPA:

> The revolutionary armed struggle which is being waged by the ZIPA forces and the Patriotic Front has forced some of the Zimbabwe women to be politically conscious. They are now conscious of the exploitation and oppression of women in the racist colony of Rhodesia, and the world at large. Those who have realised their low position in the capitalist society and have joined the ranks of the armed struggle must educate those who are still under the settler-capitalist socio-economic system that women's emancipation is not an act of charity.... Women must know that women's liberation is born out of arduous and determined struggle.[95]

However, the continuation of this radical socialist feminist discourse on women's emancipation was pacified along with ZIPA in late 1976, when the old guard and other politicians were released from prison and returned from the Geneva Conference to take over from ZIPA. Radical socialist feminism and the combined forces of ZANLA and ZIPRA were short lived. Charles Samupindi, in his novel *Pawns* described the dilemma for the *vashandi*. When "the Chief of Defense, Comrade Josiah Magama Tongogara, ZANLA supremo and Secretary for Defence in the ZANU Central Committee," (sometimes known as Comrade Cod), was released from a Zambian prison and returned to Mozambique, announces, "*Pasi neVashandi ... Pamberi na* Comrade Robert Mugabe!" (Down with the *vashandi* / Forward with Robert Mugabe).[96] After the Pacification Campaign to suppress the *vashandi,* people were afraid to be associated with ZIPA. Fear silenced the ideological impetus behind ZIPA. Many people were killed, others went into hiding, and the leaders of ZIPA were jailed in Mozambique until the end of the war. Among those jailed in 1977 was one woman, who I interviewed but asked her story not be told.[97] In the eyes of ZIPA's leaders she is a hero who paid the price for her beliefs. There are a few other women in Zimbabwe today, who were associated with Wampoa College and active in ZIPA, who have risen above their oppressions and succeeded in the public arena, promoting democracy and women's rights. These include Irene Zindi and Margaret Dongo, who both were members of parliament. However, because ZIPA and the experiences of the women involved are not discussed publicly, it has precluded a rather more liberationist ideology of women's emancipation from emerging, and has contributed to the silencing of women's experiences in war. This has happened through the conflation of ZIPA women with women in the struggle in general.

The differences between women in ZAPU, ZIPA, and ZANU are thus significant in any analysis of women in the war. Here it suffices to note that there were significant differences, which challenge the stereotypes and representations of women guerilla fighters. The problems with women in war cannot be generalized to all women who joined up. These generalizations, whether positive, negative, or glorified representations of women's participation in the struggle have obscured a clear representation of women's experiences of war in Zimbabwe. The contentions surrounding the issue of whether or not women shot at the enemy with guns is an interesting aspect to the discourse of women's equality based on their full participation in the struggle.

Endnotes

1. It is difficult to estimate exactly how many women joined up and how many were trained as most records were destroyed during the war. The significance of the numbers of women is discussed below.

2. Interview with Teurai Ropa in Christine Qunta, ed. *Women in Southern Africa*, (London: Allison and Busby, 1987), p. 148.

3. ZANU Archives Women's Affairs File: Cde Catherine at ZANU Defence Secretariat, Rally held at operational farm base on July 20, 1978, Pfutskeke Base.

4. Interview with Teurai Ropa in Christine Qunta, ed., *Women in Southern Africa*, p. 148.

5. Ibid. As seen above in her interview she "happened to be the most successful one" in the end. Perhaps by 1978, Teurai Ropa would have known that being married to Rex Nhongo, then a leading commander in ZANLA, would also find herself well placed in an independent Zimbabwe. As in her situation and the case of men, the differences in women's positions during the war were reflected in many cases after the war.

6. Ibid.

7. See Interview with Teurai Ropa in Christine Qunta, ed. *Women in Southern Africa*, p. 148. Also see Lapchick and Urdang, *Oppression and Resistance: The Struggle of Women in Southern Africa*, p. 177. And see Miranda Davies, ed. *Third World - Second Sex: Women's Struggles and National Liberation: Third World Women Speak Out*, (London: Zed, 1983).

8. "The Role of the Zimbabwe Women in the Liberation Struggle," in *Zimbabwe People's Voice* - ZANU PF (UK edition), 1979, p.11.

9. "Comrade Teurai Ropa: Women Have Total Involvement in Struggle," in *Zimbabwe News*, 10:2, May-June 1978, p. 30.

10. Norma Kriger, *Zimbabwe's Guerilla War: Peasant Voices*.

11. Lapchick and Urdang, *Oppression and Resistance: The Struggle of Women in Southern Africa*, p. 177. Apart from the latter woman's experiences in ZAPU, all of the others were married to senior male commanders within ZANU.

12. Ministry of Community Development and Women's Affairs, *Women in Construction and Reconstruction in Post-Independence Zimbabwe*, (Harare, UNICEF, 1985, p.12), cited in Elinor Batezat, et al., "Women and Independence: The Heritage and the Struggle," in Colin Stoneman, ed. *Zimbabwe's Prospects: Issues of Race, Class, State and Capital in Southern Africa*, (London: MacMillan, 1988), p. 156.

13. Norma Kriger, *Zimbabwe's Guerilla War: Peasant Voices*, p. 191

14. Ibid, p.192.

15. Naomi Nhiwatiwa, *Women's Liberation in the Zimbabwean Revolution, Materials from the ZANU Women's Seminar*, Xai Xai, Mozambique, May 1979, (San Francisco, California: John Brown Book Club, Prairie Fire Organising Committee, 1979), p. 24.

16. See Norma Kriger, *Zimbabwe's Guerilla War: Peasant Voices*, p. 191; and Sally Mugabe cited in Richard Lapchick and Stephanie Urdang, *Oppression and Resistance: The Struggle of Women in Southern Africa*, (Greenwood Press, 1982), p. 101. Also, the figures suggested would put ZANLA's total number of fighters at 66,000, however, in 1998 only 50,000 ex-combatants were eligible for compensation payments.

17. Julia Zvobgo, in Ruth Weiss, *The Women of Zimbabwe*, (Harare: Nehanda Publishers, 1986), p. 106.

18. Jeremy Brickhill, "Daring to Storm the Heavens: the Military Strategy of ZAPU, 1976-79," in Ngwabi Bhebe and Terence Ranger, eds. *Soldiers in Zimbabwe's Liberation War*, p. 66.

19. *Sunday Mail*, May 31, 1981, p. 15.

20. Interview with Joyce Mujuru, Harare, October, 1996.

21. Nira Yuval-Davis, *Gender and Nation*, (London, Sage, 1997), p. 99.

22. Interview with John Gwitira, Executive Director, Zimbabwe National Liberation War Veterans Association, August 19, 1996. Also see *Re-Integration Programme for War Veterans in Zimbabwe: A Participatory Development Plan*, (Harare: ZNLWVA, 1996).

23. Petronella Maramba, *Tracer Study on Women Ex-Combatants in Zimbabwe*, incomplete and unpublished, (International Labour Organization, December 1995). This report is missing crucial tables and graphs regarding the numbers of women involved. If twenty percent of the 50,000 ex-combatants who received compensation payments in January 1998 were women, this number of 10,000 seriously under-represents the estimated 250,000 women involved in the war, and obviously neglects a lot of men too. Furthermore, it suggests the absurdity of such a high figure of 250,000, when there are only 50,000 registered ex-combatants in Zimbabwe.

24. Robert Mugabe, opening speech "The Role and History of the Zimbabwean Women in the National Struggle," Xai Xai, Mozambique, May 21, 1979, in Naomi Nhiwatiwa, *Women's Liberation in the Zimbabwean Revolution: Materials from the ZANU Women's Seminar*, Maputo, Mozambique, (San Francisco, California: John Brown Book Club, Prairie Fire Organising Committee, May 1979) p.16.

25. Christine Sylvester, "Simultaneous Revolutions and Exits: A Semi-Skeptical Comment," p. 424, note 23.

26. For example see Michael Raeburn, *Black Fire: Accounts of the Guerilla War in Zimbabwe*, (Harare: Zimbabwe Publishing House, 1978, reprinted 1986).

27. Policy 1:3, *Report of the Workshop on the Role of Women in Social, Economic and Cultural Reconstruction of Zimbabwe*, (Harare: February 22 - March 4, 1982), organized by Pan-African Institute for Development East and Southern Africa, in collaboration with the Ministry of Community Development and Women's Affairs.

28. Teurai Ropa Nhongo, "The Constraints and Contribution of Zimbabwe Women in the Development of Zimbabwe Before and After Independence," Keynote Address by Mrs T.R. Nhongo Minister for Community Development and

Women's Affairs, in ibid.

29. Gisela Geisler, "Troubled Sisterhood: Women and Politics in Southern Africa: Case Studies From Zambia, Zimbabwe, and Botswana," *African Affairs*, 94, 1995, p. 551.

30. "Pamberi neChimurenga, ZANU WOMEN IN THE STRUGGLE" (poster by the Department of Information and Publicity, ZANU Headquarters, Maputo, Mozambique, November 1979 - *The Year of the People's Storm)*.

31. Paul Moorcraft and Peter McLaughlin, *Chimurenga: The War in Rhodesia, 1975-1980*, (Marshalltown: Sygma Collins, 1982), p. 129.

32. The *Sunday Mail*, Harare, December 24, 1995.

33. Interview with John Gwitira, Executive Director, Zimbabwe National Liberation War Veterans Association, August 19, 1996.

34. Interview with Nhamo, Harare, September, 1996.

35. Interview with Freedom Nyamubaya, Marondera, October 1996.

36. Comrade Zvisinei, "We Women Have The Right To Fight," in *Zimbabwe News*, 11:3, September/October, 1979.

37. Ibid.

38. "Rudo Hondo: Heroine of The Liberation Struggle," *The People's Voice*, March 13-19, 1994, p. 13.

39. Ibid.

40. Ibid.

41. Naomi Nhiwatiwa, "Women's Liberation in the Zimbabwe Revolution," p. 24. Nhiwatiwa was speaking to an American audience trying to get support for ZANU, and to put pressure on the U.S. Government to stop providing helicopters to the Rhodesian forces.

42. Ibid.

43. "Salisbury Fuel Depot Blown Up on Wednesday," The *Chronicle*, Bulawayo, December 14, 1978; ZANU Archives Women's Affairs File: Teurai Ropa, ZANU Women's Affairs, 1979. Interview with Joyce Mujuru, Harare, March 5, 1997.

44. Interview with Joyce Mujuru, Harare, March 5, 1997.

45. See "Joyce Teurai Ropa Mujuru: Zimbabwe's Own Woman of Substance," in *Moto*, November 1990, pp. 7-8.

46. "The Angel of Mercy Who Left Rhodesia with a Dark Secret," in *Sunday News*, (Bulawayo), February 12, 1978, p. 5.

47. ZANU Archives Women's Affairs Files: Tsatsayi Constantino, ZANU Archivist, "The Role of Women in the Liberation Struggle," (Harare: unpublished notes, 1996).

48. ZANU Archives Women's Affairs Files: Teurai Ropa, "ZANU Women's Affairs (League)," (undated but between March 1978 and May 1979).

49. Interview with Joyce Mujuru, Harare, March 5, 1997.

50. ZANU Archives Women's Affairs File: ZANU Defence Secretariat, Rally held at operational farm base on July 20, 1978, Pfutskeke Base, p. 6. No details were available which named the particular international and Western solidarity sponsors, which supplied the cars and other donated goods.

51. Interview with Joyce Mujuru, Harare, October, 1996.

52. Naomi Nhiwatiwa, *Women's Liberation in the Zimbabwean Revolution: Materials from the ZANU Women's Seminar*, (Maputo, Mozambique, May 1979).

53. See Norma Kriger, "The Politics of Creating National Heroes: The Search for Political Legitimacy and National Identity," in Ngwabi Bhehe and Terence Ranger, eds., *Soldiers in Zimbabwe's Liberation War*, pp.139-62.

54. Interview with Maria, Harare, September, 1996.

55. Interview with Monica, Harare, August, 1996.

56. Interview with Nyarai, Harare, September, 1996.

57. Interview with Nhamo, Harare, September, 1996.

58. Interview with Rudo, Harare, September, 1996.

59. Interview with Margaret Dongo, Harare, March, 1997.

60. "They Are Teaching our Women How to Murder," The *African Times*, February 15, 1978, pp. 8-9.

61. Emphasis included in original. Comrade Zvisinei, "We Women Have The Right To Fight," in *Zimbabwe News*, 11:3, September/October, 1979.

62. This phrase was explained to in an interview with Freedom Nyamubaya, Marondera, October 1996.

63. "They Are Teaching our Women How to Murder," in The *African Times*, February 15, 1978. The *African Times* was initiated and funded by Tiny Rowlands who supported Muzorewa's internal settlement.

64. Rudo Gaidzanwa, "Bourgeois Theories of Gender and Feminism and their Shortcomings with Reference to Southern African Countries," in Ruth Meena, ed., *Gender in Southern Africa: Conceptual and Theoretical Issues*, (Harare: Sapes Books, 1992), pp.112-13.

65. "Unwanted Burdens of the Revolution," *Focus on Rhodesia*, 3:3, 1978.

66. The *African Times*, January 25, 1978, p. 12.

67. "Unwanted Burdens of the Revolution," *Focus on Rhodesia*, 3:3, 1978.

68. Ibid.

69. Ibid.

70. Ibid.

71. See "Chimurenga Is Now Liberating Our Country," *Zimbabwe News*, 10:4, July-August 1978.

72. *Zimbabwe News*, July-December, 1977, p.46.

73. See Sharon Macdonald, "Drawing the Lines - Gender, Peace and War: An Introduction," p. 10.

74. Christine Sylvester, "Simultaneous Revolutions and Exits: A Semi-Skeptical Comment," in Mary Ann Tetreault, ed. *Women and Revolution in Africa, Asia, and the New World*, p. 418. She recommends we look at Ruth Weiss, *The Women of Zimbabwe*, and Kathy Bond-Stewart, *Young Women in the Liberation Struggle*, and the Zimbabwe Project, *Stories and Poems from the Struggle*, (Harare, 1981).

75. Although the status of ex-combatants in Zimbabwe today is a contested issue, many male ex-combatants have also been homogenised into a group of anonymous people. However, the men have mostly been remembered as the ex-combatants who fought for Zimbabwe's liberation. As Maramba has argued,

all ex-combatants faced hardships upon their return to independent Zimbabwe, however there are some fundamental differences between male and female ex-combatants and their reception. See Petronella Maramba, *Tracer Study on Women Ex-combatants in Zimbabwe*. It could be argued that male ex-combatants were homogenized and remain anonymous within public/government discourse, however these arguments will not be dealt with here. Nonetheless, by and large male ex-combatants achieved higher ranks during the war and thus benefited directly post-independence by being appointed as ministers and heading the top jobs. Only two out of twenty-seven ministers in the first Zimbabwean government were women.

76. Interview with Teresa, Harare, September, 1996.
77. Interview with Rufaro, Harare, September, 1996.
78. Jane Ngwenya ,"Women and Liberation in Zimbabwe," in Miranda Davies, ed., *Third World - Second Sex: Women's Struggles and National Liberation: Third World Women Speak Out,* pp. 82-3.
79. Ibid.
80. Ibid.
81. Joshua Nkomo, *Nkomo: The Story of My Life*, (London: Methuen, 1984), p. 164.
82. Ibid.
83. Ibid.
84. The extent of these differences cannot be dealt with adequately here.
85. *Vashandi* is a Shona word, meaning *workers*. Many leading figures within ZIPA were called *vashandi* in line with their Marxist ideology; however not all members were called this, including Rex Nhongo the commander of ZIPA.
86. See David Moore "The Zimbabwe People's Army: Strategic Innovation or More of the Same?" in Ngwabi Bhebe and Terence Ranger, eds., *Soldiers in Zimbabwe's Liberation War*, p. 75.
87. Ibid, p. 79.
88. Interview with Dzino, Harare, August,1996. Teurai Ropa was Rex Nhongo's girlfriend at the time.
89. Interviews with Dzino and Wilbert, Harare, August, 1996.
90. Interview with Dzino, Harare, August, 1996.
91. Interview with Nhamo, Harare, October, 1996.
92. Interview with Shupikai, Harare, September, 1996.
93. Interview with Freedom Nyamubaya, Marondera, October, 1996
94. Josephine Nhongo-Simbanegavi has discussed ZIPA and the potential for women's liberation in her PhD thesis. Her conclusions differ in some instances but support other claims made here. See Josephine Nhongo Simbanegavi, *Zimbabwean Women in the Liberation Struggle: ZANLA and its Legacy, 1972-1985*, PhD Thesis, Faculty of Modern History, University of Oxford, 1997. A version of her thesis was published after the completion of this manuscript. See Josephine Nhongo Simbanegavi, *For better or Worse? Women and ZANLA in Zimbabwe's Liberation Struggle* (Harare: Weaver Press, 2000).
95. ZANU Archives' Women's Affairs file: "The Role of Women Before and After Liberation," pp. 3-4.

96. Charles Samupindi, *Pawns*, pp. 95-6.
97. Interview with anon. ex-ZIPA cadre, Harare, July, 1996.

Chapter Eight

Sex and Equality

It was in the fighting camps that the women began to relate sexually to men in a way that went against tradition. Away from home and the constraints of social order, many of the young women took on lovers or husbands or had children out of wedlock. Having left families behind they created new ones. In the uncertainty of war what matters is the tangible clinging to life, not custom. For the men, war also meant relating to women in ways to which they were not accustomed.

- Alexis DeVeaux in *Essence*

We have seen how women's behavior seemed to be a problem for the liberation armies. Looking at the issues of sex and equality here, we continue the analysis of the contradictions and ambiguities with the representations of women in the struggle. By acknowledging the differences between women in ZANU, ZAPU, and ZIPA we are not precluded from engaging in any further discussion of a generalized "women in the struggle." In fact, with these differences in mind it is beneficial to consider the problems that women in general faced in the guerilla training camps. As we have seen above, many of these "problems" were only acknowledged after a critical look at the evidence and documents salvaged from ZANU's version of the war. That is, until the glorifications, propaganda, and representations of women in the struggle are challenged as being *representations*, the problems associated with women will continue to be obscured. Yet, the problem with any analysis of women in the struggle lies not just in the obfuscations concerning women in the guerilla training camps, but with the negative portrayal of women guerilla fighters as murderers and prostitutes juxtaposed with the image of the heroic woman warrior. DeVeaux's description makes sense of the women's behavior that became a problem for the liberation parties.[1] However, as we have seen the representations have not allowed such justifications to dominate in the discourse about the war.

As one of the key concepts behind much of the nationalist rhetoric espoused during the struggle, which was detailed in previous chapters, the question of equality raises some serious issues that support the present argument that women's liberation was not an important goal for national liberation. Hence, it should have been unsurprising what occurred after independence vis-a-vis women.

When we consider the difference in the treatment and deployment of women in the struggle, the question of equality between men and women in the training camps becomes problematic. ZIPA seemed to present a potential for equality between women and men. What possibilities did ZANU hold for women? Sally Mugabe has argued that women's roles in the liberation war were "not that of a weak feminine force of cooks, nurses, mothers and entertainers; they had been equals with the men in every role and phase of the liberation war."[2] ZANU's propaganda, which promoted women's participation in the struggle, sounded the claims of equality of treatment between the sexes in the training camps. Robert Mugabe for example stated that women fighters

> have demonstrated beyond all doubt that they are as capable as men and deserve equal treatment, both in regard to training and appointments. It is because of their proven performance that we have agreed to constitute a Women's Detachment with its own commander who should become a member of the High Command. It is also necessary ... that ... we should promote more women to the High Command.... Although in the High Command there is only one woman ... In the General Staff, there are scores of women officers, while in the Army generally several thousands of women cadres gallantly serve in one role or another.[3]

Robert Mugabe admitted that there was only one woman in the High Command, (and he does not add that she also happened to be married to a senior commander). His claims that the Women's Detachment was set up due to women's "proven performance," contrasts with Teurai Ropa's claim that the main reason for the establishment of the Department of Women's Affairs was because women had "special problems," which had to be treated separately from the party.[4] Norma Kriger points to some contradictions in Mugabe's representation of women being treated equally, especially when some women

> voiced resentment at ongoing gender discrimination: only 5 percent of cadres sent for special courses by ZANU were women; all ZANU representatives abroad were men; leadership selection was biased in favour of men even though women did much more of the work.[5]

While this gender hierarchy existed in ZANU's deployment strategies, Rudo a female ex-combatant explained that the different roles in the camps were equally important:

> There was a division of labour, I think ... okay someone is deployed on the kitchen for five years, do you blame that person that he [she] is doing nothing? Can you do that? That he didn't fight is he considered a useless person? They were equal because one could not do without the other.[6]

As ZANU ex-combatant Maria states, "I think we were just like men!"[7] For these women guerilla fighters, to be simply involved in the struggle gave them this "equality."

Women in ZAPU's armed wing ZIPRA tell a different story than ZANU women. Rufaro explained that when women were not pregnant, they were just soldiers like the men, and soldiers take orders:

> The situation, when you are staying at home, there are rules. The commanders didn't want women to have children in the bush. They treated us like their children. But there are circumstances, we can not stop anybody to do that. The women who got pregnant were sent to V.C. [Victory Camp] in Lusaka. The men didn't treat us like women. They made sure that if he says "this," you do "that." Even when we went for Judo, he would give you a man to try. But women had no say [what went on in the camps], because when you are a recruit you have no say, you just take orders.[8]

For Rufaro, equality between the sexes meant being treated just like male soldiers. Yet if the female combatant should become pregnant, she becomes more female and less fighter. She is then sent off to the women's camps. This happened in both ZANU and ZAPU training camps. Teresa explained in more detail the situation for ZIPRA women. She said that the concept of *comrade* was initially a leveling device:

> I will tell you of the position or identification of the feeling between the different sexes as we experienced it in Zambia. Initially we were told that we are comrades. And the word *comrade* was an umbrella word, which meant you are my pal, you are my brother, sister, you are everything to me, - *except sexually motivating.* We were given strong and very meaningful explanations, in the sense of accepting a comrade. Because we were supposed to look at each other as brothers and sisters, more than anything else. So the differences in the sexes was supposed to imply that we are just brothers and sisters. So that we all wore combats, trousers and a shirt, and a cap, which was military gear, and boots. You could not identify that that was a woman and that was a man from a distance, because we all looked like just a man or a woman. From a close range you could tell from the significant features - and maybe facial features. Some of them would sell you out! But for some of the comrades it would be difficult to identify, this would be a female, this would be a male. So in that same context, we would train, we would undertake similar military training, we would do everything together as comrades, as brothers and sisters. If somebody collapsed, collapsing would be either a man or a woman. Anybody would collapse. And it would not be singled out as maybe purely a feminine gesture. Though practically it was mainly females collapsing ... [I]t was at the initial stage that most females would collapse because they had not had the strength and the stamina ... to be able to withstand the harsh environment in which we gradually lived. We would wake up at 3 or 4 a.m. ... to go out to the bush to do jogging. We had to run long distances and get fit to do operations. After military training, it was uniform in most cases. You could not differentiate between the female and the male.[9]

Sekai, another woman ex-combatant, states that women carried more than men to the front, because they were better at balancing heavy loads on their heads. But she said that in the camps *all* suffered equally. When there was not enough food to go around it was divided equally amongst the recruits. Sekai stressed that the relations between women and men were equal. She said, "I had no trouble at all with the men; the soldiers were obedient."[10] Hence, it would seem that while some women voiced resentment at inequalities between men and women, other women experienced new-found equality with their male counterparts.

Yet, there was not always equality between the sexes in the training camps. One woman ex-combatant mentioned that there was equal treatment in some things, but not so equal in others:

Women were given equal treatment even when ... going through military training. We were just being mixed up with the men and if we show that military commander we can command and everybody will be saluting you and everything ... But [what] was disappointing was that they would try to fall in love with [you] or to make you love the guys and ... when you're in the hardships promising you that you can have soap, you can have ... luxury ... even sugar ... where you could go for four days without food ... so they started kind of buying out women.[11]

This claim of "sex for soap" reveals the underlying contradictions in the experiences and roles of women in the struggle. Samupindi highlights these contradictions. During the war:

Sex is prohibited, officially
It is not indulged in, officially
But apart from Nehanda there's Osibisa
Another women's base, officially
Special women's base, officially
Expecting and breast-feeding women
Sex is not indulged in, officially.[12]

The extent of equality between the sexes varied between women and men, and between different camps. Some women experienced more equality than others. Other women were able to negotiate their survival in the camps by using their positions as *women* (being available to men). To derogate women as prostitutes in this instance was to deny women's suffering and lack of choice in the camps. Equality was not so equal.

Marriage

The problems of women's alleged behavior have been discussed above as they impinged on the revolutionary process of the struggle. "Gossiping" and "jealousy" among women in the camps was cited as the main threat. However, when we examine the role and policy of marriage within the party, we see other concerns within the party that necessitated intervention and control of mainly female participants. These marriages were held away from family networks, and, as a result they directly challenged traditional customs. The couples registered with the party and were simply married. However, it was not that simple, and many problems arose.

Teurai Ropa complained of the situation in the camps of men and women wanting to be together (sexually) but not registering their intent to marry:

> If you find it difficult to stay without men come and register your love to me. These days all pens are free because people were not registering yet corruption is playing a dominant role. We agreed that people marry in the Party provided their marriage never disturbs the Party duties.[13]

Her comments suggested that the party could not control the "passions" of the young couples. The problem with this situation, for Teurai Ropa and the party, was that women were being portrayed as prostitutes - weakening the image of ZANU's forces. The corruption of women was of concern to the party. However, a party circular written toward the end of the war reported a problem even when marriages were registered and granted by the party:

> Circular
> Since its establishment, the main purpose of the Maputo Transit camp is the accommodation of comrades to and from Party Missions abroad. Thus all the comrades sent to the Transit Camp by the defence Department had been requested for by the Manpower, Planning and Labour Department for the sole purpose of taking up Party Missions.
>
> It is also important to realise the fact that the selection of comrades for party missions involves a number of considerations such as their

academic qualifications, an attempt to increase the number of female comrades in the training programmes etc.

Unfortunately it has been observed that some female comrades, whilst in transit at the camp were given permission to marry and therefore abandon their missions. This kind of thing interferes with Party missions. We therefore appeal to all Party departments to make sure that such marriages take place after the completion of missions, by comrades in question.

signed: R.D. Manyika (Department Secretary, Manpower, Planning and Labour Department).

ZANU Archives Women's Affairs' File: Zimbabwe African National Union (ZANU), Manpower, Planning and Labour Department, Circular, May 12, 1979.[14]

Married or not married, women's "love" lives affected the revolution. Women who did marry reduced the "manpower" [sic]. And women who did not get married, but had affairs or relationships with men, who used contraception to avoid pregnancy, were labeled as "prostitutes." Unmarried women, who simply did not have sex still had to carry the stigma associated with these representations.

In July 1979 ZANU produced a report *On Marriage* which argued that marriage was essential to prevent "prostitution" and the use of contraceptives. Not at odds with the above circular, this report demonstrates a concern with women's positions vis-a-vis the revolution and tradition.

On Marriage

It is consistent with our customs and it is a natural process that a man or woman who has become of age should marry, if he or she so wishes. To refuse suitable partners from marrying can have disastrous consequences, inter alia,:-
a) The rate of prostitution will escalate. Men will spoil women with the knowledge and understanding that they will not have any responsibility to bear down on them.
b) women will practice birth control to avoid having 'fatherless' children. When they have done this, they will engage themselves, freely, into prostituting.

c) The cultural value of marriage will disappear, etc.

Viewed from this angle, marrying is a convenient and unavoidable process. The question of marriage becomes a complicated issue in the course of our struggle. More often the meaning and essence of marriage is abused and the responsibilities accruing the marriage come into conflict with the commitment each individual has, to our revolutionary struggle. Some of the reasons why marriages are a failure in our struggle are, :-

1) By coming to the revolution, a majority of our youths feel freed from parental restrictions and see the revolution as something that justifies their ego for youthful mischief.

2) The presence or grouping of many girls induces infatuation which is oftenly misinterpreted as love. This brings about 'short term' love affairs and results in the changing of boyfriends or girlfriends regularly.

3) Lack of strong action to end prostitution.

4) Youths engage into prostitution whilst they are still very young and fail to be rebuked strongly by adult comrades or their responsible authorities.

REMEDY:-

Probably a remedy lies in the four headings stated below:-

a) Outline procedure to be followed before getting into marriage.

b) Draft regulation governing marriages

c) Impose penalties for breach of these regulations.

d) Intensify orientation on our culture with emphasis on marriage and 'internal discipline.'

Pamberi Na President Mugabe!
Pamberi Ne Z.A.N.U.
signed_____

MEYA URIMBO (Chief Political Commissar)

ZANU Archives Women's Affairs File: "On Marriage" Z.A.N.U. ZANU Commissariat Department H.Q. July 6, 1979 (unsigned).

The concern with marriage to prevent immoral behavior among young recruits thus seemed paramount to the daily running of the guerilla training camps. One woman ex-combatant described the situation a little more succinctly. Teresa stated that marriage within the party during the war was a necessary part of survival in the camps:

> I met the father of my first two children during the war. He was a commander, and I got with him because he was single and so was I, and I thought, I had better get hooked with someone so the other men wouldn't put pressure on me, and also my husband respected my virginity. We did not have sex until we were registered, just fondling and kissing.[15]

For Teresa, marriage was a survival tactic and a reward like "soap" mentioned above. Sex or marriage for "soap" and survival, was a choice for *some* women in the camps.

The emphasis placed on marriage in the party reveals certain contradictions about the role and position of women in ZANU's camps and in wider society. For example, a marital status form was issued in some camps.[16]

ZANU SOFALA PROVINCE/SEMAQUESA
Commissariat Department
MARITAL STATUS FORM

I   Home name
    Chimurenga name
    Date of birth
    Headman
    Address
    Rank in Party   Operation Zone
    Trained   where

II For married comrades (approved)
    Name of husband/wife   Operation Zone
    Where Married   when
    his/her home name   chimurenga name
    children   sex
    1
    2
    3
    4
    5

III Marriage still to be approved
    your husband's details
    Home name
    Chimurenga name

Date of birth   Education
Previous occupation
Chief   Headman   district
Address
Trained
Where
Pertaining to those entering second marriage
Were you married before?   To whom?
Children with previous husband/wife

Reasons for second marriage.

Filled by those awaiting approval or are pregnant
Are you pregnant
How many months
Who is responsible
his home name
his chimurenga name
Does he accept
have you ever applied for marriage?
If applied state period

Source ZANU Archives Women's Affairs File. (no date)

ZANU's Department of Women's Affairs was established so that the party did not have to spend energy on resolving gender problems during the guerilla war. The blame for these gender problems fell upon women rather than men, thus the policies made regarding marriage were in many respects ineffective.

This is demonstrated by a concern over "women without husbands." In 1977 a ZANU document listed the names of thirty-seven women who did not have husbands and the reasons why. For example, Miriri Chidarikire stated that she was no longer with her husband because he, Wallace Mpofu "said that the pregnancy does not belong to him but to Cde Chimedza; ex-boyfriend of her lover Miriro."[17] The reasons why Mellania Mutema had no husband were given:

When the girl arrived at Nyadzonia she reported that she had a boyfriend and the husband refused. The guy also said that he didn't like an ill or sick lover. The girl left for Chimoio and she didn't know that she was pregnant.[18]

196

Tawanda Magorira "refused" her second husband Cde Pisha Ngwati at Tembwe because she loved her first husband Comrade Ostern Chinembiri at H.Q. Chaminuka, and because he was her home boyfriend. Tafirenyika Vatema had been one month pregnant just before detente, and "the situation separated them so when they met the husband refused." Of the other reasons given by the women why they did not have a husband fifteen had "no reason"; five said [the man] "refused pregnancy"; one said [the man] "wants baby, not mother"; one said [he] "simply refused"; one stated that there was "no full consultation with husband"; one said "she didn't tell her husband she was pregnant"; one woman said "he refused because the girl is a witch"; one was "divorced before they both knew she was pregnant"; one woman's husband died; and one woman was divorced.[19] The document itself reveals the irresponsibility of men towards pregnant girlfriends, but was perhaps used by Teurai Ropa or other women in the Department of Women's Affairs to understand why and how women become "immoral." The point of the document was not made clear, but it is interesting that the details were recorded by the party, either to protect or control women.

Margaret Dongo explains how marriage within the party was not a guarantee of commitment from the man. She said:

> You know what would happen, it's a funny story. What would happen if someone would impregnate you, and you'd actually go to the men who are the bosses and tell them that my pregnancy belongs to so-and-so, and that person you'd know him by his chimurenga name and not his real name. And that's how the marriage goes on. He comes in, he dies, you don't know if he was in Tete Camp or if he was Frelimo or what, you just know he was Comrade Bazooka! So how do you call that marriage? Some could easily lie that I am so-and-so and there is no proof of that. Neither was there any birth certificate or ID. So I can tell you, "I'm not Margaret," and this brought a lot of hardships for women fighters because when they came back they couldn't identify the fathers of their kids. It was very difficult for them to identify them. And most of them had runaway, and most of them had died. Except for a few.[20]

Teurai Ropa argued in 1981 that many women came back from the war with fatherless children, but only because the father had been killed fighting for liberation. She said even the women who stayed behind in Rhodesia and did not join the struggle had illegitimate children so it is not just a problem with female guerillas.[21]

The concern over women's behavior in relation to the party and men was acknowledged by at least 1977. But the blame placed on women at the rally held on July 20, 1978 was misplaced, as seen in the documents *On Marriage* and *Women Without Husbands* above, the men, boyfriends, or husbands were also to blame. It is interesting that contradictions in gender relations emerge here, in the concern over women's marital status and the extent to which the party endeavored to resolve it, rather than just concentrating on military strategies - as if men and women were equal. Marriage within the party symbolized the problems of and for women in war. These problems, and the emphasis on marriage for women guerilla fighters, continued into independence, symbolizing the problem of integrating guerillas into civilian society. Further problems associated with marriage in the party and the relations between men and women manifested themselves in the thorny issue of *lobola* - bridewealth payments by the prospective husband to the wife's family.

Lobola

The issues of lobola and family planning were raised during the struggle, appearing in both socialist and feminist discourses of women's emancipation, and in the opposing calls for the maintenance of some aspects of tradition. The latter discourse, voiced in the spaces between nationalist rhetoric and desired outcomes for a future Zimbabwe, represented a lack of commitment to equality between the sexes.

On the issue of lobola, some ZANU High Command and Women's Affairs leaders espoused the eradication of lobola as an oppressive institution in order to promote the liberation of women in line with socialist revolution. Naomi Nhiwatiwa explained at a conference in Los Angeles in 1979 how ZANU had

> eliminated one of the major sources of women's oppression in our tradition, the concept of dowry, which actually entitled a man to own his wife ... [I]n the liberated areas [ZANU] arranges the marrying of people, so people get married in the party. People are getting married, and they are not getting married with the dowry system.[22]

198

However, rhetoric of this sort did not amount to much in practical commitment. Although lobola was not officially paid during the war in party/camp marriages, ZANU kept records of the marriages, so that lobola could be claimed by parents after the war.[23] Most couples who returned to Zimbabwe subsequently organized lobola payments. Julia Zvobgo explained that ZANU did not challenge African customs because they could not afford to lose the support of the traditional chiefs or parents in the countryside whose support was crucial to the success of the guerilla war.[24] Teurai Ropa, often cited as one of the most liberated women in ZANU since she was appointed to the High Command, had lobola paid for her.

> When I met my husband he was already a commander in ZANLA. But it wasn't the first meeting that we fell in love. It was after 1977. That is when we got married. It was close to four years later. We were married in the party. Yes, he paid full lobola when we came back to Zimbabwe, and we had two daughters already. Then we had a Chapter 37 [Constitutional] marriage.[25]

The continuation of the practice of lobola during and after the liberation war reflected the unwillingness of the nationalist movement to radically change the social and economic position of women. The nationalists were not committed to equality. Ruth Weiss has pointed out how in 1982 after independence when the Legal Age of Majority Act was passed giving everyone over the age of eighteen the right to vote, a minister reminded the young women that lobola still existed and young women should not get too carried away with women's liberation:

> The women dance [and march]. They reach parliament ... A minister comes out, addresses them. He shared their joy, he said, and their delight. Yet he had to remind them that ... lobola still existed, and would continue to exist. True, an eighteen year old could now marry without the parents' consent, but they were still entitled to [lobola]. Compromise. Soothing words. Giving with one hand, withholding with the other, said a cynical bystander, a white woman. Perhaps. But for the women in front of parliament, nothing could change the joy of that day. They had come of age. It was the first step towards women's liberation.[26]

Compromise. Giving with one hand. Taking with the other. There have been many debates on the continuation of lobola into the 1990s in Zimbabwe, but they cannot be dealt with here. It will suffice to say, however, that the question of lobola set by the socialist/feminist nationalists was to be the precursor to postindependence debates on marriage and bridewealth, which revealed urban/rural and literate/illiterate divides among women in Zimbabwe. In 1995 most women in the rural areas agreed that lobola was a tradition that benefited them personally and wished it to be upheld. They disagreed that it was oppressive. It was mostly urban educated women who argued that it should be eliminated in order for the oppression of women to end.[27] As a symbol of equality for women during the struggle however, the elimination of lobola was not to be women's liberator. In relation to marriage, women's positions as women were neither changed nor emancipated by the socialist rhetoric of the war. The representations made by Nhiwatiwa about women's status without lobola, could not withstand the patriarchal pressures of the nationalist forces. Women were not as liberated as portrayed. Thus in reality, women were not as liberated as the socialist/feminist viewpoint (and hopes) had represented.

Family Planning
These contradictions and the representations of women guerilla fighters can further be demonstrated by the use of family planning methods by women during the struggle, and the subsequent discussion of the practices within the nationalist parties. Briefly, some women guerilla fighters used contraception to prevent pregnancy, although access to contraceptive pills was unreliable and expensive.[28] These women did not necessarily want to become the "mothers of the revolution," and if they became pregnant outside of marriage they were blamed for what could be labeled the "problem with men." As Comrade Dadirai explained:

> Some of you are forgetting we are at war. We are taking production of children as a great contribution to the revolution. Ossibisa [sic] is now overpopulated, and there is a corrupt tendency of Biggamy [sic]. One woman having a chain of men. Really we are destroying ourselves. We are practising prostitution. Were we given the mandate by our officials to do these activities. Do you know that we are destroying the Party? Only when we conquer this weakness

can we win full respect from men ... It's a shame some will regret tomorrow.[29]

Thus is was necessary to try and get access to contraception. As Comrade Rumbidzai put it at a meeting of women discussing the "problems with women,"

> I want to add on discipline. We understood all that you said, but we would like the male comrades to have similar lessons because they are mainly responsible for the corruption.[30]

Rumbidzai points to the role men played in getting the women pregnant and suggests they should also be educated. It was assumed that women using the contraceptive pill would become "prostitutes," and women were encouraged and required to be the mothers of the next generation of soldiers.[31] However, Sally Mugabe and Naomi Nhiwatiwa, both leading ZANU women, agreed that the use of contraception was not promoted as an option for women within the party.[32]

Freedom Nyamubaya pointed to the dilemmas facing women guerilla fighters in their choice to use contraception:

> If you were going with an ordinary soldier [as opposed to a commander] it is more likely to be love. Women were treated as "mothers." They wanted more soldiers, so no family planning was allowed. If you were caught with condoms you could be put in prison. People were suspicious of all pills, oversensitive to security. For example, if you are cooking for 1,000 people you don't want to be seen with anything like poison. The men were not consciously trying to make women pregnant to make more soldiers. But when you get pregnant you are sent to Osibisa, and a vacuum is created for the guy and he just gets to the new recruits. He might have three of four babies in Osibisa. As a soldier you acquired useful skills. While it is not nice to be with someone then the next minute they are dead, it makes you value life - extra value is placed on your life. You appreciate, enjoy, make the most out of life.[33]

Planning families or pregnancies were luxuries that most women and men could not enjoy during the guerilla war. For women the risks of pregnancy were high, but the official line was not to promote contraception. When considering aspects of equality between men and women in this case, it is obvious that women were disadvantaged by party policy that encouraged them to remain pure or become the mothers of the next generation of soldiers. As Nyamubaya highlighted, in a war you cling to any kind of life. However, ZANU in particular was concerned not to represent its women being involved in such practices as contraception, because those that did use it were portrayed as prostitutes. This was a problem for women who wanted to participate in the struggle without the burden of pregnancy, birth, and mothering.

Osibisa Camp

This problem came to be associated with ZANU's Osibisa Camp in Mozambique - a camp for women and children that symbolized all that was problematic about women in the struggle. First, it was a problem because it reduced the number of able fighters. Comrade Catherine said:

> We have plenty of officers, two months' pregnant who were removed from their departments to this base Ossibissa [sic] to wait for the day of their delivery. I think that as these comrades are still fit to carry on with their duties ... they should be sent back for a month or two before they deliver.... plus some women at Ossibissa [sic] have very big children ranging to two years, can't the mothers be returned to their departments to take up duties so that we abandon a lot of corruption in the way of gossipping?[34]

Second, it was a problem because women did not want to be sent there. In a poem called *Osibisa,* Freedom Nyamubaya, an ex-ZANLA combatant, wrote of the experiences in this women's camp. Nyamubaya's account does not represent women as passively accepting the fate of being assigned noncombat duties, since they saw their duty as one of fighting, not babysitting. Although Nyamubaya only visited Osibisa for a few days, the conditions there made her angry. In an interview she said:

> I was just passing through and met the women there. When I wrote *On the Road Again* I was still angry about everything, but now I am more comfortable with things than then.[35]

The poem Osibisa appeared in her volume *On the Road Again* and expresses this anger. The main point in the first two stanzas of the poem is to highlight that women were dumped in this camp, unable to fight, and yet still vulnerable to attacks from the Rhodesians. Later, in the last four stanzas, the problems that women faced in the war are represented, pointing out the inadequacy of the glorification of women as equal with men on the frontlines. Nyamubaya's poem gives voice to the women whose experiences have been silenced by the glorifications (discussed above) and demonstrates the unequal position of women in the nationalist armies.

Osibisa

I was told it's a Chinese word:
I definitely know of one
A place of mental torture
Where women and children were dumped,
Cut off from life.
A mental prison for mothers in the war.

Mentally disconnected, but physically involved:
Of course, they received their share
Of bombs and firing - from security headquarters
in Thornhill.

They were all mothers
With the experience of labour pains
And bullet wounds on their buttocks
Fragments all over their bodies.
They were all fighters
They were all Zimbabwean
Yet they hated their womanhood.

Unknown by the world at large,
Forgotten by their male comrades
Who made them pregnant
Remembered by their distant parents,
The women still shouldered their burdens.

Fighters to defend their children
Mothers to provide child care
Mistresses to entertain the men:
Their minds sink in despair.

Osibisa, I remember well
I know there will be many to come
For Namibia and Anzania today and tomorrow.
It's sexual, mental and physical harassment
For women, mothers, in the liberation wars.[36]

Nyamubaya said that the difficulties for women were not peculiar to Osibisa. Even in the other camps, "women were treated differently.... Not different as being given respect as women, but in the sense that they were subject to more abuse."[37] As demonstrated above, women were more vulnerable to abuse by male colleagues (in "sex-for-soap" situations) and were blamed more readily for immorality than the men who also played a part in the behavior. Women who could access contraception to avoid pregnancies were labeled as prostitutes. Men remained guerilla fighters. Women's choice was to marry in the party and expect (or not) lobola to be paid after the war; but her compromise was no guarantee of support or of a future together with her husband. For many women, Osibisa became their base camp. Monica, who became a guard at Osibisa, said that she felt disappointed when she was appointed there because she

had come to fight the enemy. They always wanted people who would look after the camps, and in this case we were appointed. I think we were eighteen women soldiers trained to go. We were given our rifles to go and guard the women in the camp, Osibisa. So we went to Osibisa, I was actually one of the commanders of that group looking after the women and their children. I mean this was a war, and there were quite a number of children ... even when the other camps didn't have food that camp would have food... but still we didn't have enough education ... It was difficult. Putting mothers and children in one place wasn't easy... there weren't any creches, it was just a difficult time.... There were not many projects for these ladies. Most of them were already trained and they had to look after their children in this place. So again it was another frustrating ... I think the party found it very difficult. The mothers were trained, they had all come to the war to fight but they end up [doing nothing] ... and some of the fathers had gone away and you never know whether they are alive, or whether they'll come back. You don't know if they will ever see that baby. You can imagine what was going through those women's minds. A lot of them would ... the babies would never know their fathers. At Osibisa we then moved after a lot of threats from the Rhodesian forces planes, airforce, fly over, like every other day, recognising ... Nyadzonia had been bombed; Chimoio had been bombed; a number of other places were bombed. When the party realised that it had become dangerous for the children to remain there, we moved right back into Pungwe forest. Osibisa was a better camp in the sense that it was closer to the city, Mozambican towns ... so for mothers if we need to take children to the hospital, now we had to move the children.[38]

Teurai Ropa confirmed that many women became frustrated, and she "had tried to organize some projects such as knitting, sewing, cookery, animal husbandry and gardening,"[39] in order to engage them in something productive. However, because of the war and the movements of people this had been difficult to establish.

Julia Zvobgo stated that at another camp especially for pregnant women, new attitudes among the women were developed, and new strategies were undertaken to keep the women busy:

Pregnant women were sent to Ambuya Nehanda camp for protection. At first they used to scream and refused to go there, as they felt it was a place where wicked women were dumped. We worked very hard to improve conditions at the camp. We started sewing classes, and pulled apart clothes that had been donated to get material to make baby clothes. Later on we got donations of baby clothes. We also opened a typing school. It was very difficult because everyone needed help, but we did what we could and spent a lot of time at the camp showing the young women that we were with them. Ambuya Nehanda camp produced new attitudes. The girls with older children were armed and did patrols to defend themselves. They became tough and independent and felt they could do everything.... Women learnt revolutionary thinking in the camps and you cant pull it out.[40]

Despite Julia Zvobgo's claims that Nehanda Camp inspired revolutionary thinking, the general view is that women suffered terribly in all of the camps, more so than men. From my interviews with ZANU and ZAPU women ex-combatants it can be seen that the women had similar misery. The following kinds of experiences are excluded from mainstream nationalist representations of women in war.

Rudo, who was also in Osibisa Camp supported Monica's view that women were not happy being sent there:

> At Osibisa Camp it was important for ... women to look after a child. There are couples still around today who had babies in [from] the war. Everybody was interested to come home. This is why they are saying that some women are refusing to go to Osibisa, they wanted to come to the front [located in Zimbabwe].[41]

Margaret Dongo, an ex-combatant and now Independent Member of Parliament, explained that it was not easy for women to be at Osibisa, especially during attacks:

> If you fall pregnant they'll take you to a special camp for women who were pregnant - Osibisa Camp, and life was very difficult in that camp. One - in the event of any attack, you have your baby, you have clothes for your baby, you have the food for your baby, you have your gun and ammunition, and the material to protect yourself. Women suffered. Also during the times of the attack you would see some people take clothing and put it in the mouth of their kids. They cried, if they cried they would know where you are. Trying to stop a kid from crying so that, you know once the kid cries these people know, and you'll know you and the kid are going to die. If it tries to cry you put something in its mouth. There was no special porridge [*sadza*] for these people. How would they get their food, they would sell the little clothes and goods that they had. Then they get on the queue to get it. They would tear [their clothes] to make [sanitary] napkins. It was terrible.[42]

Third, Osibisa came to symbolize the corruption of women in the guerilla training camps. The head of women's affairs in ZANU, Teurai Ropa, tried to tackle the problems of women's "alleged" behavior:

> The question of discipline in the military wing is not satisfactory. I tried to instruct women of Ossibissa [sic] to write their love autobiographies because most of them seem to lie. They don't want to say the real father of the kid so I think this solution will work because I will then enquire from the mentioned husband and put the record straight.... We also appeal to Welfare Department to look for creche because women with grown up children should go back for duties and they are willing to do so.[43]

Again, women's corruption is considered to be of their own making. Men's actions are not taken into account. Teurai Ropa did attempt to solve some of these problems, but in a war resources to solve "women's problems" were not a priority. As an experience of the war, life in Osibisa camp for many women was not pleasant, and thus it symbolized the negative side of the war for women. This perspective, however, was rarely included in mainstream/nationalist representations of women in the war, as it contradicted the image of the "mother of the revolution" - baby on her back carrying a gun in her hand. If Osibisa had become a symbol of the nation, the nation would have been difficult to forge. Instead, representations of women were glorified to obscure these problems. The issues of sex and equality in the guerilla training camps highlight the problems for women in war. However, as we have seen above, the representation of women guerilla fighters was not clearly glorified nor was it clearly negative.

Endnotes

1. Alexis DeVeaux, "Zimbabwe Woman Fire!" in *Essence*, July 1981, p. 111: Also see "Liberation the Real Reward," in the *Sunday Mail*, November 29, 1981.
2. Sally Mugabe, "Women's Struggle for Liberation" - Roland Buck interviews Sally Mugabe, wife of the prime minister of Zimbabwe, in *West Africa*, 1981, no. 3336, pp. 1531-32.
3. Robert Mugabe, "The Role and History of the Zimbabwean Women in the National Struggle," p. 78.
4. See Christine Qunta, *Women in Southern Africa*, p. 48.

5. Norma Kriger, *Zimbabwe's Guerilla War: Peasant Voices,* p. 193.
6. Interview with Rudo, September, Harare, 1996. She is referring to both "he" and "she" here.
7. Interview with Maria, September, Harare, 1996.
8. Interview with Rufaro, September, Harare, 1996.
9. Interview with Teresa, Harare, October, 1996.
10. Interview with Sekai, Harare, September, 1996.
11. Anonymous female ex-combatant, interviewed by David Moore, Canada, April 26, 1994. Here the reference to love means "having sex with."
12. Charles Samupindi, *Pawns,* p. 100.
13. ZANU Archives Women's Affairs File: Teurai Ropa at ZANU Defence Secretariat, Rally held at operational farm base on July 20, 1978, Pfutskeke Base.
14. I was unable to photocopy the original document to include here, so I have reproduced it here in similar fonts and layout. The original document was signed and stamped.
15. Interview with Teresa, Harare, September, 1996.
16. Marital Status Form lodged in the ZANU Archives Women's Affairs Files. However, it is not clear how successful this kind of data collection was, or if the surveys were ever used to support lobola payments or to track down missing spouses. Notably, a document also appeared written in Shona, which would have made it more accessible to the rank and file. It was on the rules and procedures of marriage. See ZANU Archives Women's Affairs File: *Nhando Dzekuroora,* ZANU Commissariat Department H.Q. August 16, 1978.
17. ZANU Archives Women's Affairs File: Z.A.N.U. (ZANU) Z.A.N.L.A. Headquarters, Chimoio, November 14, 1977, *Women Without Husbands.*
18. Ibid.
19. Ibid.
20. Interview with Margaret Dongo, Harare, March, 1997.
21. "Liberation the Real Reward," in The *Sunday Mail,* November 29, 1981.
22. Naomi Nhiwatiwa, Interview by Carol B. Thompson, in *Women's Studies International Forum,* 5:3-4, 1982, p. 249
23. Angeline Shenje-Peyton, "Balancing Gender, Equality, and Cultural Identity: Marriage Payments in Postcolonial Zimbabwe," *Harvard Human Rights Journal,* 9, 1997, p. 115.
24. Norma Kriger, *Zimbabwe's Guerilla War: Peasant Voices,* p. 193.
25. Interview with Joyce Mujuru, Harare, October 1996. In an interview with Christine Qunta, Mujuru stated that she was a "servant to Rex," as well as being a mother and a member of Parliament. See Christine Qunta, *Women in Southern Africa,* p.150. Under the Zimbabwean Constitution, Chapter 37 of the Marriage Act provides for a civil marriage based on Christian beliefs and monogamy. It is at odds however with customary marriage which requires *lobola* and allows for polygamy. See *Zimbabwean Government Gazette Extraordinary,* 71:27, April 27, 1993, for a review of the inheritance and marriage laws in Zimbabwe

26. Ruth Weiss, *The Women of Zimbabwe*, p. 115.
27. W.N. Tichagwa "Lobola and Women's Status and Role in Society," *Culture Survey, Zimbabwe Women's Resource Centre and Network*, Harare, February, 1995.
28. Amy Kaler, *Fertility, Gender, and War: The "Culture of Contraception" in Rhodesia*, Ph.D. Dissertation, University of Minnesota, 1998. Amy Kaler, "Gender and Fertility in a Postcolonial Moment: the Prohibition of Depo-Provera in Zimbabwe 1981," paper presented at *Gender and Colonialism in Southern Africa*, International Conference, University of Western Cape, South Africa, January 1997.
29. ZANU Archives Women's Affairs File: Comrade Dadirai, at ZANU Defence Secretariat, Rally held at operational farm base on July 20, 1978, Pfutskeke Base.
30. ZANU Archives Women's Affairs File: Comrade Rumbidzai at ZANU Defence Secretariat, Rally held at operational farm base on July 20, 1978, Pfutskeke Base, p.7.
31. It is important not to confuse this designation of women as mothers of new soldiers with the "mothers of the revolution," who have importantly been acknowledged as the unsung heroines of the liberation struggle through their roles as women and mothers in the rural areas supporting the guerilla fighters. See Irene Staunton, ed., *Mothers of the Revolution*.
32. Sally Mugabe, interview by Roland Buck, 1981; and Naomi Nhiwatiwa cited in Ruth Weiss, *The Women of Zimbabwe*.
33. Interview with Freedom Nyamubaya, Marondera, October, 1996.
34. ZANU Archives Women's Affairs File: Comrade Catherine, ZANU Defence Secretariat HQ July 29, 1978 Department of Women's Affairs - REF DSWS/01, Minutes of Central Committee, High Command General Staff Meeting (Female Comrades) held July 27, 1978, p. 5.
35. Interview with Freedom Nyamubaya, Marondera, October, 1996.
36. Freedom Nyamubaya, *On the Road Again*, (Harare: Zimbabwe Publishing House, 1986), pp. 66-7
37. Interview with Freedom Nyamubaya, Marondera, October, 1996.
38. Interview with Monica, Harare, August, 1996.
39. ZANU Archives Women's Affairs File: Teurai Ropa, ZANU, Department of Women's Affairs, "Report for the Year Ending December 31, 1978," pp. 1-2.
40. Julia Zvobgo, Interview, in Kathy Bond Stewart, *Independence is Not Only For One Sex*, (Harare: Zimbabwe Publishing House, 1987), p. 34.
41. Interview with Rudo, Harare, September, 1996.
42. Interview with Margaret Dongo, Harare, March, 1997.
43. ZANU Archives Women's Affairs File: Teurai Ropa, ZANU, Department of Women's Affairs, "Report for the Year Ending December 31, 1978," pp. 1-2.

PART FOUR:
RE-PRESENTING THE PAST

Chapter Nine

Women, the Nation and the Domestic

Women have a great role to play in uniting the nation because they
are the household builders, mothers of the future generations and
wives to the rulers. The more women cooperate, the more
prosperous will be our nation. - Teurai Ropa

As the above quote by Teurai Ropa suggests, despite women's
actions in the struggle for liberation, the perception is that
they will only ever be the wives to the rulers, and never the rulers.[1]
Women will always be breast-feeding the leaders, but they will never lead.
To praise women's political and practical roles and achievements as just
part of their "natural" roles, for which they do not need military training,
results in a lack of recognition for women's military service. Women's
military roles are reinscribed into domestic roles as mothers, which denies
them the benefits of political independence and the benefits granted to
(male) citizens based on their military and political/nationalist roles. This
reinscription has occurred on many levels.

Women and Nation
In order to understand the impact of the representations of women and
women guerilla fighters in the liberation war on the actual women it is
necessary to look at the postcolonial, independent nation and see how the
nationalist project included gendered identities. Anne McClintock has
argued that "all nationalisms are gendered" and "cannot be understood

without a theory of gender power, [which can] bring ... into historical visibility women's active cultural and political participation in national formations."[2] She argues:

> All nations depend on powerful constructions of gender. Despite many nationalists' ideological investment in the idea of popular unity, nations have historically amounted to the sanctioned institutionalisation of gender difference. No nation in the world gives women and men the same access to the rights and resources of the nation-state. *Rather than expressing the flowering into time of the organic essence of a timeless people, nations are contested systems of cultural representation that limit and legitimize peoples' access to the resources of the nation state.*[3]

In independent Zimbabwe, women and men have had different access to the resources of the nation in terms of political representation, legal rights, land acquisition and income. Despite the calls for women to participate equally in the nationalist struggles for independence, and despite calls for *unity*, the nation-state has legitimized inequality based on gendered differences. Women were not granted full citizenship rights after independence, despite their role in the nationalist struggle.[4] According to Cynthia Enloe this is not surprising when nationalisms and nationalist movements

> have rarely taken women's experiences as the starting point for an understanding of how a people becomes colonised or how it throws off ... domination. Rather, nationalism typically has sprung from masculinized memory, masculinized humiliation and masculinized hope.[5]

In Zimbabwe, "masculinized memory" explains how the early nationalist movement arose from the actions of men and was based on their agendas for the future of Zimbabwe. We have seen how women's role in the 1961 protests was relegated to cheerleading a male-led movement and how independent single women in Harare were raped by some bus boycotters when the women "failed to appreciate" the methods of nationalist action. Hence, as McClintock argues "the representation of male *national* power depends on the prior construction of *gender* difference."[6] That is, women as women have no access to power within the nation because nationalism is defined by men as men.

Women, on the other hand, are only symbolic of the nation or appear as metaphors.[7] McClintock writes that women are

> excluded from direct action as national citizens, [and] ... are subsumed symbolically into the national body politics as its boundary and metaphoric limit: "Singapore girl you're a great way to fly." Women are typically constructed as the symbolic bearers of the nation, but are denied any direct relation to national agency.[8]

As symbols of the nation Zimbabwean women (here we conflate ex-combatant women with civilian women) have not escaped the tedious and ambiguous location of themselves as metaphors for masculine citizenship. After independence the representation of women symbolizing the nation became a site of contestation, which saw various images of women being juggled in the public domain.

Competing against the (colonial hangover) legacy of women guerilla fighters as "prostitutes" and "murderers" tensions arose in the discourse on women in Zimbabwe. The durability of the "guerilla girl" was quickly eroded. The "prostitutes" were rounded up.[9] Trained "female murderers" were disassociated from any women in the struggle in Zimbabwe. The voices of women ex-combatants were silenced - their experiences and "problems" were drowned in a sea of propaganda.

Miss Zimbabwe

One of the images of Zimbabwean women is illustrated by the 1981 "Miss Zimbabwe" competition to find the perfect woman to represent Zimbabwe at the Miss World Beauty Contest. In this example, women themselves were divided on how to represent themselves as symbols of the nation. Joyce "Teurai Ropa" Nhongo, then the Minister for Community Development and Women's Affairs, argued that her ministry would not recognize any present or future Miss Zimbabwe, although she could not stop the reigning Miss Zimbabwe, Juliet Nyati from Bulawayo, from appearing in the Miss World competition in London.

But I would strongly urge that she does not go as a representative

215

of Zimbabwe, as Miss Zimbabwe. My opinion and the opinion of my ministry is that she goes to London as plain Miss Beauty on behalf of those who wish to commercialise her physical assets ... In the concept of African tradition, culture and morals a woman's body was solely for her husband and herself.[10]

Nhongo stated that instead of promoting the physical beauty of Zimbabwean women her ministry would be working towards

the principle and policy of creating an image of a Zimbabwean woman based on hard work, sound morals and discipline ... our real Miss Zimbabwe is the special breed of woman who works hard and who sweats to improve her life and the lives of her community and her nation ... a woman's contribution to the improvement of the standard of life of her society is the yardstick to measure the crowning of Miss Zimbabwe. We shall encourage our girls to dress properly, look nice, have decent morals, and be dignified, and disciplined.[11]

Zimbabwean girl, you can fight for your country's liberation, carry a baby on your back, hoe the fields and cook *sadza* for your family. However, this "moral, dignified, and disciplined" female representative, who, by the way, was not recognized for her ability to take up arms and fight for national liberation, could not withstand sixteen years of independence and Western-influenced commercialization and capitalist development. In 1997, the Zimbabwean woman's position as symbol of the nation was challenged by Air Zimbabwe's staffing problems reported in the local media: "Air Zim Hostesses Too Fat and Must Lose Weight!"[12] Miss Beauty has reared her (ugly) head.

Thus, for all of the debate on nationalism and the desire not to import Western feminisms - that a) Zimbabwean women should not want to be liberated like their Western sisters, and that b) any gains made for women was due to the nationalist movement; in postindependent Zimbabwe, women may have become the focus of "national symbolism," but through the issues raised by Miss Zimbabwe symbolizing the nation, there are no historical connections to her role and experiences of women in the liberation war. Beauty has no demand for women's emancipation based on participation in a socialist revolution or national liberation struggle. Yet, the concern over how and why a woman should represent the nation illustrates both the centrality of women in the national discourse and the construction of her silence.

Dresses

Women only embody the nation so far as they do not disrupt masculinized discourse. National unity or a sense of nationalism is evoked by the visible mark of women as symbolic bearers of the nation. However, national unity is often associated with a "vigilant and violent discipline [characterizing] ... the intense emotive politics of dress."[13] At the same time that the new national flag was unveiled to mark independence a new national dress had started to appear.

> This is a wrap-around cloth with a picture of the Prime Minister, Mr. Mugabe, and the party symbol - a cock. Mrs. Regina Chiwape, a stall holder, said she will be wearing the wrap-around cloth and a T-Shirt with "I Voted ZANU(PF)" written on it. In addition women will wear head scarfs of the same material as the wrap-around cloth. But Mrs. M. Marime said, "The majority of the young people who cannot afford the material, and those who will not be able to get the material, will be wearing T-shirts bearing all sorts of ZANU(PF) slogans." Most women in the Salisbury area are in favour of the wrap-around cloth as a national dress. They hoped the government would encourage this type of dress. But Mrs. Joyce James hoped that the method of going about this would not be that adopted in some countries where women were forced to wear the national dress. Men also thought it a good idea if women turned more and more to a national type of dress rather than the Western styles. But they were quick to point out that this process must, if it is adopted, be voluntary.[14]

Although this new national dress was popular among women in ZANU(PF), it did not sweep across the nation. It was a design for women only to represent the nation. While ZANU(PF) party women continue to wear Mugabe print cloth at official ceremonies, (usually to welcome President Mugabe at Harare International Airport), the impetus for such a national dress waned after the initial independence euphoria. In 1996 the government claimed that it was not its role to develop a national dress.[15] Yet, women are still under pressure to wear clothes that will portray a sense of the nation. The difficulty with this is the ambiguity of how this can be achieved. As a result, women's freedom to choose what they want to wear is constrained. Standards of attire remain contentious.

Trousers

At the University of Zimbabwe in 1992 the politics of visibility for women came under fire when a woman's attire challenged the male (nation) perception of an appropriate female symbol of the nation. There is a

> belief that only prostitutes wear trousers and miniskirts ... [however] as women have become economically and politically empowered, male backlash, it seems, has grown more vicious.... At the University of Zimbabwe, in 1992, a young woman in a mini-skirt was attacked and almost raped by a group of male students. The episode ... did not pass unchallenged. The University's female students responded en masse by marching through the campus in protest wearing mini-skirts and shorts [and trousers].[16]

Mini-skirts, shorts, and trousers worn by women were associated with women's liberation and Western influences. This example illustrates the male backlash to attempts at female liberation, highlighting the view that women are not supposed to be *that* liberated after national independence; they are to remain within the limits of national (male) boundaries. Women, it seems, are still expected to carry the burden of being the "visible markers of national homogeneity."[17] Women cannot achieve this in mini-skirts or trousers because men cannot conceivably control them.

Statues: The debate

The tensions surrounding women's dress at the University of Zimbabwe can be linked to the debate about the outfit worn by the woman guerilla fighter depicted by the *Statue of the Unknown Soldier* at Zimbabwe's *National Heroes' Acre*. Standing side-by-side with two male fighters she was constructed wearing a long skirt, despite the fact that women guerilla fighters were renowned for wearing trousers.[18] The female guerilla depicted in the statue is one of the only successful female ex-guerilla fighters represented at Heroes Acre. However, while it is a contentious underrepresentation of women in the struggle, the main site of contention in this analysis is not the number of women but what she is wearing. As Gaidzanwa points out, although it is rather obvious, the woman is wearing a skirt, and this contradicts many women's experiences of being guerilla fighters in the liberation war. (See Plate 4)

Plate 4 The Statue of the Unknown Soldier - Heroes Acre (Photograph by the author)

For example, Nhamo said that "we were wearing Chinese green uniforms, which included trousers," and Rufaro stated that she wore trousers, and this made an impact on how she felt in relation to men:

I used to think that women were not supposed to be soldiers. But when I went to Zambia, when I first saw these ladies, and I was told they were soldiers, well trained soldiers, and they were putting on nice camouflage uniforms from Russia, I was very attracted. When I was wearing the uniforms I felt that I was equal to men excombatants. If given the chance I could do whatever he could do.[19]

According to Sarudzai Churucheminzwa, a member of ZANLA, being given trousers and a gun did not automatically mean you were equal to men. She describes her experiences of joining up and training with ZANLA to the *Zimbabwe News*:

A small ground was prepared for us to practice the handling of a gun and the tactics of guerilla warfare. The male comrades lent us two pairs of trousers for the training. A sense of pride grew in us, being the only women in the camp of men and being in possession of a weapon. We moved proudly up and down the camp. The comrades soon realized this misconception within us and occasionally took our guns away from us.... One of the commissars told us: "A gun is not an object for you to use as an instrument of showing off; neither is it a certificate that you are equal to men comrades. A gun is only for killing the fascist soldiers of Ian Smith and the eradication of racial discrimination, capitalism, and exploitation in Zimbabwe."[20]

With a gun and a pair of trousers the woman ex-combatant was able to feel almost equal to the men, but as her commissar reminded her, a gun did not make her equal to men. However, both men and women feel that wearing trousers is a powerful symbolic gesture of such perceived equality in fighting for a common cause - liberation. In *Zenzele*, Maraire describes Linda's metamorphosis from woman to warrior when she puts on the trousers of war.

By day she was a primary-school teacher, but at night she huddled in smoky kitchens, helping to plot the demise of the 'forces of apartheid.' She would strip off her starched white blouse and long navy-blue skirt to don khaki trousers and a guerilla-green camouflage beret. I envied her this ability to metamorphose ... her lifestyle frightened me and I cautioned her often of the perils of her underground activities, but she would laugh and cluck at me, '*Aluta continua*, Sisi Shiri. The struggle is ours to fight; these boors [sic] are not going to hand us our independence.'[21]

Wearing trousers was as significant as taking up arms against the enemy. During the war women wore trousers and whatever else was donated to them by sympathetic international organizations. A common sight after the war was of women returning from the struggle wearing trousers. Nyarai stated that "in 1980 I was very happy, wearing trousers, shirts, boots, [and] my parents didn't have a problem with this."[22] However, many women ex-combatants came back wearing skirts as a sign of respect for their families. Women were also considered by many to be too rough if they wore trousers. One letter to the editor in 1980 encapsulated this attitude against women in trousers:

Our women who are working side by side with men will be given the same salaries. I say Amen. I would like to remind them that they are not as good as men in reality. A woman must know that a man is a man not only because he puts on a pair of trousers but because he is also the backbone of the family.[23]

Women who wore trousers were considered to be like "prostitutes" or "too liberated." The designers of the statue (seven Korean and ten Zimbabwean artists), sculpted the woman wearing a skirt. The ideological reasoning behind this is not clear, but one casual but serious commentator on this statue stated that they had to put her in a skirt otherwise it would have been too difficult to tell it was a woman.[24] During the war, nationalist rhetoric suggested that there was not supposed to be any distinctions between men and women. After the war, however, significant features of difference are not nearly enough. As Teresa stated:

We all wore combats ... trousers and a shirt, and a cap, which was military gear, and boots. You could not identify that that was a woman and that was a man from a distance, because we all looked like just a man or a woman. From a close range you could tell from the significant features - and maybe facial features. Some of them would sell you out![25]

In 1979, Teurai Ropa stated that women guerillas wearing trousers confused some people:

> Our increased role in combat in Zimbabwe as soldiers, was unimaginable. Many old man [sic] could not believe that our women comrades in military uniform were in truth female. Many doubting older women dispelled their disbelief when our female comrades invited them to carry out physical examination of the comrades.[26]

Perhaps to avoid these disbelieving physical inspections upon a statue, the statue of the woman ex-combatant wears a skirt. More importantly however, it is suggested that men were to be the ones to "wear the pants" in liberated Zimbabwe. The woman is reinscribed in the traditional domestic role of women. Her role, fighting side by side with men, is removed from being equal with men and placed instead within the traditionally gendered realms of women in Zimbabwe. In Zimbabwe today most women still wear skirts as a kind of uniform, although the younger female generation are increasingly wearing jeans.[27] Yet, as seen above in the case of the University of Zimbabwe protest, the violence associated with challenges to accepted dress standards remains the tightest constraint on both ex-combatant and civilian women's (wardrobe) representations.

Hence, one could sum up the problem as single-trouser nationalism in a patriarchal state, where women are expected to be the symbols of the nation in long skirts, and men are supposed to wear the pants. This expectation for women to be the (female) symbols of the patriarchal nation, certainly frustrates those women who felt they fought equally with their men in the liberation struggle. The freedoms won by women guerilla fighters who wore trousers in the war, were not translated to young women in Zimbabwe today. Instead, as we shall see, media portrayals and public monuments in Zimbabwe show that women ex-combatants have been forced back into domestic roles as traditional women. Their roles as guerilla fighters have been silenced in the discourse of Zimbabwean independence.

Demobilization

In 1980, when women who had fought in the war to liberate Zimbabwe returned home to their villages and families, many found that they did not receive the warm welcome they were expecting. This negative reception was perpetuated in their communities by both their families and the media.

The representation of their war time experiences in the mainstream discourse about the war obscured their voices and any sense of pride or reward that had inspired their struggle. One example of the negative portrayal of women ex-combatants emerged in media reports about the "demobilization process." Women guerilla fighters were labeled as "prostitutes" and thus not deserving of demobilization pay-outs. One headline reporting "Prostitutes Got Army Pay," detailed how fifty to sixty "high class African prostitutes" were

> rushed by high-ranking party members in official cars to ZANU(PF)'s Grazely Farm Camp at Arcturus, near Salisbury, to pose as guerillas and claim $100 a month pay.... Mr. Landau said it was an impossible situation to control when there was no means of positive identification of the ex-guerillas.[28]

In response to these allegations,

> Mr. Mugabe also criticised former Army Pay Corps Director Lt. Col. W.G. Leen who told the Public Accounts Committee that he had had to pay prostitutes among guerillas at Grazely Farm. Colonel Leen told the committee that the army expected to pay about five hundred guerillas at the farm, but when they counted them the number was nearer two thousand. Mr. Mugabe described Col. Leen's evidence as a "dishonest" expression of what transpired. "If in fact he was satisfied that there was a group of prostitutes, why did he proceed to pay them. I ask you?" Col. Leen would have to answer for his actions, Mr. Mugabe said.[29]

It is most likely that the women who received payments were actually ex-guerilla fighters and thus deserved payments. However, to label the women as prostitutes signifies male reluctance to accept their wartime roles as guerilla fighters. As a result, women guerilla fighters were stigmatized after the struggle. Musemwa explains how women faired poorly compared to men during and after demobilization:

> While ex-combatants generally faced problems of rehabilitation, female ex-combatants faced problems associated with conservative traditional customary belief about the social and marital position of

women in Shona society. The status of women in Zimbabwe was generally subsumed to that of men in the household and in the community, especially before independence.[30]

With such conflicting perceptions of women's roles and experiences brought to the foreground by the war, women guerilla fighters' experiences of demobilization led to a series of problems. For some, this resulted in being ineligible for marriage. The question became, "How many among our conservative folks would want such a woman for a daughter-in-law?"[31] Shupikai, a female ex-combatant described how her marriage fell apart after independence:

My husband's family (he was also an ex-combatant) didn't like me and said I was too much of "an ex-combatant." Maybe they meant I was too strong? The family tried everything, even witchcraft. They cut my back at night [meaning stabbed in the back] until eventually my husband divorced me, although he was very apologetic about it. It was his family - not him! I am a small woman but strong. I have brought up my two girls by myself on a teacher's salary.[32]

Portrayed as "prostitutes" in the media and seen by many as "too strong to be a female," the women ex-guerilla fighters found it difficult to adjust. Women's hopes and status were further dampened by the "brutal view expressed by most men asked ... about marriage prospects for the former freedom fighters."[33] As Musemwa noted,

Those [women] ex-combatants who wanted to be married found the civilian men unenthusiastic to marry them. There were some mixed, real and imagined, perceptions about female ex-combatants prevalent in Zimbabwe at independence. Some men were of the opinion that female ex-combatants were too haughty to be married.[34]

Other men felt that "Zimbabwe's women guerilla are too independent, rough, ill-educated and unfeminine to make good wives."[35] One example of this male bias is seen in the case of

Charles Cheveru [who] was forced to "ditch" his ex-combatant girlfriend because he found it difficult to deal with "such a wild lover." Cheveru stated that even though they loved each other she never ceased to say: "I can do without you" ... She used to boss me around and would tell me about her adventures during Chimurenga to intimidate me into fearing her. She gave me many warnings about crushing me if I failed to keep appointments.[36]

Musemwa concludes from Cheveru's statement that "when certain things were not working in their favour, women took recourse to their status as ex-combatants to defend themselves or intimidate."[37] He does not conclude as Michelle Faul did that "the problem seems to be rooted in [male] fear, materialistic social values and antiquated male chauvinism."[38] Furthermore, Musemwa concludes from the report in the *Sunday Mail* on December 6, 1981, that there seems to have been a "popular belief" that ex-combatant women must be lacking in "decency and propriety," because they had spent time with "men in the bush": "They must have slept around a lot."[39] These views were expressed by two young Zimbabwean men in 1981:

Mr. Max Matavire, a twenty-two-year-old charge clerk said men were not interested in marrying the women "because they came back from the bush with many children." He also believed they considered themselves equal to men. "They think just because they have taken part in the war that they are on the same level as the man"... he said he would happily marry a former combatant "if she is educated and earning some income." A twenty-six-year-old clerk said it's not economic reasons but "I think it's their behavior. Most of the women are rough. I would not want to marry a woman who doesn't respect me and my parents." Due to her training she'll fight you in a row!"[40]

Two women ex-combatants interviewed by *Moto* magazine in 1990 located their perceived behavior and actions within their own experiences of women having returned from the bush as trained guerilla fighters and trying to adjust to civilian society:

The two lightheartedly recounted hilarious anecdotes of the adventures of sexually starved female guerillas who "prowled" the areas around their assembly point, abducting "unfortunate" men and "demanding" to be made love to. "We were hungry!" Sithembiso (not her real name) said as she tried to justify what the civilian society in the "affected" areas must have regarded as grossly immoral conduct.[41]

Musemwa admits, despite the generalizations that were made about women ex-combatants,

The majority were well behaved and dignified. It is by and large people's uninformed perceptions, which made it difficult for female ex-combatants to integrate comfortably into the society.[42]

Not all women "wrecked marriages in lower Gweru" nor behaved like "nymphomaniacs."[43] Most women just tried to get on with their lives in independent Zimbabwe. Yet the prospects of doing this were hindered by their time away as fighters, the perceptions of their roles, and rumors of their behavior. Isaac Khumalo, a twenty-six-year-old, male ex-guerilla pointed out that

men are not interested in marrying the girls from the camps because they prefer to marry women who are working as bank-tellers, secretaries or typists who can help bring some money in and take care of them. They don't want a parasite.[44]

Having fought for liberation, the women were going to be left behind! Not all men feared these women however. One man, a thirty-one-year-old teacher, accused the men who feared marrying a woman ex-combatant of being "reactionary" and holding materialistic values. He pointed out that there are differences between those who fought under the influences of socialist values and those who remained in Rhodesia and were subjected to colonial oppression. The teacher recommended that the young men needed re-education.[45]

Teurai Ropa, the Minister for Women's Affairs in 1981, attempted to shift the focus away from women ex-combatants and the debates of marriageability, and highlight the goals of liberation. She stated that:

The liberation of Zimbabwe and the attainment of Independence was the supreme reward sought by the girls who fought in the guerilla war ... the article [by Michelle Faul] made it seem as if the guerilla girls sought to be rewarded by being married ... had the guerilla girls held marriage as the ultimate achievement they would never have joined the liberation struggle.... They gave their lives without counting the cost to themselves, toiled and sought no rest, and laboured for no other reward but the liberation of their people and country.[46]

Nonetheless, the "battle for acceptance" continued. Women ex-combatants in 1983 still complained of being discriminated against because of their experiences in the war. "Most of them complain that men are not prepared to marry them because they regard them as loose and self-asserting."[47] It was suggested by some men that the only role women had in the struggle was as "mistresses to the male combatants," making the women unsuitable for marriage. These views we have seen continued for seventeen years after Independence in Zimbabwe.

Crochet

Furthermore, in contrast to the above images of women ex-combatants there was an attempt to rehabilitate them into more traditionally feminine roles. One headline in the news reported: "While They Wait They Learn To Crochet."[48] Their military roles in the war were underplayed in the media and popular history. Initially, in Zimbabwe's newspapers, women ex-combatants were represented as more "equal with men" than "traditional" women who had not joined up. For example, in May 1981, the *Sunday Mail* reported that "if Zimbabwe's Women Libbers wish to prove the point that women are equal to men, they only have to point at one place - Assembly Point Tango."[49] There were 1,800 former ZANLA women guerillas demobilized from active guerilla service from Mt. Darwin, Mtoko, Buhera, and other areas in May 1980 at the demobilization Assembly Point Tango in the Manyene area. The women at Tango were all in school from grade one to seven and were running all aspects of the place:

But the girls are tough, healthy and fit: indeed some look tough enough and strong enough to take on Langton Schoolboy and to hold their own in a rough house with Muhammed Ali. They have muscles that would be the envy of a good many nightclub bouncers.... Until the girls are all rehabilitated, life will go on at Tango with an efficiency that adds weight to the argument that, given the opportunity to prove themselves, women can, and do, provide as good leadership as men.[50]

Focusing on women's physical strength suggests the view that women are not just equal, but a potential threat to men.

After six months rehabilitation in the demobilization camps many women were reabsorbed into civilian life.[51] However, this reabsorption was at the expense of women's skills learned during the war, which were neither mentioned nor explained. Instead of being groomed for more public roles, many women ex-combatants were taught how to crochet, among other domestic skills. At Melfort Women's Education Centre at Bromley, (funded by a Netherlands non-governmental organization), located 40 km from Salisbury (Harare), Michelle Faul spoke to twelve women who "lead a sheltered, isolated life learning such skills as dressmaking and crocheting and attending literacy classes to prepare them for the final plunge back into "civvy" street."[52] The women hoped to find work and marry like any other Zimbabwean woman. Miss Margaret Kunjonga, a twenty-one year old unmarried mother said that she might have "some difficulty getting back into the mainstream of life."[53] Eunice Mupezeni said, "Sometimes [the parents] might think that because we have been outside Zimbabwe for some years we do not know the proper culture, but this is not true."[54] She said it was nonsense that we are too independent. "We are just the same as other girls. There is no difference."[55]

Sara Maitland summarizes these difficulties for women ex-combatants in her fictional account of women in the Zimbabwean struggle:

But after Independence Day there came a difficult time for Neme. Men had been frightened of the Women's Corps and did not like to remember that.... Those who had daughters looked at these women and looked at their cookpots: two thousand women who knew how to fight better than they knew how to cook. It was alarming ... they all felt that women should not be like these women, that it was not a credit to the Nation. A civilized Nation took care of its women. The women were heroes of the Nation. They were redundant heroes. They were offered rehabilitation, which meant secretarial training, but it did not suit many of them, and afterwards there were no jobs. 'There are no jobs,' Neme thought, 'for a woman trained in the handling of high explosives, who has commanded others to kill, who has killed herself, who has a disease and a blind child.'[56]

This image of the "redundant heroes" represents the combined problems and conundrum for women ex-combatants in Zimbabwe. Once again, fiction could speak louder than they can; but in this case, the story was limited by publication restrictions and distribution. Not available in Zimbabwe this account cannot tell the story of women ex-combatants.

Returning then to popular images in the Zimbabwean media we hear The (Bulawayo) *Chronicle* reporting in November 1981 that, "Girls Abandon Guns to Fight Peacetime Battle." Two hundred and twenty women "were learning to use a typewriter in place of their more accustomed weapons of war," as part of a secretarial training course sponsored by Lonrho and the Ministry of Local Government, to prepare the women to work for sixty district administrators.[57] The women ex-combatants wanted and needed to be re-inscribed in more domestic roles in order to be accepted by society. Although an analysis of a follow up and tracer study of women ex-combatants since demobilization would enable a clearer picture of women's pursuits after the war, for the purposes here, it suffices to say that the rehabilitation focus for women ex-combatants was mainly in traditionally gender-specific, acceptable roles for women.[58] Women were further reinscribed in domestic roles through national symbols.

Operation Clean Up

Later in October 1983, the image of women ex-combatants as "prostitutes" was revived in a sweeping abuse of human rights in Zimbabwe - "Operation Clean Up." A woman ex-combatant wrote about how unjust the police action was to women:

> Zimbabwean women were subjected to the shameless, degrading, and totally unjustifiable humiliation at the hands of the police and soldiers who forced, beat, and generally mishandled women on the dubious allegations of being prostitutes ... [W]omen found travelling alone, unaccompanied, or in a group are defined as [prostitutes]. The only common factor among these women was their sex. To our disgust there is silence from the politicians and concerned citizens who preach equality and socialism. Does equality mean that one can be randomly picked from a street, shop, theatre, [or] flat and be

bundled away on the pretext of being a prostitute. Our national press again was nowhere to be heard and found except the "Sunday Mail" which condemned the arrests. ZBC and ZTV were silent as graves ... I thought women also fought to liberate this country from tyranny and arbitrary laws, or am I dreaming? Please someone tell me I am dreaming.[59]

Recognition for the roles women played during the war of liberation were again shattered when over 6,000 women were swept up by police in an attempt to remove, whom they considered to be "prostitutes" from the streets. "The majority of the detained women were housewives, secretaries or simply unemployed women,"[60] and not necessarily women ex-combatants. All women were considered suspect. Yet as the above letter to the editor demonstrates, it was widely viewed that all women should have benefited from women's roles in the war. Instead, most of the women swept up were sent to a detention camp in the Zambezi Valley.

In a letter to the editor of *Moto*, Geoffrey Mafukidze, from Zhombe Mission, argued that prostitutes were all sorts of women; mothers, school children, employed women, and married women, thus it was not unfair of the police to pick them all up:

If equality of the sexes is leading our country into a cultural downfall, then for survival's sake, deprivation of rights becomes justifiable. Remember my dear comrades - the enraged female ex-combatant in particular.[61]

Again, we come back to the representation of women guerillas and ex-combatants. Which image is he asking us to remember? It would be those which portray her as "haughty," "unfeminine," and "too strong," to be female - one who "slept around in the bush." Not that image of the heroic woman warrior fighting against Rhodesian forces. In a response to Mafukidze's letter, Benny L. Moyo, from Maphisa, suggested that men who used prostitutes should have also been arrested:

A Democratic government pledged to socialism which embraces equality of the sexes more than any other social-political system should not have used compulsion in tackling such a sensitive issue as 'cultural downfall' ... because it only breeds suspicion, mistrust and hatred. It is very painful to recall that our womenfolk bore the brunt of the anti-colonial struggle and provided an inexhaustible and reliable supply of chimbwidos ... Female comrades cheer up! Some men support you! The struggle has just begun. You are still the vanguard of the revolution.[62]

Moyo's expression of solidarity points to the pain and suffering many women had already experienced in the course of the war for the sake of liberation. Why make them suffer even more? Apart from this view, however, the "uninformed perceptions" of women by (mainly) men, served to remind women that they were not equal citizens in the country that they had helped to liberate.[63]

Nehanda Maternity Hospital

Taking us back to the representations of the military role of Nehanda leaves some questions surrounding the postindependence monuments chosen to honor her name. David Lan has pointed to the celebratory poster of Robert Mugabe as the first democratically elected Prime Minister in Zimbabwe. Charwe, the spirit medium of Nehanda, is featured above Mugabe's portrait as she "bequeaths the authority of the ancestors" to him. Despite her role and her authority as spiritual leader, she continues to be remembered as a grandmother of the nation.

Rudo Gaidzanwa has argued that women's roles in the liberation struggle have been through a process of redomesticization.[64] She argues that the renaming of the Lady Chancellor Maternity Hospital in Harare after *Mbuya Nehanda*, suggests that women's roles in the two chimurenga were being associated with the "natural" biological functions of women. Would it have been more appropriate to acknowledge women's courage and participation as soldiers, guerillas, and freedom fighters during the war than to celebrate their maternity? Sylvester suggests that a military unit should have been named after Nehanda, because she was a military adviser during the first Chimurenga.[65] Kwanele Ona Jirira argued that "although historical documentation puts her [Charwe's] age as under forty-years-old, the denotation *Mbuya* (grandmother) is a biological-physical mis-representation which has, nevertheless, been a useful theoretical tool in terms of 'maternalising' her in the public sphere."[66]

However, Beach has documented that Charwe did in fact have children, and he points to the historical confusion on the statues of the Nehanda spirit mediums:

> In January 1896 Charwe claimed to be thirty-six-years-old, a relatively young woman. (The first connection of the word *mbuya,* old person, with the name Nehanda seems to have been in connection with a later medium in 1959).... She was married and had two daughters and a son, but the name of her husband is not recalled.[67]

Charwe, the Nehanda medium in 1896-97, was a mother, and she is famous for her leading role in the First Chimurenga. Robert Mugabe argued that Nehanda was an exceptional woman. He stated:

> Our society has always feared and respected women possessed with spirits or medicinal power. They strike the men with awe and invoke in them a subservience that no doubt contradicts their general traditional attitude to women. It is in those rare circumstances that our women have sometimes commanded men. It was indeed in those circumstances that Nehanda was able to demonstrate her powers and to command the respect of men.[68]

A woman could not have such public, political power, unless she was "possessed" by some higher force. Nehanda was exceptional. She was a rare case of woman wielding power, possible only under even rarer circumstances - as a spirit medium. Most women, he reassures the men, will not be invoking male subservience, and there have not been female leaders of that same stature in Zimbabwe since. Yet, we have seen above that although women did not rise to leadership roles, they were nonetheless playing significant roles in the nationalist movement.

It must be noted that during the war an operational zone was named after Nehanda, and in 1986 *Air Zimbabwe* named one of its Boeing aircraft *Ambuya Nehanda,* which is (significantly) not associating Nehanda with maternal functions, but it does follow the masculine tendency of naming aircraft and ships after women! It is also worth noting that the Princess Margaret Hospital in the same area of Harare was named after Sekuru Kaguvi, Nehanda's male counterpart.[69] This demonstrates a lack of intention in the reinscription of Nehanda and other women into the domestic sphere, because here a male spirit medium known for his military involvement in the First Chimurenga, also had a hospital named after him. There are also two streets in downtown Harare named after Kaguvi and Nehanda, along with the other streets named after liberation heroes, like Robert Mugabe, Julius Nyerere (the President of Tanzania who supported ZANU), Herbert Chitepo and Josiah Tongogara. There are no streets named after any female war veterans or heroes other than Nehanda. Nonetheless, by referring to Nehanda as *Mbuya*, and naming a maternity hospital after her means she is remembered as a mother of the revolution, rather than a military adviser, leader of a rebellion, or indeed as the inspiration for a post-war siege at Great Zimbabwe.

Today in Zimbabwe, as Beach has argued, it is fashionable to remake Nehanda into a "feminist heroine," as "a plausible case can be made for Charwe as a feminist victim of men."[70] However, without making claims for her victimization by the judicial system 100 years ago, Nehanda has still become an important role model for contemporary Zimbabwean women.[71] Yet, over the last one hundred years, her so-called military role has been reinscribed in the domestic, despite the observations made by Ona Jirira and Sylvester.[72]

Zimbabwe National Heroes Acre

Zimbabwe National Heroes Acre, located 7 kms outside of Harare, is a national monument dedicated to the heroes of the liberation war. Overlooking the high density suburb of Warren Park, it is guarded by the army and is not open to the public. Special permission is required from the Ministry of Information to visit the national heroes. *A Guide to the Heroes Acre: Zimbabwe*[73] states that "independence was a product of profound service, suffering and supreme sacrifice by her patriotic sons and daughters." Zimbabwe is depicted as the motherland produced by both men and women fighting equally for liberation. Heroes Acre symbolizes the sacrifices and the struggle that was made for Zimbabwe.

> Those buried at Heroes Acre distinguished themselves in that struggle. They gave everything they had, including their own lives, to the cause of the young nation. Their names are written here on the rock of the nation's history; more importantly, they are written in our hearts.[74]

Yet, within this national maternal relationship - Zimbabwe the motherland born of her sons and daughters - favoritism has emerged. Aside from political alliances, the favorite child remains "the son of the soil." For all of their efforts during the liberation war, the daughters, mothers, sisters, and wives have only been represented in pictures and statues at the National Heroes Acre, in the two wall murals and the statue of the unknown soldier (discussed above), which is an anomaly at the site.

Very few women were able to reach the higher ranks in the guerilla armies, for the many reasons discussed above, including lack of education and being relegated to women's camps and detachments. Unable to gain senior positions during the war, those women remain the unsung heroines. Of the two dozen heroes buried at this national site so far, only one is a woman, and that is Sally Mugabe, the late first wife of President Robert Mugabe. Sally Mugabe is the only national liberation war heroine officially sanctioned by the state. As the first First Lady of Zimbabwe, she was heralded as the "mother of the nation" by many Zimbabweans.[75] Ironically, the presidential motorcade sped past the National Heroes Acre on the main road to Bulawayo, while I was visiting the site in 1996. The President did not make the 1 km detour to replace the dried flowers by the First Lady's unkempt graveside. (See Plate 5)

Plate 5 Sally Mugabe's Grave Site at Heroes Acre (Photograph by the author)

Heroes Acre is not there to challenge ZANU(PF)'s construction of history and the discourses of war, but serves to support it. Hence it should not be surprising that only one woman is buried there. As the *Guide* states:

> Heroes Acre is a product of historical reality.... It focuses attention on permanent natural values upheld by the masses of Zimbabwe, distinguishing these values as a heritage because of their importance and the continuity of history.[76]

Sally Mugabe was not a guerilla fighter, but fought for Zimbabwe's independence through nationalist political protest.

The Two Wall Murals

Another major feature of the Heroes Acre site is two high walls flanking the statue "on which are engraved and painted various scenes of the armed struggle and these murals bear witness to the rich and diverse culture of the country."[77] Completing the peaks of each wall mural, the statues of the stone birds found at Great Zimbabwe, sit overlooking the public seating arena of the National Heroes Acre (see Plate 11).

The symbolic pride in Shona history reflects the political dominance of the ruling party ZANU(PF) in postindependence Zimbabwe. There are six panels, each one telling part of the history of the war pictorially. The first three panels flank the left side of the Statue of the Unknown Soldier. In the first panel a mother with a baby on her back is being attacked by a dog and Rhodesian forces: The men are in chains and are beaten away. The people are being oppressed. (See Plate 6) The second panel illustrates the nationalist political stage of the struggle. Both men and women listen intently to a male nationalist leader. (See Plate 7) The third panel depicts the beginnings of the armed struggle against the settler regime. Two women (wearing skirts, not trousers) join the eight men in taking up arms to fight. Out of these three panels there are six women and twenty men depicted, plus two Rhodesian policemen and a dog. (See Plate 8).

The artistic representations at a national symbolic site dedicated to the liberation war are significant in the telling of Zimbabwean history. As it we have seen women were much involved in Zimbabwean nationalism and the armed struggle. Zimbabwean women have also been central to much discourse about the war. Their positions as women have been used in the propaganda war. The First Panel (Plate 6) is uncontroversial as it depicts the mother and child, symbolic of the nation, being oppressed by the Rhodesian forces and colonialism. The Second Panel (Plate 7) is also accurate in depicting women and men's involvement in the nationalist political stage of the struggle, and of the mobilization of the masses. However, it does not encompass or summarize the nationalist agency of women, for example, during the 1961 women's protests. Instead of the often-cited figure of one-third of the armed forces as having been women, the Third Panel (Plate 8) depicts only one-fifth of the fighters as women guerillas (in skirts). The men outnumber the women in the first three panels of the wall mural. This contrasts with popular history in which women and men were equally involved in the struggle. This wall mural confirms that women's roles as *mothers* is symbolic of the nation, yet they are undeserving of equal recognition for their military service. Trained women guerilla fighters are simply underrepresented.

Flanking the right side of the statue are the last three panels that continue the pictorial history of the war. In the Fourth Panel, the armed struggle is in full swing. Four male guerillas lead the battle with their guns and grenades, while a woman wearing a skirt follows at the rear carrying supplies on her head. (See Plate 9) By the Fifth Panel we have victory. Three male guerillas jump for joy with their guns in hand, while a fourth hugs a small child, his son. A woman leading the celebration, running in front of the group, carries a small child up in her arms. (See Plate 10) The Sixth Panel portrays the postindependence period, where Robert Mugabe (seen standing above the people) remains the president of Zimbabwe. (See Plate 11)

The Fourth Panel (Plate 9) is a typical representation of the division of labor in the war, reflecting traditional gender roles - men as warriors, women as supporters. The Fifth Panel (Plate 10) reaffirms the birth of the nation, using the symbol of mother carrying her child forward into national liberation. The female guerilla is expected to lay down her guns and trousers for babies and skirts, to be the mothers of the new nation. The final panel (Plate 11) confirms the transformation of the politically and militarily trained women guerillas. The women are reinscribed in their skirts, striving for equality with men. They are proud, and they should be. Women were essential to the success of the guerilla war. President Mugabe however, presides over the people as the father of the nation. The people follow him into liberation and independence. The symbolism of the mother as the nation is rejected in favor of the father. She is again silenced in the discourse about war.

Fiction

Charles Samupindi's novel *Pawns* is sensitive to the gender issues of the war, but he nonetheless represents the woman guerilla fighter as fundamentally domestic, even in her desires. For example, Samupindi has the women fighters packed up and ready to go home before they have even begun to fight. In his narrative he describes the nationalist rhetoric that promoted the need for women in war:

> ZANU is now a national, liberation party whose immediate task is to fight. As for ideology this can be decided after independence ... the war is to be intensified. Women, for perhaps the first time, will also be dispatched to the front.[78]

As we have seen in previous chapters the role that women played in the war was significant and necessary in order for the war to succeed. However, Samupindi cynically describes how the men watched as the now enthusiastic women danced and sang about going to join the struggle:

> They dance, home is round the corner
> Home, for to fight
> Home is near
> The girls dance[79]

They are struggling only so they can go "home," but home is the domestic sphere, and not the liberated or emancipated location that ZANU's rhetoric promised. Samupindi refers here to the period just after the demise of ZIPA in early 1977, which it was argued above, also signaled an end to a radical perspective on women's emancipation. Domestic aspirations appear to have dominated at a time when women were being offered their first opportunity to break with tradition and fight their oppressions. Some of the women ex-combatants I interviewed emphasized "love" and "children" as the important highlights of the war. Women's domestic dreams are explained when "Fangs," Samupindi's main male character, meets Angela

237

at a guerilla training camp over the border. We find even in her words the desire to reconcile with tradition:

> I sincerely hope this war is coming to an end. I would like to start leading a normal life. And what exactly is a normal life? I don't know, every woman dreams that one day she will have her own home, raise her own children and family, participate in something which grows, something creative.[80]

In Samupindi's *Pawns*, Angela is silenced in the most cruel and brutal way possible. In the aftermath of a Rhodesian attack on their training camp Angela becomes the singular expression of the "pain and insanity" of the war. Fangs searches for her after the attack. Graphic description of nameless victims precedes the discovery of Angela's body, which makes the war personal:

> Her body was dangling from a tree, a metre from the ground. He walked towards it and then carefully touched it, as if it could still suffer pain. She had been hit in the intestines and hurled by the violence of the impact into the air and on to the branch. She must have died slowly, through loss of blood. Tears had dried on her cheeks. Her body was already beginning to decompose. He lifted the body carefully and laid it on the ground. Maggots wriggled in and out of the gash in her stomach ... Ants crawled on her face. He wiped them off with his open hand. Agony was inscribed all over that face. He picked her up. With his gun strapped on to his left shoulder, he carried the body on his right and started to walk. He walked. Then the weight of the reality hit him! His mind exploded and he began to bark.[81]

Fangs then attempts suicide, but is saved by his comrades, only "to live a better life" after the war as a vagrant in the streets of Harare, an occurrence not unfamiliar to many ex-combatants, both male and female. In Angela's case it is notable that even the "feminine" dreams of living the life of domesticity are to remain unfulfilled. She is a victim of a war over which she had no control.

In contrast to Samupindi's *Pawns,* Freedom Nyamubaya offers a poem, *Daughters of the Soil,* which centers women, victims of the same atrocities of war, within the actions of war. As in *Pawns* with Angela's death, Nyamubaya's woman warrior dies a horrific agonizing death. Her death is for the revolution, she dies brave, shouting, "Long live the suffering masses." But as she shouts, no one hears her, no one listens to her cries; her voice echoes away. She is the epitome of Spivak's subaltern woman, who cannot speak simply because no one will listen to her.[82] Yet, Freedom in her poem hears the subaltern's voice and hence speaks on her behalf - "I saw her cry, I saw her die," just as the woman as subaltern of the revolution disappears and is reinstated as a guerilla fighter in the discourse about war.

Daughters of the Soil

Suddenly it was dark
The air was breathing hard. A thick layer of helicopters hovered
Like vultures ready to attack
Did I know sand would bubble?
In the flames, I saw her perish.

One of the warriors Africa provided
Her blood spurted above the trees
Like the gushes of a bomb fire
I saw her cry - like a woman dying in agony.
Yet she was laughing the laughs of pain
Screaming: long live the suffering masses.

She had shouted and shouted
for the world to hear
Cried and Cried to alarm the public
Fired shots to open their ears.

Oh sister! There was no world to have heard
No public to have alarmed
Not even ears to be opened.
In the timeless went the daughter of the soil.

A sister of the motherland,
Who sought freedom
Justice for her people
In the hot air , her soul burnt away
Above the angry mountains, her voice echoed
      away.
Yet she had ventured to join the brave
Who had given their lives
In the dark smoke that swallowed my sister.

Feeling defeated but sure of victory
I saw her die kicking in protest.
In the flames disappeared the freedom fighter.[83]

Another attempt to let her voice be heard in the din of male accounts can be found in Nozipo Maraire's novel *Zenzele: A Letter To My Daughter*, which offers a romanticized account of women's roles in the liberation war. Her narrative allows for women to become the heroines of the revolution, and yet the story focuses on how the ex-combatants become silenced - like Spivak's subaltern - because no one is interested to hear their stories. Maraire acknowledges that they were not valued in the newly independent society. Tinana and Linda are female freedom fighters. As a commander in the liberation forces, Tinana becomes an undercover spy, finding a job with a Rhodesian military commander. Linda laughs as she remembers what happened: "If only he could have known that it was his poor innocent little maid [Commander House Girl] who was the one passing on information to *us* and planning the next day's strategy in Mazoe Province."[84] Their sister Sisi Shiri is relieved to hear that Tinana had not given up the struggle, since it appeared that she had become a domestic worker for a white family. While the women recount their stories to each other Sisi Shiri marvels at the other two. "So these were the women of the struggle. These were the women who by their bravery and sacrifice would become the heroes of the future."[85] The women freedom fighters in Maraire's novel transcend the domestic and feminine to encompass the revolutionary cause of the nation as a whole.

Tinana recounts her reasons for joining up. As a young girl she had seen a dress in a shop window that she had wanted to buy. She worked hard to save the money for it and her mother took her back to the shop to buy the dress. The "European lady" behind the counter shrieked at them to "[g]et out now! It is your stubborn impudence that is ruining our country! Get out! I don't want your dirty kafir money!"[86] This scene of injustice and humiliation for her mother was what she carried with her "that night when, without a word, [she] crept into the bush and joined the freedom fighters."[87] Then an opportunity for revenge arose:

> You know, one night, many months later, when our regiment came into town from the bush to spread the gospel of Chimurenga, we passed by that shop. I saw the dress still hanging there and told the story to one of the comrades. He wanted to smash the store and burn it. But I told him no, that we should save our ammunition for the bigger struggle. I did not want to buy the dress; I wanted to own it and every other thing that was of my sweat. Through the teaching of the struggle, my ambitions had grown beyond the little outfit to encompass the nation.[88]

However, for all her sweat and toil, "owning" the nation does not follow her transcendence to the revolutionary. To remain the female heroes that they may have become during the war was as remote as their chances of being of interest to later generations. Sisi Shiri, says to her daughter:

> When next you are home, you should ask Auntie Linda about her fighting years. She does not talk much about it now; I am not sure why. But it is all there inside her and I know she would be flattered to have you interested in the revolution. So few of the young people are nowadays. Freedom is something you all take for granted. Yet fifty - no, even twenty years ago - it was a dream we dared not even dream.[89]

Without anyone to hear their story, no matter how romanticized or how realistically it is told, the experiences of the women guerillas will remain silenced in history, like the fate of the mothers of the revolution. In the process of reinscribing women in the domestic through national symbols and national expectations, the representations of women as mothers, fighters, and heroines have actually silenced the voices of women and their experiences in the discourse about war.

Photos from the National Heroes Acre

Plate 6: First Panel of Wall Mural at Zimbabwe National Heroes Acre.

Plate 7: Second Panel of Wall Mural at Zimbabwe National Heroes Acre.

Plate 8: Third Panel of Wall Mural at Zimbabwe National Heroes Acre.

Plate 9: Fourth Panel of Wall Mural at Zimbabwe National Heroes Acre.

Plate 10: Fifth Panel of Wall Mural at Zimbabwe National Heroes Acre.

Plate 11: Sixth Panel of Wall Mural at Zimbabwe National Heroes Acre.

Endnotes

1. Interview with Teurai Ropa, in Zimbabwe Women's Bureau, *Black Women in Zimbabwe*, 1981, p. 10.
2. Anne McClintock, *Imperial Leather: Race, Gender, and Sexuality in the Colonial Conquest*, (New York and London: Routledge, 1995), p. 355.
3. Italics in original. Ibid, pp. 352-3.
4. For example, despite the Legal Age of Majority Act (1982), which gave all people over eighteen the rights of majority, Zimbabwean women could not gain citizenship rights for their foreign husbands, whereas Zimbabwean men could gain citizenship for their foreign wives. In 1996 women's organizations challenged this law, Amendment to Constitution, Bill 14. The end result, however, was that neither male nor female Zimbabweans could gain automatic citizenship for their foreign partners.
5. Cynthia Enloe, *Bananas, Beaches,* p. 44, cited in Anne McClintock *Imperial Leather: Race, Gender, and Sexuality in the Colonial Conquest*, p. 353.
6. Anne McClintock, *Imperial Leather: Race, Gender, and Sexuality in the Colonial Conquest*, p. 353.
7. Elleke Boehmer, "Stories of Women and Mothers: Gender and Nationalism in the Early Fiction of Flora Nwapa," in Susheila Nasta, ed., *Motherlands: Black Women's Writing from Africa, the Caribbean and South Asia*, (London: The Women's Press, 1991), pp. 5-6, cited in ibid p. 355.
8. Anne McClintock, *Imperial Leather: Race, Gender, and Sexuality in the Colonial Conquest*, p. 354.
9. Operation Cleanup 1983.
10. "Nhongo Calls for Ban on Beauty Contest," The *Sunday Mail*, September 27, 1981.
11. Ibid.
12. "Muckraker," *The Zimbabwe Independent On Line*,<www.samara.co.zw/zimin>, November 28, 1997.
13. Anne McClintock, *Imperial Leather: Race, Gender, and Sexuality in the Colonial Conquest*, p. 365.
14. "National Dress Makes Its Debut," The *Herald*, March 28, 1980. The power of dress was illustrated in late 1997 when it was reported that street vendors selling PF-ZAPU T-Shirts in Bulawayo (seen as opponents to the ruling party) were allegedly harassed by CIO officers for allegedly inciting ethnic division.
15. "National Dress Not A Priority," The *Herald*, September 6, 1996.
16. Green, M., Lloyd, F., and Makwenda, J., "Multi-Trouser Democracy! Clothes and Identity in Southern Africa," in *Women in Culture in Southern Africa*, Diary Notebook, (Harare: WICSA, 1996), pp. 55-7.
17. Anne McClintock, *Imperial Leather: Race, Gender, and Sexuality in the Colonial Conquest*, p. 365. Also, an interesting example from Uganda was a "decree in 1973 regulating female attire asserted that Ugandan women should look dignified like 'our mothers,' and was premised on the belief that women

who wear tight or short dresses are morally loose." See Christine Obbo, "Sexuality and Economic Domination in Uganda" in Yuval-Davis and Floya Anthias, eds., *Women-Nation-State*, (London, Macmillan, 1987).

18. Rudo Gaidzanwa, "Bourgeois Theories of Gender Feminism and Their Shortcomings with Reference to Southern African Countries," in Ruth Meena, ed., *Gender in Southern Africa: Conceptual and Theoretical Issues*, (Harare: Sapes Books, 1992).

19. Interviews with Nhamo and Rufaro, Harare, September, 1996.

20. ZANU Archives Women's Affairs File: Sarudzai Churucheminzwa 'Why I Joined ZANLA Women's Detachment," pamphlet, reprinted from *Zimbabwe News*, June 1974.

21. Nozipo Maraire, *Zenzele: A Letter to My Daughter*, (Johannesburg: Ad Honker, 1996), pp. 125-26. It is interesting that "apartheid" and "boors" are part of South African discourse and they appear here in a text about Rhodesia and Zimbabwe.

22. Interview with Nyarai, Harare, September, 1996.

23. Letter to the editor by L.E. Chisiri - Seke, in The *Herald*, Monday, June 2, 1980, p. 8.

24. Comments by Heroes Acre army (tour) guide, Harare, July 1996. He was able to quote *The Guide* word for word, but also offered his own commentary on the cause of death and worthiness of the heroes buried there. He could not explain why there were not any more women buried there. See *A Guide to the Heroes Acre: Zimbabwe*, (Harare: Zimbabwe Ministry of Information, Publication, June 1990).

25. Interview with Teresa, Harare, September, 1996.

26. ZANU Archives Women's Affairs File: Z.A.N.U. Women's Affairs (League): Document unsigned by Comrade Teurai Ropa (Secretary for Women's Affairs) member of National Executive of Central Committee of ZANU, p. 4.

27. Christine Sylvester pointed this notion of a skirt being a uniform for Zimbabwean women and a need especially for foreigners to respect this: Women's Studies Seminar, Adelaide University, May, 1996.

28. These claims were made by Mr. John Landau the Chairman of the Committee of Public Accounts in the House of Assembly. The *Chronicle* (Bulawayo), January 31, 1981, p. 1.

29. "Army Officers Told: We Wont Look For Scapegoats," The *Chronicle* (Bulawayo), February 4, 1981, p. 1.

30. Muchaparara Musemwa, "The Ambiguities of Democracy: The Demobilisation of the Zimbabwean Ex-combatants and the Ordeal of Rehabilitation, 1980-93," in *Transformation*, 26, 1995, pp. 31-46.

31. "A Luta Continua," in *Moto*, 94, November, 1990, p. 4.

32. Interview with Shupikai, Harare, September, 1996.

33. Michelle Faul, "Are Men Fighting Shy of Marrying the Guerilla Girls?" The *Sunday Mail*, November 22, 1981.

34. Muchaparara Musemwa, "The Ambiguities of Democracy: The Demobilisation of the Zimbabwean Ex-combatants and the Ordeal of Rehabilitation 1980-93,"

in *Transformation*, 26, 1995, pp.38-39: see *Sunday Mail*, December 6, 1981.

35. Michelle Faul, "Are Men Fighting Shy of Marrying the Guerilla Girls?"
36. Muchaparara Musemwa, "The Ambiguities of Democracy."
37. Ibid, p. 39.
38. Michelle Faul, "Are Men Fighting Shy of Marrying the Guerilla Girls?"
39. Muchaparara Musemwa, "The Ambiguities of Democracy," p.3 9.
40. Michelle Faul, "Are Men Fighting Shy of Marrying the Guerilla Girls?"
41. "A Luta Continua," in *Moto*, 94, November, 1990, p. 4.
42. Muchaparara Musemwa, "The Ambiguities of Democracy," p. 39.
43. "A Luta Continua," in *Moto*, 94, November, 1990, p. 4.
44. Michelle Faul, "Are Men Fighting Shy of Marrying the Guerilla Girls?"
45. Ibid.
46. "Liberation the Real Reward Says Nhongo," The *Sunday Mail*, November 29, 1981.
47. "Another Battle for Women Ex-combatants," *Moto*, March 1983, p. 31.
48. Subheading in "Are Men Fighting Shy of Marrying the Guerilla Girls?"
49. "Tough, Disciplined ... They're Eager for a Role in the New Society," The *Sunday Mail,* May 17, 1981, p. 15.
50. Ibid.
51. The women demobilized from Assembly Point Tango received Post Office Savings Books with a guarantee of two years payments. see The *Chronicle*, December 4, 1981.
52. "Are Men Fighting Shy of Marrying the Guerilla Girls?"
53. Ibid.
54. Ibid.
55. Ibid.
56. Sarah Maitland, "Justice and Mercy," in *Women Fly When Men Aren't Watching*, (London: Virago, 1993), pp. 144-45.
57. "Girls Abandon Guns to Fight Peacetime Battle," in The *Chronicle*, November 30, 1981
58. See Petronella Maramba, *Tracer Study on Women Ex-combatants*, ILO unpublished report, 1995. Unfortunately the report is incomplete and fails to establish what rehabilitation and training for women ex-combatants was actually received.
59. Anonymous, *"Enraged by Police Blitz,"* Letters to *Moto*, 19, December 1983/ January 1984.
60. See Ruth Weiss, *The Women of Zimbabwe*, (Harare: Nehanda Publishers, 1986), p. 124.
61. Mafukidze, G., *"In Support of Operation Clean Up,"* letter to *Moto*, March 1984, p. 3.
62. B. Moyo, *"Blitz on Women Retrogressive,"* letter to *Moto*, May 1984, p. 3.
63. See for example, "Operation Clean-Up Takes Women's Lib One Step Back," in *Moto*, December 1983/January 1984, pp. 5-9, and letters to the editor in the same edition.
64. Rudo Gaidzanwa, "Bourgeois Theories of Gender and Feminism and their

Shortcomings with reference to Southern African Countries."

65. Christine Sylvester, "African and Western Feminisms: World Traveling the Tendencies and Possibilities," *Signs*, Summer, 1995, pp. 941-69.

66. Kwanele O Jirira, "Our Struggle Ourselves: Shaping Feminist Theory in our Context: The Zimbabwe Scenario," in *Southern African Feminist Review*, 1:1, 1995, p. 77.

67. David Beach, "An Innocent Woman, Unjustly Accused? Charwe, Medium of the Nehanda *Mhondoro* Spirit, and the 1896-7 Shona Rising in Zimbabwe," University of Zimbabwe, Department of History Seminar Paper, no. 98, 1995, p. 4.

68. Robert Mugabe, *Our War of Liberation: Speeches, Articles, Interviews, 1976-1979*, (Gweru: Mambo Press), 1983, p. 73.

69. See "Hospitals to be Renamed after Heroes," in The *Herald*, April 15, 1981, p. 7.

70. David Beach, "An Innocent Woman, Unjustly Accused? Charwe, Medium of the Nehanda *Mhondoro* Spirit, and the 1896-7 Shona Rising in Zimbabwe," p. 27.

71. Ruth Gabi, "The Secret Cave," in Norma Kitson, ed., *Zimbabwe Women Writers Anthology 1994, (*Harare: ZWW, 1994), pp. 60-3.

72. Rudo Gaidzanwa, "Bourgeois Theories of Gender and Feminism and their Shortcomings with Reference to Southern African Countries," pp. 92-125.

73. *A Guide to the Heroes Acre: Zimbabwe.*

74. Ibid.

75. In 1996, four years after Sally Mugabe's death President Robert Mugabe remarried. As the new First Lady, Mrs. Grace Mugabe stated, "There can only be one first lady!"

76. *A Guide to the Heroes Acre: Zimbabwe.*

77. Ibid, p.3.

78. Charles Samupindi, *Pawns*, p. 102. See also Tanya Lyons and David Moore, "Written in the Revolutions: (Mis)Representations, the Politics of Gender and the Zimbabwe National Liberation War," in Peter Alexander, P., et al, eds., *Africa Today: A Multidisciplinary Snapshot of the Continent in 1995*, (Canberra: Humanities Research Centre, Australian National University, 1996).

79. Charles Samupindi, *Pawns*, p. 102

80. Ibid, p. 174.

81. Charles Samupindi, *Pawns*, p.182.

82. See Gayatri Spivak, "Can the Subaltern Speak," in Gary Nelson and Lawrence Grossberg, eds., *Marxism and the Interpretation of Culture*, (Chicago: University of Illinois Press, 1988), pp. 271-313.

83. Freedom Nyamubaya, *On the Road Again*, (Harare: Zimbabwe Publishing House, 1986), p. 3.

84. Nozipo Maraire, *Zenzele: A Letter for My Daughter*, p. 138.

85. Ibid, p. 139.

86. Ibid, p. 163.

87. Ibid, p. 164.

88. Ibid, p. 164.
89. Ibid, p. 167.

Chapter Ten

The Telling of History in Zimbabwe

It all began with silence. We deliberately kept silent about some truths, no matter how small, because some of us felt that we would compromise our power. This was how the lies began because when we came to tell the history of the country and the history of the struggle, our silences distorted the story and made it defective. Then the silence spilled into the everyday lives of our people and translated itself into fear which they believe is the only protection that they have against imaginary enemies whom we have taught them to see standing behind their shoulders. They are no longer able to say what they want.

- Alexander Kanengoni in *Echoing Silences*

Representations

K anengoni's description of the silences in history and the lies that are told speak to the general problems in Zimbabwean politics and the history of the liberation struggle. While all of these problems cannot be dealt with here, one important aspect of them concerns the lives of women ex-combatants. "We deliberately kept silent about some truths" and the "silences distorted the story" are true for them. A women's history has been told, but only through "silences" and "lies." Nationalist rhetoric has glorified women's roles and "distorted" their experiences of war. Rhodesian propaganda negatively stereotyped women in the war. The difficulties that women faced were obscured by the representation of women, which announced equality, but practiced the opposite; which romanticized women warriors, but failed to consider definitions of frontline military action involving women; which promoted women's natural roles as mothers, but accused them of prostitution; which used images of women to symbolize the new nation, but reinscribed women in the domestic sphere, despite their active and full participation in the liberation struggle.

This chapter and indeed this book began with the "silences" but will end with the voices of Zimbabwean women ex-combatants speaking out against the treatment they received during and after the war. Both fiction and film in Zimbabwe have challenged the "silences" in the discourse about the war. Like Spivak's subaltern, when the women speak they are no longer subaltern. In Zimbabwe much of this effort to eradicate the subaltern position has been carried out through fiction, and in one case a film has also succeeded in doing this. First however, it is necessary to discuss some of the previous attempts to make a film about the liberation struggle.

Attempts to capture the experiences of the liberation war on film have been surrounded in controversy since independence. For example, in 1981 Zimbabwe's Minister for Information, Dr. Nathan Shamuyarira, prevented a South African production of a film about a guerilla war from being filmed in Zimbabwe. The film was to be based on Nadine Gordimer's short story *Oral History* about the

> dilemma of a chief caught up in a black liberation struggle in an unnamed African state. Guerillas come to his kraal to hide their guns and seek shelter. The chief after much soul searching - tells the whites, who destroy his village. When the chief returns home and finds the kraal razed to the ground he commits suicide.[1]

Shamuyarira stated that the filming could not go ahead because "re-enacting scenes from a guerilla war would reopen old wounds in Zimbabwe."[2] An attempt was made to make a definitive film about the war in the mid-1980s, but this also failed:

> A block buster movie on the liberation struggle, which would have been financed by the French government, which was prepared to invest $US one million, was aborted because some people in power

thought the subject was still too close to the bone. Three local writers were recruited to write a script, which is gathering dust on some government shelf.[3]

The masculinized discourse about the war was disrupted when a Zimbabwean film company dared to challenge the representations of women in war in order to expose their "true" experiences. The end result of their efforts - another representation of women in the war - is a film called *Flame*. As Desiree Lewis has pointed out, another representation, even though tainted by the personalities and autobiographies of the writers and producers, can still be useful to present the contradictions, ambiguities, questions and conundrums of previous representations. *Flame* highlights the difficulties women have talking about their experiences of war. *Flame* was released in Zimbabwe in a climate when ex-guerilla fighters were demanding compensation for their war roles, and registering as an ex-combatant depended upon being recognized (usually) by a male commander. Women ex-combatants were unlikely to speak out about their experiences of war publicly, if this meant speaking out against these same men who had been with them in the training camps across the borders, and who may have abused or raped them. *Flame* spoke for the women without silencing them.

Flame is the most profound attempt to articulate women's war experiences. From its conception, *Flame* was more than just a "fictional" account of women's roles in the liberation war. It is the first feature film about Zimbabwe's liberation war and offers a profound challenge to the construction of the war story dominated by ZANU(PF) rhetoric within the discourse of war. As one independent newspaper in Zimbabwe has argued, "History, they say, is the propaganda of the victors, and the Patriotic Front comprising ZANU(PF) and PF-ZAPU has been rewriting Zimbabwean history with a bias towards their own achievements, that is after the 1987 Unity Accord, because before that Zimbabwean history was ZANU history."[4] *Flame* is not just an articulation of women's or feminist's concerns but poses a challenge to the way Zimbabwean history has been told. Film has the potential to reach a very wide audience and in the case of *Flame,* "provides such a powerful and convincing representation of reality, [the] film has also had a profound effect on members of its audience psychopolitically."[5] As we will see below, much of the concern over *Flame* was that it would be seen as "a decal of the reality [it] represents."[6]

As the film opened in cinemas in Harare, the audience heard how "this story of two friends is one of many," narrated by the character Liberty, at the beginning of the film. It is a story about Liberty and Flame, two young women who join the struggle for the independence of Zimbabwe to make life better for their parents and themselves. When Flame's father is arrested by the Rhodesian forces in 1975, after being "sold out"[7] by the local shop owner for not paying his bills, the two girls run away to join the comrades in Mozambique, "to rage like the flame of a bushfire." Flame secretly hopes that she might also meet up with Comrade Danger who gave her a wrist bangle, as a token of "friendship and commitment" at a village *pungwe* (meeting with guerilla fighters), when he urged her to join the struggle and be by his side.[8]

Their story is similar to many women's stories of joining the struggle. They would travel for days in the general direction of Mozambique and often be taken to ZANLA refugee and training camps by Frelimo soldiers. There is no mention of political parties or names of camps in the film, but it is obvious they are ZANLA because of the location and training techniques. When they arrive at the camp they are questioned about where they came from in case they are spies, but they are accepted by the camp commander after their reasons for joining are heard. At first they are not trained and suffer hardships, especially hunger, and the film shows specific difficulties women faced like irregular menstrual cycles due to malnutrition, as well as issues of contraception and pregnancy. One girl, who complains of missing a period, is reminded that "at least you won't get pregnant." This is a subtle reminder that many women negotiated their survival in what is called the "sex-for-food-or-soap" syndrome.

Despite reference to this particular problem for women, the film does not dwell upon the more personal hardships like being unable

> to wash often, so that when we were menstruating things were difficult; we wore jeans or those heavy uniforms, and just imagine, with your periods it's not comfortable. Anyway, things come and go, we still had to proceed, so we had to manage. With time you get used to the whole thing.[9]

Freedom Nyamubaya criticizes this omission because "[a]fter three days walking the girls were still clean. Their hair etcetera would have changed."[10] The film does not show the grime or weariness of the women after such a long journey.

In the film the women are eventually trained to use guns and fight. However, during the training period the leaders of the camp invite a few of the women comrades to join them at a party to drink alcohol. Flame and Liberty enjoy the chance to relax. However, when Liberty refuses the sexual advances of a male comrade, he hits her across the face. Flame on the other hand goes with a senior officer, Comrade Che, back to his tent. He announces to her, "I love you!," and rapes her. It is this scene, shot in slow motion, with the camera panning around the hut (rather than graphically showing any visual detail of the rape), that has stirred up the controversy about the film and the role and experiences of women in the war. This scene acknowledges that Zimbabwean "guerilla girls" were raped by their male comrades. However, it has also rekindled the "colonial hangover" perceptions that women "slept around in the bush," that women guerilla fighters were prostitutes.

Much of the film's audience responded to the rape scene during the screenings in Harare as if it was a romantic encounter, whistling and cheering. However, some could have been laughing from fear. When Flame forgives Che for raping her in a later scene, some vocal male members of the audience yelled out in Shona, "She's coming back for seconds!" The fact that the negotiating skills of Flame are subtly unspoken in the film was lost on moviegoers, who are a product of a patriarchal society, which encourages the sexual subjugation of women.[11] This attitude might reflect what the director of the film Ingrid Sinclair stated was a male belief that to have women for sex "was their 'right' or 'reward,' given the tough life they led."[12] However, as she pointed out,

As usual they choose to ignore that women have an equally tough life. The other (male) way of looking at the rape of female combatants by senior male combatants was that it wasn't rape at all. The way it's presented in *Flame* (which was rewritten on set by the male actors) *is* a rape to my eyes but not to theirs. To theirs, and to men who have seen the film, what happens in *Flame* is not a rape but an average normal way of making love to an African woman.[13]

255

When Liberty accuses Flame of being immoral because she did not return to her own bed that night, Flame tells Liberty that "he was too strong." She didn't enjoy it and was upset because she loved Comrade Danger (who had seen her coming out of the senior officer's hut thus ruining her chances for a future with him!). Liberty tells Flame to "fight back," but Flame could not report Comrade Che because she was afraid, and took months to recover. Sinclair said in an interview that in this rape scene

> Flame does not fall in love with Che, but when he asks for forgiveness, she decides it's better to [forgive him] ... rather than keeping herself as a victim, but that is not spoken in the dialogue. It's true what actually happened to people was far nastier than what happened to her.[14]

For example, Honour a ZANLA woman ex-combatant stated that she

> was in Mozambique and it was a different situation to that for ZIPRA, in V.C. in Zambia. When there was not enough food, to me it was a surprise because you'd see boys falling down, but the women were strong. And in our camp, if you spoke to anyone who was in Mozambique and ask them which was the best, strongest, where I was, Tembwe, people died there because of hunger, well for women again myself, I was very unlucky. There was Comrade Nyadza, he was very very cruel when the female comrades joined the struggle. Say this one comes to the camp to do [something], he will go to the girl and say "I want you!" what, what, - but we used to refuse, and he would hit you thoroughly. Myself I even got a few injuries ... he would hit me and say I'm a sellout, but I refused. But he never had me.[15]

Freedom Nyamubaya confirmed that what happened to women in the camps was "not nice:"

> The armies were ruthless. There was sexual torture, seduction, co-optation and rape by any means. When no one in the camp has eaten for three days, a chef [commander] might have food and offers it to you. After you have eaten it, it is a privilege and hence you are obliged to have sex with him. "In terms of authority it is difficult to say no!" Also some women may think they can get

somewhere by sleeping with a guy. You might get to go overseas
for education! As a wife of a chef you have less problems.[16]

Nonetheless, Freedom Nyamubaya criticized *Flame* for not being realistic,

The rape scene was no rape as in a rape a jaw could get broken for
example. It is usually vicious! Commanders had a lot of power,
they ruled the roost. They could ask for anything. There are many
children with fathers who hold high positions that don't want to
acknowledge them.[17]

The production of *Flame* thus created waves in the (male) mainstream
version of the war story, because it created a space for "her-story" to be
told for the first time in the popular discourse about the war. Ingrid Sinclair
maintains that the script is fictional, but was based on extensive interviews
with women ex-combatants over a seven year period.[18] It started out as
a documentary project, but none of the women wanted to appear in it
because of the extremities of their experiences, and because

the women didn't have a very good reception when they came
back to Zimbabwe as women ... Women during the war were given
a great deal of freedom, far more than what they had back home,
and when they came back society didn't really welcome that, and
in that respect ... (women just stopped talking about it because it
became synonymous with a bad experience) ... If you haven't talked
about it ... to then stand up and admit it is quite dangerous ... but
psychologically ... people might think [you] have lied to them in the
past. They couldn't say the sorts of things we [want them] to say
[because] they are too contentious; they are not part of the glorious
history. They [her informants] weren't interested in simply
contributing to a history of the war, they wanted to talk from the
point of view from today. I think they wanted people to see how
difficult it was for them.[19]

In the making of *Flame*, fiction was used to disguise the identities of those
involved, to protect their realities, but at the same time used to promote a
reality that was experienced by many people. As Sinclair stated in a letter
to me, "I know fiction is different from academic research, but the principle
of using information given by others for your own work and publication is

surely the same."[20] The only difference is that *Flame* as a fictional movie will reach a much wider audience than any publication from the University of Zimbabwe, Zimbabwe Publishing House, Baobab Books Harare, or indeed a foreign Ph.D. dissertation lodged at the National Archives.

Flame itself almost became an untold story when the War Veterans Association attempted to have the film banned in Zimbabwe.[21] By attempting to ban *Flame* the ZNLWVA created a controversy, which also gave much free publicity for the film. On January 12, 1996, The *Herald* reported that:

> Police in Harare ... seized the negatives of the film based on Zimbabwe's liberation war, *Flame*, from the producer's offices after allegations that it contained subversive information and some of its parts were pornographic. Armed with a search warrant, detectives stormed the premises at about 5 p.m. ... and after a thorough search, took the film away for further investigation.[22]

The film was incomplete at this stage, and so only the rushes (unedited shots) were seized. After being viewed by police and the censorship board the film was given back to the producers because there was nothing pornographic in it. On January 18, 1996, The *Financial Gazette* reported that the police raid was a "spectacle," and that "it seems that war veterans and politicians are attempting to sanitize the story of the liberation war to suit their immediate needs ... [this] is a shocking reflection of the politicization of the police force and a very serious abrogation of constitutional rights to free expression."[23]

The controversy erupted after the Black and White Film Company, which produced the film, chose to have a policy of "transparency" regarding the film's production, acknowledging the politically sensitive nature of anything to do with the liberation war. Hence, before the film was confiscated, rough cuts were shown to the Director of Information, Bornwell Chakaodza, officials from the army and ZNLWVA (including John Gwitira), the Central Intelligence Organization, the artistic director of the Zimbabwean Association of Community Theatre, and Dr. Tafataona Mahoso, a historian and cultural activist.

According to Ingrid Sinclair some of these people were unaware of the extent to which it was a rough cut, and how much was intended to be cut out as a matter of editorial and artistic integrity. Nonetheless according to the *Sunday Mail*, December 24, 1995, the group "unanimously" objected to the negative portrayal of "liberation efforts." They,

> felt that the film portrayed the liberation struggle in a bad light showing such scenes as new war recruits being locked up in underground dungeons for interrogation [this scene was cut from the final screenplay], girls exchanging sex for food, rape, the camps being bombed by Rhodesian jets, freedom fighters burning down a shop in revenge, fearing to engage a truck load of Rhodesian forces at an ambush, drinking and womanising, without depicting anything positive about the liberation struggle.[24]

John Gwitira (by conflating love with sex and rape) argued that *Flame* misrepresents the liberation war because:

> Our war was not about love. We summoned the director of the film here but after discussions with him we did not agree. We want to have the film banned because it has stirred concern within our members and even at a higher level.[25]

However, only a few weeks before the first screening of *Flame* in Harare,[26] the director Ingrid Sinclair explained to me what the problems were with these scenes, and why their inclusion was misinterpreted by some of her "opponents." She also explained why some of the contentious scenes were eventually cut out and justified the story and its "negative" aspects. She said that the film represents what happened to the women she spoke to, despite the fact that their stories do not correspond with much of what has been written in Zimbabwe about the war so far. This is why *Flame* is such an important challenge to the dominant discourse about the war. What has been written and what has been spoken about, or rather what can be said about women's involvement in the liberation war, often stands at odds to what women really experienced and what women are prepared to talk about. *Flame* challenges both the glorifications and the misrepresentations.

Furthermore, John Gwitira stated that the only reason he "let the film go ahead in the end" was because of the final scenes of the film, which portrayed the ex-combatants remaining unrecognized for their efforts and even being forgotten on National Heroes Day (August 12th) in Harare. The group of comrades who fought together are seen watching on television the ceremony and parades at the national sports stadium, because they were not invited to attend the parades to be publicly acknowledged for their efforts.[27]

The Rape Debate

The release of the film *Flame* was followed by a debate on the experiences of women guerillas and the question of rape. The power of representations to influence the history, desires, lifestyles, and futures of women ex-combatants - to change the way history is told - is demonstrated by the development of the public debate on the question of rape in the struggle that was sparked by the release of the film. This debate is significant, for both the above reasons and to help heal the wounds of war that many women ex-combatants have carried in silence. Since independence, women's war experiences were silenced - obscured by the glorifications; reinscribed in the domestic; and muted by the shame of rape. As symbols of the nation, women could not be the victims of rape, perpetrated either by the enemy or indeed by their own comrades. As seen in the Rhodesian attacks on the women's camps above, an attack on women strikes at the very heart of (male) nationalism. Some women have used this rape debate to demand recognition of their violent experiences of war.

When talking to some women ex-combatants about their experiences the question of whether some women were raped seemed very controversial. While the interviews I conducted were not specifically about rape in war, because of the release of *Flame,* some of the women wanted to make it perfectly clear that there was no rape in the camps, although "some people fell in love and had babies"[28]:

> Of all the women who had children during the struggle, most of them we cannot say it was a rape case, some of these were being real agreements. Some of which they are married, married up 'til today. So we cannot say it was a rape case, they were in love. We cannot rule out that one. They were women and children with fathers also. Of course most of the parents, either the mother or the father, died during the struggle. But it was not rape, we can rule out that one completely.[29]

However, Shupikai, an ex-combatant, said that rape *did* happen like in any society, but she was censured by other women in the group interview. Later and privately, she described how she was raped by comrades in the ZANLA training camps and said that so were most of the girls she was with:

> There was rape happening in the camps all the time, especially among new recruits. The men commanders would just send for a girl and she was told to go and 'sweep' his hut - which meant she wouldn't be doing any sweeping. They would demand sex and rape the woman - as their right! I was raped by a comrade. It happened to me! Also if the newcomers to the camp didn't sleep with the guys they'd be accused of being spies - "If you were not sent here to spy you will sleep with me!"[30]

Alexander Kanengoni describes the abuse of women guerillas in the training camps in his novel *Echoing Silences*. Here Munashe a male guerilla fighter asks a woman guerilla who she is, and she replies "Nobody ... My life is the war." Kudzai tells him her story:

> "I was raped by the bastard for over a year! I couldn't run away. I had no option but to abort [she had three abortions]. I *hate* men. I *hate* the war."
> "Why didn't you refuse him?"
> "Rape? Refuse? That was why you saw me in prison at Tembwe."
> "Was there no one to help you?"
> Her laughter was sarcastic. "Who?" ... "Can you report a superior?"[31]

Despite this fictional portrayal of one woman's experience in the struggle as well as the evidence of women ex-combatants above, John Gwitira, the executive director of the ZNLWVA stated in 1996 that the rape scene in *Flame* was an unfair portrayal of the situation in the camps because it did not show that there were punishments in place for perpetrators of such crimes. He mentioned that in one case a comrade who allegedly had been raping village women, was actually beaten to death by other comrades who convicted him "beyond doubt."[32] However, Gwitira ignores the problems that women guerillas like "Flame" and "Kudzai" faced in reporting senior commanders for rape, not just during the war, but after the war.

That these two women are fictional representations of women guerilla fighters is significant.

Despite the existence of the Department of Women's Affairs in ZANU, there did not seem to be many avenues for women to complain or receive justice. According to Joyce "Teurai Ropa" Mujuru, the women did not tell her what was going on at the time so she could not act against it, but when they did tell her and if she did act the men complained to her. She said:

It was unfortunate that I was their leader and no one came to me to report about those cases. It is very unfortunate. What I know is that the majority of them went by consent. To tell you the truth. It needed a strong character because along the way you think 'I have been raped,' and yet, you were not that strong to really stand and defend it yourself.... I can't say 100 percent that there were no rape cases, but I didn't get told about them. But I know exactly what used to happen. I almost got into trouble by cautioning them [the men]. That I can say in front of many. I almost got into trouble! Because when we used to have these counselling sessions, they were going back to their boyfriends. You see and threats were coming to me. Of course, it's not a lie. From the boyfriends, some of whom were married men, going with young girls. And these were the young girls I was trying to counsel, who used to go back and report. So, now it's good for them to say all these things, I really can understand. Some went by consent. That is my point. Most went by consent. Because if you are raped, you can't continue to go there and get raped ... how many times do you get raped? You can see where the truth of it is. I am not saying totally that no one was raped, but I didn't get them. But for most it was by consent.[33]

During the early years of the liberation war there were guidelines and practices espoused by the spirit mediums. One of these was to refrain from having sex.[34] However, as the war intensified and more and more young men and women were recruited, discipline was more difficult to monitor. Mujuru said that the women were just as responsible as the men in cases where sex happened. She cannot agree that rape was the order of the day.

Yes [to obey the spirit mediums on abstaining from sex] that was supposed to be done. Characters change, my dear. Understandings change, and backgrounds speak a lot to an individual. From where I come from sex is illegal until you are married. And most of these people from where they came from sex was nothing. You can see the conflict already. You try and counsel that person, she will come back and say, "Who are you? You are not my Auntie! or my Mum! or any relative!" I wasn't any of these except that I was a comrade. What else should I do. No power, nothing. Let her go get pregnant. Tomorrow she is crying, "I have been raped!" Ah! What type of rape case. You go to this man, you go to that man, seeing you moving on your own two feet, all of those going for rape cases. If you had kept yourself away, let them come there and drag you, then we call that a rape case. But you go there willingly, you are called, you go there, you are coaxed into discussion, you also contribute, when it gets to real sex you also to some extent give in, but you know it's a wrong thing when a bad thing comes as a result of that. You say, "I was raped!" I don't agreed with that.[35]

In this case, Mujuru agreed with the male actors and some of the men who have seen *Flame*, whom Sinclair referred to, who claimed that Comrade Flame was not raped but made love to. However, as Margaret Dongo has pointed out, it was not easy for women to admit that they had been raped by the men, and if they did, despite Gwitira's claims above, there was only "jungle law" for justice:

Women suffered. To make matters worse, some of us and some of other women, when you hear that there was a rape, there were! There was no mother to tell that someone has abused you. There was law, where there's justice, where you could say, I want to report in the courts. There was what we call "jungle law." You're unhappy - that's it - you keep quiet to yourself. To tell other people would be an embarrassment. And the so-called chefs that we talk of, they'd actually see a beautiful lady: "Where does she, what does she do? She's a nice [woman], or she's under training - please after training can you go and pick her I want her in my room." Just like that![36]

Freedom Nyamubaya contributed to the debate by speaking out about her rape. She argues that she was raped and that is the truth. A society which denies the truth cannot develop or move forward. And for me to say I was raped is a kind of therapy. We must accept the truth and show what happened.[37]

It was not just guerilla girls who were subjected to rape or sexual abuse during the war. Alice Armstrong has argued that during the struggle women

had difficulties from both sides. The soldiers, stationed far from home and without their women around, often demanded sexual favours from them, and - with the power of the gun on their side - were easily able to force compliance. The guerillas, although firmly instructed not to, also demanded that women contribute to the struggle by satisfying their needs.[38]

One woman reported that "[a]s you know, you could not deny sexual intercourse to a 'mujiba' [young male messenger or carrier] or to a 'comrade.'"[39] To do so would result in accusations that you were not supporting the struggle. Women's roles in war were to be available for men's support and comfort. Armstrong provides evidence that women who were voluntarily sleeping with guerilla boyfriends might claim that they were "forced" into sex "to avoid prosecution for 'harbouring a terrorist,'"[40] if they were caught.

Sarah was not a guerilla fighter but lived in a village in Mutoko District. She was repeatedly raped by one of the comrades over a two-week period. She "soon discovered that other girls were having the same experience," and also that she had become pregnant. Later, she was also raped by a white Rhodesian soldier who also made her pregnant. She describes in detail how the rapes happened, and said that

what happened to me was painful and unforgivable. Sometimes I think about it and get sick and very sad. It pains me more that many years after independence nothing much has been said about the experiences that some of us, women and girls had - from both sides in the war. I am not saying all the comrades were like this, but let us talk about what happened in certain cases. We often talk about reconciliation and forgiveness. I will never forgive and forget.[41]

The use of rape by Rhodesian security forces was terrifying for women in Zimbabwe. For example:

> Three female patriots from St. Michael's Mission Mhondoro, reported to Comrade Tonderai Nyika ... that African schoolgirls are raped by enemy troops/mercenaries, most of whom suffer from chronic venereal diseases ... The mercenaries tell their victims that they fought against the people of Vietnam, Mozambique and Angola ... some are Malawians, American Negroes, British, Red Indians and Israelites.[42]

In another case it was reported that on October 12, 1978

> a bunch of terrorist Smith troops shot in cold blood a civilian woman after raping her. The incident took place in the Makoni District. However, the three gunshots they fired in their barbaric act, were the very cause to their exposure to the ZANLA forces. The one enemy troop among them who survived the ZANLA ambush confessed all their crimes to a people's court that later tried him, including revelation of the murder of the woman patriot. He was sentenced to death by an all female firing squad.[43]

During Zimbabwe's liberation war, as in many wars, rape was used as a tool by all sides involved in the fighting. However, this one recorded instance of a female firing squad was not enough to satisfy the need for revenge for all of the women abused during the war. For example, Kanengoni's character of Kudzai is finally murdered brutally by South African commandos. Not even Munashe could protect her; neither was he able to revenge her death:

> Munashe stood back and saw the mutilated breasts and the twisted legs and the blood smudges between the thighs and the single bullet hole through the forehead. But above all, he saw anger that only he could understand in her half-closed eyes and the impudent scowl on her blood-spattered lips. And he knew she had not died silently. "The bastards raped her before killing her!" the other guerilla said angrily. "Let's go!" he shouted, but Munashe remained standing, looking down at the angry corpse of his beloved Kudzai wondering what sort of fate it was that condemned her to a life of perpetual

rape. It seemed it was all that she had ever known of the war and it was ironically the last ritual that she endured before her unceremonious death.[44]

Carolyn Nordstrum has noted that "rape is one of the most common terror tactics employed in war, yet it [did] not ... constitute a formal war crime"[45] until the United Nations Security Council legislated against war rape in 1996. Rape has been a military strategy for millennia. But as Nordstrum argues rape as an "atrocious" act of violence "has been largely silenced in the history of academic and military discourses."[46] Nordstrum's research on rape in war is crucial in understanding the impacts of war on women. She argues that some feminist attention given to rape in war has recently focused on the "Korean 'comfort women' abused by the Japanese military in World War II, and the genocidal rapes taking place in former Yugoslavia," [47] but she argues that

> The same violations have occurred, and continue to take place, in armed conflicts throughout Asia, the Middle East, Africa, and Latin America. They are not restricted to any form of warfare: conventional war, low intensity conflict, state-sponsored repression, and communal conflict have all employed rape as a core tool of terror-warfare ... [thus, we need to] recognis[e] how entrenched and legitimised, the tactic of sexual violence is in systems of militarisation worldwide.[48]

Nordstrum illustrates how such rapes are a "time-bomb left ticking in society - one that will last well beyond the signing of the peace accords and the firing of the last bullet."[49] Speaking to Mozambican women who had given birth to children from rape during the civil war, Nordstrum said

> So how does a child grow up both loved and hated - as we love our children and hate how they were conceived ... they are the war, as they grow, they carry the idea of the war into the future.[50]

According to Nordstrum, the purpose of war rape "is to break down the fabric of society," and hence it is not just restricted to women and girls as the victims. Many boys and men are also raped. It is a "dirty war strategy, thus to break down political will and resistance. It is a form of war that equates de-humanization with control."[51]

Women carry the burdens of war in their wombs, as biological women, as mothers, and as victims to dirty war tactics. However, women in this instance are still viewed as passive victims of a male war strategy. Rape is an act of aggression and power, which is not only an attempt to destroy the woman, but is an attack on men's abilities to protect their women. As Kanengoni has written:

> Munashe made the shameless resolution that, come what may, the war that he was going to fight would be for no one else but Kudzai and the other woman with the crying baby on her back whom he had battered to death for something that he did not know had happened, to atone for their deaths which represented the chilling absurdity of war.[52]

Munashe could not protect Kudzai from being raped both by senior nationalist commanders and the South African commandos fighting for Rhodesia. The questions of women's agency and negotiating skills during such horrific acts of violence like rape and war are rarely asked in the mainstream media, and emerge even less in the subsequent analyses of war. As a result the victims of both circumstances of war become "guilty" and must carry the burden within.[53]

Thus, when Flame negotiates her survival by allowing Comrade Che forgiveness, she is seen as being weak by Liberty, and accused of being a prostitute. Her situation gave her some agency and choice, and yet the stigma attached to her actions identifies her as the wrongdoer. Kudzai, however, is silenced by her death. She had no choice and no agency in war. Kudzai's sister concludes then that "[w]omen seemed to have been helpless in the war, not allowed to make any decisions, exercise any choice."[54] Furthermore, Armstrong has noted that the military rapes of women in Zimbabwe

> continued during the period after independence, when the soldiers remained in some areas and the dissidents simply replaced the freedom fighters. Women in unsettled times of war are therefore, the pawns of both sides, and are allowed little sexual choice by either.[55]

Yet, compensation for such atrocities depends upon women speaking out about their abuses. Many Zimbabwean women have been hesitant to admit that they were victims of rape, and often deny its existence. To admit to rape should negate any accusations of prostitution, however, as one woman ex-combatant explained,

> Women do not want to admit that there was rape in the camps because after the war, ex-combatant women were accused of being prostitutes, and found it difficult to get married, because they had obviously been sleeping around. So many women didn't want to admit being ex-combatants. These women who are denying there was any rape are just trying to protect their images as women.[56]

It is important to recognize here that the women ex-combatants should have the right to protect their images as women, to be able to express some control over how they are represented. However, the correlation between rape and prostitution can only be eroded once the veil of silence has been lifted.

Forgive and Forget

In the film *Flame*, a foreign journalist photographs Flame and Liberty holding their guns on the steps of a hospital in Mozambique. Flame keeps a copy of this photograph and on the back of it writes "Forgive and forget!" to remind her to get on with the future. None of the women ex-combatants interviewed for this book had been to see or intended to see the film. Some of their reasons included that they could not afford the time and money to see it, and that they did not want to see a film about rape; rather, they wanted to forget because there was no time for forgiveness. Joyce "Teurai Ropa" Mujuru the Minister for Information, Posts, and Telecommunications stated:

> I haven't found time to go and see the movie *Flame*. They [the Black and White film company] have approached me. I want to go and see it, but simply because my appointment in this ministry has just been made so busy, by the time I am free to see it I am a finished cockroach. But I have indicated that one of these days I will go and see it.[57]

In keeping with the political line espoused by the ZNLWVA, even without going to see it, some women ex-combatants said that *Flame* was a terrible portrayal of the war, and others said they had not even heard of it, so did not want to comment. It would seem that the topic of rape during the war is still a sensitive issue in Zimbabwe and that women, in particular, are not enthusiastic to discuss it. The (now defunct) Feminist Studies Center in Harare agreed that it was necessary to organize a panel discussion on the film and to invite the director of the film and women ex-combatants to discuss it.[58] Margaret Dongo said:

> For today, for women to be where they are, we fought for it, we suffered; right now there was a film featured about *Flame*. They were not happy about the rape aspect coming up. They are condemning it and they are refusing it. But they did that! In fact the film doesn't have much from what I have heard. It doesn't have much. I wish that it had of portrayed exactly what happened. I wish it would. If it would have exactly portrayed the picture then Zimbabweans would have, even Zimbabwean women would have, learned exactly what it was. Because right now if you talk to any politician who has gone through the liberation struggle, they will try to moderate, make it as nice as possible, so that they would remain these trusted and so-called party cadres. They don't want this country to have the proper history of what actually transpired during the war. This is one thing I am not happy about! If in actual fact if women could be honest enough some of those women who were victims of rape, some of those women who were victims of abuse, and the name won't come up because they are now joining the system. But at the expense of other women who the few of us who'd actually be talking to them about our experience. Also telling them how to move forward towards our fight.[59]

For the ZNLWVA women ex-combatants and others who argued that *Flame* was not a good portrayal of the war, and wanted it to be banned, to look into the mirror of history is to challenge the concepts and basis for established norms. The sensitivity of Zimbabwean public discourse about the liberation war is revealed by the powerful subject matter of the film. The producers have emphasized on more than one occasion that *Flame* is a story about friendship and the war was a backdrop to this. It was not supposed to be a documentary history of the entire liberation war, summing up the perspectives of the powers that be. Yet, *Flame* remains the most poignant representation of women's history in the national liberation war.

Flame broke the box office records for a Zimbabwean film screened in the country, with packed audiences at every screening since it finally opened in Harare in August 1996, after an eighteen month debate about its credibility. At the 1996 Southern African Film Festival in Harare *Flame* was awarded the prizes for Best Director, Best Actress, and the prestigious OAU Award in recognition of "both the Pan-African ideal and the role that women have played in the history of [African] society." While it is not possible to say that *Flame* has made women visible in a particularly heroic or glorified way, it has opened up the space for a debate on their war experiences. It asks many questions and requires women to speak on their own behalf to answer them. Unfortunately, not many women ex-combatants can afford to or "care to" see it. It has made an impact on the dominant masculinist/nationalist discourse, disrupting its precarious foothold in Zimbabwe's history, even if only momentarily. The representations in this film may eventually replace lived reality especially for the younger generations, who are increasingly less interested in those with first-hand experience of the war. Perhaps this is why the ZNLWVA and various political interests are worried about its content and wanted to control what it portrayed. It is this younger generation that will eventually take over the reins of the country, and there are already signs that a politician's war record is not enough to keep him or her in office. In Zimbabwe today, the younger generation are becoming less impressed by politicians' war experiences, reducing any leverage this might have once held. As Priscilla Misihairambwi has said, "Gone were the days when what you just needed [was] a record of participation in the Chimurenga."[60]

The 1997 Rape Revelations
It is important to note that while the debate about rape in the war could arguably deny it happened, claims that women guerilla fighters were raped or consented to sex outside of marriage were not new in the public discourse of the war in Zimbabwe. In 1994 the *Daily Gazette* reported that

> some of the women [who joined up] were raped, others forced into sexual relationships by the situation and others genuinely fell in love

- the result: thousands of children born out of wedlock and in a war situation.[61]

One woman ex-combatant stated:

At the time we were forced to sleep with senior party officials and bore children with them. When we came back from the war, most of them refused to look after their children, saying these children were not theirs. Today some of the fathers of these children are ministers and senior government officials... Having a relationship with a chef meant you had access to food, clothes and other luxuries that were not available to many other girls at the camps.[62]

These claims highlight one of the mains concerns that women ex-combatants faced when they returned from the war - aside from the issue of whether they were raped or not. There was still the question of who was going to help them look after their children and families. Petronella Maramba has reported that many female ex-combatants were single mothers and that this status thwarted their possibilities of being reeducated, retrained, or rehabilitated after the war.[63] In many cases where the father either perished during the war, or denied parental status, women ex-combatants faced a difficult time at independence because of the responsibility of child care.

In 1997 the debate on the rape of women during the war by their comrades heated up when accusations emerged that some ministers and other people had claimed false War Victims Compensation payments. The connection between the misappropriated War Victims Compensation payments and women's experiences of being raped by male commanders was revealed in April 1997 when

some senior female members of the ruling party threatened to go public with allegations that they were raped by some members of the present government during the liberation war should the government press them to refund the monies they had received from the fund.[64]

In a brief examination of the scandal that saw the depletion of $Z forty-five million in eight months, which was intended as compensation for ex-combatants injured during the war, it will be shown how the women ex-combatants secured their payments. In late April it was reported that

> investigations into the multi-million dollar War Victims Compensation
> Fund scandal have become highly sensitive ... [and] could
> dramatically shake up President Robert Mugabe's government as
> some female beneficiaries of the fund now claim they were raped
> during the war by some senior government members.... Most female
> ex-combatants who received huge amounts of money from the fund
> as compensation for injuries sustained during the war had threatened
> to open a "Pandora's box" if investigators continued to harass them
> ... [They said] they were either raped or forced into marriages of
> convenience during the war.[65]

A high ranking ZANU-PF woman ex-combatant in government argued
that

> most of us were raped during the war and we suffered.... If they
> [the investigators] continue to harass us or if they entertain the idea
> of having us payback the money or are contemplating prosecuting
> us then we will tell the whole world how some of them raped us
> during the war.[66]

Another woman ex-combatant said that "some young girls of ten years
were raped, and we know the culprits. Some of them are very senior
government officials - right at the top there - or have top jobs in the army,
the police, or in other sectors."[67] Some women, as young as twenty had
allegedly claimed and withdrawn huge amounts of money from the fund,
meaning they would have been babies in the war, not ex-combatants.
While a senior ZANU(PF) official and cabinet minister said they would
not be intimidated by these women threatening rape claims, it was also
alleged "that girlfriends of high flying officials had also illegally benefited
from the fund."[68] A ZANU(PF) official and ex-ZANLA combatant, Oppah
Rushesha, challenged the process:

> We survived rapes and all the suffering associated with the liberation
> war and this [the inquiry] is what we are now being asked to go
> through?" Rushesha "accused senior politicians of maintaining a
> conspiracy of silence over the fate of young ex-combatants who
> were raped by male colleagues during the war and the welfare of

the children they gave birth to" ... She said, "Many of these former combatants have been disowned by their own families and now live as misfits who had taken to drug and alcohol abuse because the government failed to provide counselling services for them after the war.[69]

The threats made by some women ex-combatants, and notably, those involved with the ruling party, suggests that rape did occur in the training camps, and senior commanders who now hold top jobs in the government were involved. However, that the women traded silence on this matter for continued financial assistance reflects a disappointing conclusion to the attempt to let women speak out about their wartime experiences. It could be argued that no matter how valid their claims for payments based on rank and injuries sustained are, it does suggests that women are still negotiating their survival in postindependent Zimbabwe, as they did during the war. It also suggests that these women felt they had a strong bargaining chip. The women who threatened to speak out, did not. No senior ministers or government officials were publicly accused of raping female comrades. One female ex-combatant who wrote to the *Financial Gazette*, argued that

> rape did take place, [but] for 90 percent of the women who bedded chefs, it was *by choice*, and we [women ex-combatants] would like to emphasise that.... [She asks that] if at all you were abused, do speak out, on the other hand, if you benefited wrongly from the War Victims Compensation Fund, then by all means do the honourable thing and return the money.[70]

The whole issue of rape between comrades during the struggle has indeed been a Pandora's box. There is no closure on the horizon with, for example, a "Truth and Reconciliation Commission."[71] The emergence of the debate about rape as it developed from the release of the film *Flame* surpassed the content of the film and how the issue of rape was dealt with. Thus, *Flame* does not do justice to the violence that women suffered in the camps, but instead broaches the topic with the intent to create debate and dialogue in Zimbabwe. Women ex-combatants, however, are divided on how the discourse about the war should deal with the topic. Women ex-combatants have an opportunity to speak out and make their own

273

representations. Yet, as Shupikai said when asked how she would like her story to be told:

> I am a small woman, but strong. I have brought up my two girls by myself on a teacher's salary. I am poor, but proud and a Christian. I would like to write a book about my life. Even my brother encouraged me, but there is just no time. I was involved with the Zimbabwe Women Writers [a women's writing group in Harare], but there is no time anymore.[72]

As a direct response to the controversy over *Flame*, in 1997 those who were disgruntled because the first film about the war focused on women and "love,"[73] vowed to produce their own films and popular history, perhaps to challenge the representation. An editorial in The *Herald* pointed out that "[t]he history and the story of the liberation war has largely been written or told by outsiders, rather than by those who actually fought and won the Second Chimurenga.[74] As a response to the need for those involved in the war to tell their own stories the ZNLWVA created the concept of the "Historical Documentation Project" in August 1996:

> The Department of Historical Affairs in the association has designed a valuable proposal whose main objective is to educate the people of Zimbabwe and the world at large, especially the young ones, about the Zimbabwe national struggle for self determination. There is need to explore the political past and draw out important lessons in order to appreciate the future.[75]

The "plan of action" as outlined in the report stated:

> The first stage shall be to produce an anthology of war veterans autobiographies, which will explore hitherto neglected aspects of the struggle such as:
>
> ? The point of view and experience of the fighters themselves.
> ? The difficulties of crossing into and out of the country.
> ? The lives of pioneer guerillas who spent long periods in prison.
> ? The life in camps in Zambia, Mozambique, Tanzania, Botswana, and Angola during the war.

- The experience of fighters leading up to and following the ceasefire, particularly their lives in the assembly points.[76]

The ZNLWVA stated that it had started collecting short autobiographies of its members as part of the Registration and Vetting exercises (a war veterans census). These autobiographies would be used as a basis for collecting more detailed autobiographies at provincial levels of the association. After collecting the autobiographies, the aim is to have qualified personnel at the University of Zimbabwe edit them. The edited material will be presented to the Ministry of Education and evaluated for possible use in schools throughout the country either as historical literature or as "history." Notwithstanding the doubtful credibility of stories being told in association with claiming ex-combatant status and compensation for injuries, such an undertaking is ambitious. Nonetheless a

> concerted effort is under way to shoot films of some of the stories emanating from the autobiographies. The publication and dissemination of the anthology [wi]ll be a first step in writing true history to our nationals and the world as a major contribution to future generations.[77]

Aside from the ZNLWVA's planned attempts to make history and tell the story of the war, another film about the war was being planned in 1997. If it goes ahead, *Tormented Soul* will be the sixth feature film to be produced within Zimbabwe and the second film about the liberation war. It is planned to be a completely indigenous production (*Flame* was highly criticized for being produced by a white team.) The director, Rudawiro Katsande, wants to promote Zimbabwe's local film industry and not have the film's script "diluted" by overseas funding. Kenneth Chikwekwe, the film's research coordinator, said:

> Our aim is to put the history of the liberation struggle into perspective. We want to tell the history as it is because we feel we owe it to ourselves as sons and daughters of this country to tell our own story.[78]

However, getting funding from both public and private interests in Zimbabwe to the tune of $Z twenty million has yet to succeed, and reflects the industry's calls to outside donors in the past. If the film does go ahead it will be interesting to note how it will portray women compared with the film *Flame*, and if the issue of rape is discussed. The efforts to tell the stories of ex-combatants is an important contribution to the discourse of war in Zimbabwe. Each story is just one of many.

A film about two young women who joined the struggle to liberate their country spoke to break the silence, which had developed about the history of the war. Fiction was used to tell the history of the war from a female perspective, because the women ex-combatants did not want to expose their lives to a mass-media audience. As an attempt to present a women's history of the war, *Flame* also struck a raw nerve among Zimbabwe National Liberation War Veterans who tried in vain to ban the film in Zimbabwe. The subsequent media attention to the film guaranteed its box office success. In reaction to this success other war films have been planned in an attempt to balance the representations of the war. After all, the war was not just about love! More importantly however, the release of the film resulted in attention to women's experiences of rape in war. Rape is an extreme example of the particular experiences of war that women suffered compared to men. Here it has been used as an example of the complexities surrounding the silences of women in the discourse about the war. Some women denied rape happened, while other women admitted that they had been raped. Furthermore, some women were unlikely to accuse a commander of rape if they relied upon him to recognize her during the vetting procedures required to be registered as an official ex-combatant. The political maneuvering of some senior-ranking ruling party women ex-combatants, who threatened to expose those "comrades" who had raped them during the war, was an attempt to guarantee their financial compensation. Unless the commission of inquiry probing these women for alleged abuse of war compensation funds was called off, the women's threats would be carried out. This suggests that these women ex-combatants felt they had some negotiating power in Zimbabwe in 1997 because they were raped during the war. However, these women have not carried out their threats and have remained silent. Most women ex-combatants have not been in a position to make such a challenge or even have a choice about remaining silent. Their silence arises from the specific ways in which Zimbabwe's history has been told. However, the film *Flame* has enabled these silences to be noticed, so that women ex-combatants no longer are "subaltern".

Endnotes

1. "Guerilla TV Film Dropped," The *Sunday Mail*, October 11, 1981.
2. Ibid.
3.. Olly Maruma, "Flame: The Ownership of History," *Southern African Political Economy Monthly*, February, 1996, pp. 30-1.
4. Nevanji Madanhire, "Liberation History Much More Complex Than Hitherto Portrayed," in The *Financial Gazette*, July 7, 1994.
5. James Monaco, *How to Read a Film: The Art, Technology, Language, History, and Theory of Film and Media*, (revised edition) (New York: Oxford University Press, 1981), p. 217.
6. Ibid, p. 218.
7. To be "sold out" in this case meant that the local shop owner reported her father as being a nationalist/guerilla sympathiser to the Rhodesian security forces. A "sell-out" is someone who allegedly covertly supports the enemy.
8. See David Maxwell, "Local Politics and the War of Liberation in North-East Zimbabwe," *Journal of Southern African Studies*, 19:3, September 1993. Maxwell investigates the relationships between the guerillas and the villagers and their reasons for joining up.
9. Nyasha, in "Four Years in the Armed Struggle," in Miranda Davies, *Third World - Second Sex: Women's Struggles and National Liberation: Third World Women Speak Out*, p. 104.
10. Interview with Freedom Nyamubaya, Marondera, October, 1996.
11. And also an audience that is used to mainstream Hollywood movies which subtly also condone violence against women. The audience's responses to the these scenes were similar on three separate screenings I attended in Harare.
12. Correspondence with Ingrid Sinclair, August 30, 1996.
13. Ibid. emphasis in original.
14. Interview with Ingrid Sinclair, Harare, 1996.
15. Interview with Honour, Harare, September, 1996.
16. Interview with Freedom Nyamubaya, Marondera, October, 1996.
17. Ibid.
18. Martin Mhando, a Tanzanian filmmaker wrote the first screenplay for *Flame*. He stated that the character of *Flame* was based on a compilation of three women's stories. Interview with Martin Mhando, Southern African Film Festival, Harare, September 1996.
19. Interview with Ingrid Sinclair, Harare, 1996.
20. Correspondence from Ingrid Sinclair, August 30, 1996.
21. It is important to note that it was the War Veterans Association that complained about the film mis-representing 'reality.' ZNLWVA's mandate is to represent ex-combatants, to seek rehabilitation and compensation from the government. However, there are no women in the hierarchy of the association, despite the

acknowledgement that women war veterans have special needs.

22. The *Herald*, January 12, 1996.
23. Brian Raftopoulos has also stated that the sanitization of the war has been persistently attempted by sections of the nationalist leadership: See Brian Raftopoulos, "Gender, Nationalist Politics and the Fight for the City: Harare 1940-1950s," in *Southern African Feminist Review*, 1:2, September/October, 1995, p. 42.
24. The *Sunday Mail*, December 24, 1995.
25. The *Sunday Mail*, 20, August, 1995, cited in Brian Raftopoulos, "Gender, Nationalist Politics and the Fight for the City: Harare 1940-1950s," p. 42.
26. A charity screening for the Zimbabwe Junior Chamber of Commerce, with donations to a children's home and a women-war-veterans-project.
27. Interview with John Gwitira, Harare, August 29, 1996.
28. Interview with Teresa, Harare, September, 1996.
29. Interview with Ruth, Harare, September, 1996.
30. Interview with Shupikai, Harare, September, 1996.
31. Alexander Kanengoni, *Echoing Silences*, p. 56.
32. Interview with John Gwitira, Harare, August 29, 1996.
33. Interview with Joyce Mujuru, Harare, March, 1997.
34. See David Lan, *Guns and Rain: Guerillas and Spirit Mediums in Zimbabwe*, (London: James Currey, 1985).
35. Interview with Joyce Mujuru, March, 1997.
36. Interview with Margaret Dongo, Harare, March, 1997.
37. Isabella Matambanadzo, "Women's War Story Causes a Stir," *Mail and Guardian* (South Africa), December 8, 1995.
38. Alice Armstrong, "Women and Rape in Zimbabwe," *Human and People's Rights Project*, Monograph no.10 (National University of Lesotho, Institute of Southern African Studies, 1990), p. 26.
39. Ibid.
40. Ibid, p. 27.
41. "Focus on: Sexual Violence and War: When Will We Tell Our Own Story? A Woman Called 'Sarah,'" in *Social Change and Development*, 40, July, 1996, pp.25-6.
42. No further information on the significance of this all female firing squad has been found. See "Chimurenga War Communique, No. 19, September - October 1978, quoted in David Caute, *Under the Skin; The Death of White Rhodesia*, (London, Allen Lane, 1983), p. 108.
43. *The Zimbabwe News*, 10:5, September-October 1978, p. 23. Thanks to Amy Kaler for this reference.
44. Alexander Kanengoni, *Echoing Silences*, p. 69.
45. Carolyn Nordstrum, "Rape: Politics and Theory in War and Peace," in *Australian Feminist Studies*, 11:23, 1995, p. 147.
46. Ibid. p. 147.
47. Ibid. Also see *Vukovar*, a film set in the former Yugoslavia which tells the story of a Serb and Croat couple, from the perspective of the woman's experiences,

which included being gang raped by mercenaries. This is the film that *Flame* in Zimbabwe could have been given completely different cultural and political circumstances.

48. Ibid. p.150.
49. Ibid. p.152.
50. Ibid.
51. Ibid.
52. Alexander Kanengoni, *Echoing Silences*, p. 72.
53. Turshen, Meredeth and Clotilde Twagiramariya, eds., *What Women Do in War Time: Gender and Conflict in Africa*, (St. Martins: Zed Press, 1998)
54. Alexander Kanengoni, *Echoing Silences*, p. 75.
55. Alice Armstrong, "Women and Rape in Zimbabwe," p. 27.
56. Interview with Shupikai, Harare, September, 1996.
57. Interview with Joyce Mujuru, March, 1997.
58. When I presented a paper to the Feminist Studies Center in Harare entitled "Gendered War Talk: Interrogating Contemporary Discourses of War," the issue of *Flame* and rape came up during question time. The women agreed there was need for a panel discussion. However, the center was soon closed by the government due to the use of the word *feminist* in its name and its policy to exclude men unless invited by a woman, which was deemed to be unconstitutional.
59. Interview with Margaret Dongo, Harare, March, 1997.
60. Priscilla Misihairambwi, "Where Patriarchy is Institutionalised," in *Southern African Feminist Review*, 1:2, 1995, p. 60. It is interesting to note that Misihairambwi stood as an Independent candidate in Ward 6 (the Avenues) council election in 1996, but lost to the ZANU(PF) candidate after much scandal. She was too young to have been in the war, and too young to stand for election. The minimum age is thirty, she was allegedly only twenty-nine years old, although this was unsuccessfully contested with affidavits from priests and her parents.
61. The *Daily Gazette*, August 15, 1994.
62. Ibid.
63. Petronella Maramba, *Tracer Study on Women Ex-combatants*. However, while she concludes that *most* women ex-combatants are single mothers, her statistics show that 84 percent of the women are married mothers. It is not clear whether they were single now or at independence. Overall, the report has some dubious statistical reporting, so it needs to be considered with caution.
64. *The Financial Gazette*, May 1, 1997, p. 1: Also see "Brace Up for Stunning Revelations from War Victims Compensation Scam," in *Zimbabwe Standard*, May 4-10, 1997, p. 11.
65. "Shocking Revelations of War time rape emerge as War vets Fund Scam Turns Ugly: Female beneficiaries threaten to sing," The *Financial Gazette*, April 24, 1997, p. 1.
66. Ibid.
67. Ibid.

68. *The Financial Gazette*, May 1, 1997, p. 1.
69. Noteworthy here is that "Rushesha spent three weeks in a Mozambique hospital following a road accident in which former ZANLA commander Josiah Tongogara was killed in 1979." Tongogara was notorious for abusing women in the camps. See "Ex-combatants Cry Foul as Inquiry Unfolds," in The *Financial Gazette*, August 28, 1997.
70. "Female Combatants: Raped or Consented," letter to editor, The *Financial Gazette*, May 15 1997, p. 7.
71. Media reports on the findings of Justice Chidyausiku's Commission of Inquiry into the administration of the War Victims Compensation Fund have recently revealed: "Some soldiers at the Zimbabwe National Army headquarters [had] abused the vetting system by issuing clearance certificates 'through the window' to persons who were not ex-combatants and certifying a rank higher than they held by the claimant at the time of the alleged disability. This abuse was particularly obvious in the case of those female ex-combatants interviewed almost all of whom were certified as holding commander rank." See The *Financial Gazette*, August 20, 1998.
72. Interview with Shupikai, Harare, September, 1996.
73. John Gwitira, Executive Director, ZNLWVA, Interview, Harare, September, 1996.
74. Editorial, "War Veterans Must Tell Their Story," in The *Herald*, (no date supplied) 1995, (ZIANA Library, Harare).
75. Zimbabwe National Liberation War Veterans' Association (ZNLWVA), *Re-integration Programme for War Veterans in Zimbabwe: A Participatory Development Plan*, (Harare, August 1996), p. 41.
76. Ibid.
77. Ibid.
78. The *Financial Gazette*, Harare, May 1, 1997, p. 12.

Conclusion

First there are tears. They will dry. There will be dreams.
They will evanesce. There will be memories, but these too,
with time, will fade away like stars.
  - Charles Samupindi in *Pawns*

This book has attempted to surmount the dilemmas of doing research on African women in Africa from the position of being a white, Western female. The first dilemma was the possibility that any research might silence African women. However, African women who are speaking their voices are not valued in most academic circles. If no one listens to these voices, African women will remain subaltern. However, when we do consider their voices to be important they become audible through the cracks in the hegemonic discourse. Yet, even with the recognition that these subaltern voices are present, we were faced with a second broader dilemma - how to project that voice to a wider audience. As John Beverly asked, what would be the point of representing the subaltern as subaltern?

The aim here has been to avoid representing women guerilla fighters and women ex-combatants as the silent voices in history, while acknowledging that they have been located in that position vis-à-vis Western academic discourse. My aim was to project their voices so they could claim their agency in the history of the Zimbabwean national liberation struggle. How was this achieved? I established a dialogue with women ex-combatants who shared their stories; and I privileged these stories within historical and academic discourse. Within this latter discourse, women ex-combatants and their experiences of war had been constituted as subaltern. Throughout this re-presentation they have not been represented as subaltern, but have been reconsidered as the subjects of history.

There is a third dilemma, however, in this process of re-presentation. Are the efforts to challenge Orientalist - Africanist discourse from a postmodern, postcolonial, feminist perspective, a simple rehashing of the same exotic image of the "other," not for the purposes of contributing to the rehabilitation of the subject, but for placing them again within the focus of the Western gaze, with all its implications of power and control? Why is it important to re-tell this story of the "guerilla girls," and how can such a voyeuristic Western gaze be avoided? When answering these questions posed by the subject of this research there was a fourth dilemma to consider. Are motivations for this study based on a power relationship that can be eliminated simply by declaring its presence? To counteract these dilemmas I have declared my position vis-à-vis the subject, and I have also privileged women's oral history, noting how easily such histories can simply collect dust or be silenced if not valued within mainstream academia.

Finally, there was a fifth dilemma to consider. Have these women's voices simply been used to garnish the main course of my (Western academic) book? I have tried to use my research to represent them so that they could shape (or contribute to a reshaping of) their own image.

From this position, in the present study I formed an understanding of what the liberation war meant to the women who fought side by side with men as the "guerilla girls," how these same women represent themselves as women ex-combatants, and why women ex-combatants in Zimbabwe fared poorly compared to men after liberation, despite their "combat" roles. Many women ex-combatants had not had the opportunity to talk about their experiences of the war, especially where they could be heard above the din of stereotypes and negative images. The focus and forum of this research has enabled the women ex-combatants to speak out with their histories of the struggle.

It was easy to identify the group of people called "women in the struggle" or "guerilla girls," as this was one identity out of many that was constructed during the struggle. Thus, it was simple to search for their presence in the discourse about the war, when we had on gender-sensitive lenses. However, the women interviewed here did not identify themselves in terms of a collective identity or as a group of people called "women ex-combatants." The construction of such a group remains tenuous when there is no political representation of and for women who fought in the struggle in Zimbabwe.

Yet the subjects of this history have multiple layers of identities. These women survived to tell their histories, which had been generalized, stereotyped, glorified, and negatively constructed around the identity of the so-called "guerilla girls" and later the "women ex-combatants." As such, the women ex-combatants interviewed here were no longer the "guerilla girls," but the women ex-combatants re-representing their history of the "guerilla girls." Their power to represent their histories challenges the discourse about the war and how and why particular histories have and have not been told. The conflicting interests of foreign researchers and African women were raised here to illustrate that indeed some women were simply more concerned with the urgent needs of day to day survival. Nonetheless I hope to have shown that the way that women are represented is important to their daily existence. Desiree Lewis identified the process whereby opinions are based on representations that may misrepresent the subject. As such, the power of representation between subject and audience determines the impact of the representations on the subject of history.

Thus, one of the most important points to establish from the outset was the confirmation that women were involved in the liberation struggle and anticolonial wars. Within wider academic debates on women in war, it is clear that women have always been involved in wars. What women *do* in wartime is another matter. In the discourse about war what is common across space and time, is that their war roles are constructed as being an extension of their natural feminine functions. After wars then, they are encouraged and seen to be happy to return to the normality of the feminine - domestic sphere from which they had merely taken leave, but had never left permanently. Women are thus portrayed as secondary to the main event of war. However, for women ex-combatants in Zimbabwe such expectations and portrayals are of concern when equal citizenship is linked to military action. To gain the "fruits of independence" with men, Zimbabwean women needed to be able to legitimate their gendered roles in the liberation struggle. These roles were unraveled in the analysis of the competing representations of women guerilla fighters.

An analysis of Zimbabwean feminism and nationalist rhetoric demonstrated that in order to secure women's support, women's emancipation was linked to nationalist discourse, in particular in the mid-

1970s, which coincided with the United Nations Decade for Women. Women fighting wars in Africa's liberation struggles were made exceptions to a feminist rule that women should have nothing to do with war because they are the nurturers of society. Against the formidable oppression of colonialism, however, African women were heralded internationally as the vanguard of feminist strength - fighting two forces of oppression, patriarchy and colonialism. Subsequently, women's equality was driven by women's actions as guerilla fighters. All of the rhetoric about women espoused during the struggle was aimed at getting women to rise up and fight for national liberation - the "carrot" was women's emancipation.

In a critique of the attention that has been paid to the post-revolutionary demands for women's liberation, it was seen that researchers have made common assumptions that women's roles in wars of national liberation are unproblematically equal with men's, and as a result the women are disappointed after independence when equality is not secured. We needed to shift the focus away from this disappointment and focus instead on what women did during the struggle. Women worked alongside male nationalists and guerilla fighters supporting national liberation.

However, from a gender-sensitive view of the location of women in the discourse about war, it was noted that there is a large blank space concerning women in the struggle. Both academic literature and Zimbabwean fiction reveal an absence of the stories of women as guerilla fighters. This is a significant absence when one needs to legitimate military action. Instead, women's stories and histories of their war experiences have been relegated to women's issues rather than issues of war.

There have been attempts (by non-Zimbabwean, foreign researchers) to proclaim women's roles as militarily inspired, and yet these attempts have relied upon evidence supplied by only a few (elite) women in the struggle. The present book challenges these over-cited views and the subsequent assumptions arising from them. As Ngwabi Bhebe and Terence Ranger have argued, "There have been too many attempts to produce a 'heroic herstory,'" and as I have argued not enough attention has been paid to the "shit of war" that women endured, justifying their more inglorious tasks as equal with men.

Zimbabwean women's perceptions of emancipation as they unfolded during the war were investigated. Some women ex-combatants stated that they rarely discussed the issue of women's emancipation during the struggle. It was seen that this discourse was reserved for the educated elite women in ZANU and ZAPU, who promoted these views on the international stage. The women guerilla fighters were interested in women's issues, such as getting access to sanitary protection for menstruation and other matters of comfort and survival, but their main reason for joining up was to liberate Zimbabwe and not to fight against men for sex equality. If any sense of equality did emerge it was because the women were subjected to the same or similar training as men were. Any challenges to traditional gender roles were limited to the challenges that fighting any guerilla war would have on anyone. Despite the rhetoric espoused by some elite women, theories of feminist liberation did not appear to be involved, and thus we should not be surprised by the outcomes of national liberation on both the development of feminism and on the position of women. Any gains that were made for women in Zimbabwe, and there were some, were accredited not to feminism - which had by now been associated as a foreign import - but instead to the powers of the nationalist movement.

What is interesting, however, is that while the Minister for Community Development and Women's Affairs, Teurai Ropa, was denying there were any connections between women's post-independence demands for equality and western feminism, there was no reference to women's actual war experiences. These experiences were effectively silenced in order to secure a (safe) position for women back in the feminine - domestic sphere after the war.

In an effort to gain a picture of the progress that was denied to women, we have to turn our historical gaze back over one hundred years of Zimbabwean history to gain an overview of women's roles in anticolonial struggles. While the specific motivations of women were not dealt with, an overview of their "military" roles in the First Chimurenga and a gendered analysis of Zimbabwean historiography revealed the importance of women's roles.

In the 1890s women were forced out of traditional gender roles, by circumstances surrounding the implementation of colonial policies. They became involved in what Elizabeth Schmidt has called military actions in defiance of unjust laws. As we saw, however, women did not just need to act more like men to be considered exemplary and included in the historical account of that period. Women were also recorded as being "pawns" in the colonial game - used as hostages by the colonial officials in an attempt to achieve their colonizing outcomes. Schmidt pointed out that even as "pawns" the women acted with strategies of resistance. Women certainly were involved in the First Chimurenga, but they were rendered invisible by Rhodesian historiographies - they were effectively written out. However, as Ranger has argued, a total history cannot be achieved without a history of women.

Nonetheless, the history of the First Chimurenga was drawn upon to inspire the second anticolonial struggle in the 1960s and 1970s, and thus how this history is remembered is significant. Within this transaction between the First and Second Chimurenga, only one woman emerged prominently. This was Charwe who was the spirit medium of the royal ancestral spirit of Nehanda. The history of the Nehanda mediums was used here as a tool to further our understanding of a critical gendered view of the liberation war. However, Nehanda was not the only female figure in Zimbabwe's anticolonial struggles and history. Many women were involved at various times and in various ways. These aspects of women's involvement were highlighted here in relation to the 1956 bus boycotts, the 1961 women's protests and the 1972 Pearce Commission, in order to demonstrate the complexities of women's involvement and the fact that they were indeed central to nationalist action. Yet because of the hierarchies of significance in many historical accounts, these women's roles have remained obscured in mainstream academia and Zimbabwean history.

During the armed struggle, however, the involvement of women became increasingly difficult to relegate as insignificant. Many young women actively supported the guerilla fighters, often defying parental advice to keep away. The guerillas in turn sought female support in the rural areas - regarding their services as essential for the struggle. The brief biographical accounts of three key women in the struggle demonstrated the silences surrounding the experiences of women who did not gain senior ranking positions in or after the war. Thus it was necessary to listen to the voices of women ex-combatants remembering their reasons for joining up and fighting for national liberation.

When women's emancipation is connected to nationalism, and citizenship depends upon the taking up of arms, women's involvement in war as actual combat fighters becomes paramount. When we heard about women's experiences of fighting, however, we found that most of these experiences occurred while they were in their training camps - often ill-prepared and untrained for combat. The attacks on women in the training camps demonstrated the blurred boundaries between front and rear during wars of liberation. In particular they also demonstrated the gendered distinctions in the experiences of war, where women's participation is important and necessary, but often inglorious.

While the role of women in the anticolonial armed struggle was the main focus here, we also saw that both black and white women challenged traditional gendered roles to become involved in the war. Both the nationalists and the Rhodesians used constructions of women as soldiers, on the one hand to bolster the image of (male) nationalism and on the other hand to destroy it. While both sides required women's support, they both criticized the other side for including women in their ranks. By juxtaposing the representations of both black and white women's roles in the war, and by reviewing their voices when spoken, we gained a gendered perspective of the war.

Such a perspective however cannot be completed without looking at the roles of women as mothers. This detour from the theme of women as "guerilla girls" was necessary because a) it highlighted the important role that women played in the rural areas that helped win independence, b) it pointed out how difficult it is for "natural women" in war to be recognized as playing a military role, and thus suitably appreciated, and c) it demonstrated the difficulties women had in representing themselves and their stories because of the horrors and suffering they endured and were expected to endure in silence. On this latter point, fiction has enabled some of these horrors and unresolved issues that mothers, in particular, endured, to be articulated. It has enabled Zimbabweans to question and reassess romantic notions they may have had about the war, and has represented the reality for many women. Outside of these few fictional exceptions women as mothers came to symbolize the nation. All this did, however, was to obscure their voices by glorifying their maternal roles.

Mothers became powerful metaphors for Zimbabwean nationalism, but were located between the violence of both sides of the war. Important contributions such as Irene Staunton's *Mothers of the Revolution*, should be the beginning of a reassessment of the representations of women's important contributions to the national liberation struggle. That mothers have only gained recognition and restitution through fictional accounts, is a significant consideration in the discourse about the war.

287

However, women as mothers were not just the women who remained behind inside Rhodesia watching the war destroy their families and lives. When the "guerilla girls" eventually became "mothers" they were not used to symbolize the nation. Instead they became a "problem" for the liberation forces. In order to understand these problems in relation to women in the war, it is necessary to examine the range of women's actions in anticolonial struggle. A women's history of the war, however, cannot ignore the problems associated with the inclusion of women as guerilla fighters. These problems tended to be side stepped in general accounts of women's involvement in the struggle, as they do little to promote an "heroic herstory."

The point of discussing these problems was to enable a more accurate representation of women's experiences of war. The aim was not to discredit women's military roles but to create an avenue of understanding between women's experiences of war and the way that they have been represented - both heroically, negatively, and ambiguously. (Mis)representations of women were central to the propaganda of war, but these images obscured gendered problems between the members of the guerilla forces. The (mis)representations of women portrayed a veneer of equality between men and women. We heard how this veneer was constructed with exaggerated claims of the numbers of women involved as guerilla fighters in combat, and how these claims hindered an accurate description of women's participation. We also heard how the assumptions of women's equal roles were perpetuated by the constructed representations of women fighting side by side with male comrades. Women guerilla fighters were glorified as gun carrying warriors. Stories of women's brigades attacking enemy targets were perpetuated within the stories of women's involvement during the struggle, but there is very little evidence to support the claims that women were frontline fighters. This is significant for issues of citizenship within feminist and nationalist frameworks, and stems from the contradictory and ambiguous representations of women guerilla fighters during the struggle.

When the film *Flame* portrayed a woman guerilla fighter attacking the enemy, these contradictions and ambiguities about women's roles overtly surfaced in Zimbabwe's war discourse. Whether or not women shot at the enemy is insignificant, compared to the energy put into the denials that they did. Where available, evidence of women attacking the enemy was provided, however, as in the case of the attacks on the training camps, most women's experiences of fighting were restricted to defense and survival.

The glorified image of the women as warriors was examined because these images contributed to the assumptions that women would be emancipated with national liberation. Women performing combat duties, it was assumed, would be a precursor to their liberation. These glorified representations peaked at the ZANU women's conference held at Xai Xai in 1979. So near to the end of the war, these representations ultimately led to the betrayal and disappointment felt by feminists and Zimbabwean women hoping for women's liberation with national liberation.

What has prevented women ex-combatants from speaking out about their experiences of frontline action to either confirm or deny the glorifications or misrepresentations? The women ex-combatants interviewed here were uncomfortable about discussing any frontline actions, but emphasized they were mainly used for carrying weapons. There can be no clear answer to the question, "Did women fight like men?" but it is undeniable that women's roles were supportive of the nationalist struggle and some form of recognition and compensation was deserved.

However, this is where the Rhodesian propaganda came in to play a role in post-independence Zimbabwean society. Women guerilla fighters had been constructed as murderers and prostitutes within the propaganda. These representations thus competed with nationalist portrayals of women as for example, heroic "mothers" breast-feeding the revolution. The propaganda from the Rhodesian perspective was intended to create resistance to the nationalists. The centrality of women in these competing representations led to many of the problems women faced after the war, particularly in regard to lack of recognition. With the "colonial hangover" of images of women, many women ex-combatants endured negative stereotyping into those Rhodesian-constructed categories. This was fueled by the conflation of all women in the struggle into one category of women ex-combatants, creating a homogenous group of anonymous women.

We hope to have dispelled the myths of these conflated categories by pointing out the significant differences between women's experiences of the war depending on which party they had joined - ZANU or ZAPU, as well as during the period of ZIPA. Thus, the problems associated with women in the struggle cannot be generalized as applying to all women who joined up. Without acknowledging these differences, an accurate representation of women in the war is impossible. The question of women's equality with men is thus further obscured in the shadows surrounding those competing representations. When the issues of sex and equality were examined in more detail it became obvious that in the Zimbabwean case, women's liberation was not a priority goal or pursuit of the nationalist liberation armies.

For example, when the issues of deployment to the frontlines for women guerilla fighters was considered it was found that this was not a gender-neutral process. Acknowledging the differences does not negate women's important roles (such as carrying weapons, but not shooting), but it identifies the key focus for the unequal treatment women guerilla fighters experienced. We examined the policies on marriage and family planning within the parties to illustrate the waning commitment to equality for women. These policies contradicted much of the feminist and socialist rhetoric espoused on the international stage, which attempted to promote women combatants as equal with men.

An oral history of women's experiences in the training camps would contradict the representation of women warriors carrying a gun in one hand and a baby in the other. The glorifications of women guerilla fighters served to obscure the problems with women in the struggle. Furthermore, because there has been negative stereotyping of women guerilla fighters there has not been a clear definition or representation of the experiences of women in the struggle that would satisfy the feminist researcher from a postcolonial perspective. Instead, when we consider the two perspectives we can only begin to explore what kind of impact such contradictory representations would have on women ex-combatants in Zimbabwe today. This task should be taken up by researchers concerned with the rehabilitation of women ex-combatants in Zimbabwe.

It should not be surprising, then, that after national independence women were not granted the equal status with men that many feminists expected. We have argued that the nationalist movement was "gendered" and women's experiences were not considered necessary as starting points to understand the anticolonial struggle and national liberation. Women were used as symbols of the (male) nation, but this required the conflation of women guerilla fighters with civilian women, which ultimately contributed to the silencing of the former. As a result of competing representations, "women" in the independent nation became a contested site, with various images of women being juggled in the public domain. As a result of this competition, women ex-combatants' voices were drowned out by the noise from the sea of propaganda and misrepresentation.

One example of this noise was manifested in the debate over women's wardrobes. From Miss Zimbabwe to Miss Beauty, the dignified and disciplined female representative of Zimbabwe was unable to completely surface. Women's wardrobes were of concern because women guerilla fighters were renowned for having worn trousers during their military training and were basically asked to remove them after liberation because of their symbolic power. Many women ex-combatants associated wearing trousers with being equal with men. After liberation however, many women realized the need to return to their traditional long skirts, to return to some kind of normality. Being "equal with men," even symbolically, was considered to be threatening to this drive toward "normality." Not surprisingly then, the commemorative statue of the unknown soldiers at Heroes Acre in Zimbabwe depicts the woman guerilla fighter in a skirt. What this artistic license achieved was a symbolic reinscription of women's roles and experiences of war into the feminine - domestic.

Women only symbolize the nation in so far as they are *women* and not women guerillas fighters. This is a problem for women ex-combatants, because it further negates their experiences of war and erodes many of the gains they may have made during the struggle - for the nation and for themselves. The demobilization of women guerilla fighters was the precursor to much of the (symbolic) reinscription that occurred on many fronts after the war. Women ex-combatants were labeled not as heroines, but as "prostitutes" and "murderers," a view kept alive in the wake of the colonial hangover. They were portrayed as being too strong, unfeminine, and therefore unsuitable for marriage.

As a result, many women did not tell prospective husbands or even their children that they had fought as "guerilla girls" in the struggle. The women ex-combatants in some cases, chose to silence their own voices and history. Thus the reinscription process began with a series of modulating representations:

a) Negative portrayals of women ex-combatants occurred so frequently in media accounts of their exploits and experiences, that in 1981 Teurai Ropa came to the defense of women guerilla fighters, by stating:

If Zimbabwe was in danger again, it would recall the former guerilla girls to its defence. They would willingly stay without husbands all their lives in its cause, if need be. To describe them as rough, ill-educated and unfeminine is therefore, the supreme insult, not only to the guerilla girls, but to the entire nation.[1]

b) After abandoning their guns for the independent nation they waited (for marriage) by learning to crochet. If the women received rehabilitation, it was of the sort to encourage them back into domestic duties and civilian roles.

c) If indeed there was any recognition for women's wartime roles at all, this was curtailed in 1983 during the officially sanctioned Operation Clean Up. The police sweep of "prostitutes" was condemned by feminists and human rights activists, who argued that women had fought equally in the struggle and such a move demonstrated the lack of respect for women's rights and their independence. Operation Clean Up was an example of a violent reaction to women's gains since national liberation.

d) The reinscription process also occurred in more subtle ways that had symbolic rather than a direct effect, for example, the renaming of a maternity hospital after Nehanda; the statue of the unknown soldiers depicting the woman guerilla fighter in a skirt; the stereotypes of women's roles portrayed in the two wall murals; and the fact that only one woman has been buried at Zimbabwe National Heroes Acre. Any experiences that women had that did not equate with a suitable image for Zimbabwean women as symbols of the nation, was thus either silenced or reinscribed into the domestic.

e) Some Zimbabwean fiction depicted the silencing of women guerilla fighters. Their violent deaths symbolized both the personification of war and the brutal silencing of their voices. If these characters had made it back to Zimbabwe their silence was guaranteed because there was no audience to hear their voice. The woman as guerilla fighter disappeared in the flames.

However, by acknowledging her voice, her role and history can be reinstated in the discourse about the war instead. She need not be reinscribed into the domestic. As in Nozipo Maraire's and Alexander Kanengoni's fiction, the silencing of women's voices is linked to the history of lies in Zimbabwe. Both fiction and film in Zimbabwe have been able to challenge these silences and lies. They have been able to remove women ex-combatants, if only momentarily, from the location of subaltern. In particular, the film *Flame* succeeded in doing this. Although it created its own representation of women in the war, it also served to challenge the contradictions, ambiguities, questions, and conundrums of the competing representations of women guerilla fighters. The film was able to speak for the women ex-combatants without silencing them, despite the women ex-combatants unable or unwilling to see the film. The point was that a representation of their stories had been told in Zimbabwe and internationally.

The controversy surrounding the content and production of the film, and the ultimate media impact it had on Zimbabwean audiences, demonstrated the centrality of representations of women in the discourse of war. At the same time, however, it acknowledged the powerlessness of women to construct and represent their own histories. The film brought to the foreground the issue of rape by male comrades, and the questions left un-answered surrounding the problems of including women in the struggle. *Flame* demonstrated that the representations of women's war roles and experiences were contradictory and ambiguous. While the question of rape in particular by male commanders was not entirely new within public media commentary on women's war roles, the release of *Flame* increased the intensity of the debate. The problem for women had been that both during and after the war, they could not freely admit to what they had suffered. Admitting rape has been linked to the accusations of prostitution during the war. For women ex-combatants to admit that they were in the struggle could have led to assumptions that they were involved in rape and prostitution.

The intention of *Flame's* director was not to make a film about rape, but by its very attempt to create a space for "herstory" in a mainstream medium, thus problems could no longer be ignored. Like the shit of war endured by the mothers, it was only through fictional characters such as Flame, Liberty, and Kudzai (the fictional characters) that women's experiences of rape could be spoken of. Since the release of *Flame* some women ex-combatants have been able to speak out about their experiences of rape in war - with their voices putting an end to the misrepresentations of women during the struggle. Understanding the impact on women that rape has, especially during national liberation wars, is crucial in any history of war.

Importantly however, while women ex-combatants' ability to represent their own histories gives them control over how they are seen, until the veil of silence has been lifted, the correlation between prostitution, rape, and women guerilla fighters will remain. *Flame* provided a mirror, in which women ex-combatants and Zimbabweans in general could look into and review the liberation war history from a gendered perspective.

Here we focused on the events in Zimbabwe in 1997 when some women finally threatened to speak out against the men who they said had raped them during the struggle. The credibility of their stories was questioned in terms of their claims for financial compensation. The women ex-combatants threatened to open a "Pandora's box" in which the truth would be revealed. However, while the publicity surrounding their claims put their voices and history into the media spotlight momentarily, the women's claims were negotiating strategies for gaining compensation - they were trading their continued silence for financial reward. With *Flame* and similar representations of women guerilla fighters, including the above claims for compensation, women's voices have challenged the discourse about war in Zimbabwe. It is no wonder that other film producers have been encouraged to try and tell the (real) history of the war from a more "balanced" (not female) point of view. The debate about rape in the war, sparked by the release of *Flame* is an example of the complex and often ambiguous silences of women represented in the discourse of war in Zimbabwe.

For the women guerilla fighters and other women in the struggle, the process of constructing representations of the past and the present enabled the formulation of a public history that essentialized and reduced women's experiences of war - in all their differences and complexities of history - into just a few main images: the guerilla girl, the woman warrior, the mothers of the revolution, and the women fighting equally with men. All of these representations, while contributing some order to the past, were negated, reinterpreted, and reinscribed by the assumptions based on some other layers of representations including the construction of women guerilla fighters as prostitutes, murderers, and unfeminine. The result of these negative stereotypes contributed to the representation of women guerilla fighters as having not fought equally with men, and therefore as not being the women warriors. This process removed them from the problems associated with the "guerilla girls" and instead reinscribed them into traditional feminine roles in war that did not undermine conservative gendered expectations.

The role of women in the liberation struggle demonstrates the contesting representations and interpretations of who or what is most convincing in constructing the past. There cannot be one hegemonic history of Zimbabwe's liberation war. There are thousands of stories to be told. Varying representations have followed women through the struggle, like a burden on their shoulders, demonstrating how women were silenced in the war via the process of representation. The contest over representations has continued past independence - albeit haphazardly - through mediums such as fiction, film, and public protest. Women ex-combatants can be represented and they can represent their own stories. They can challenge the current discourse about the war. They can ensure their voices are not lost within the rhetoric of history.

We have journeyed through the roles, experiences, representations, and histories of women in the liberation struggle. Finally, to ensure the prime directive is observed, it is important to acknowledge once more the voices of the women ex-combatants who were interviewed. They have demonstrated control over their own representations - what they think of themselves now and then. Some have chosen to remain silent. Others have spoken out on various subjects. In light of the contested representations of women in the struggle it may be said: "Hope for the nation is born out of the intensity of newly created memory."[2] This hope is also born out of how women ex-combatants choose to represent themselves. When asked if they considered themselves to be the heroines of the struggle, this is what some of the women stated (note their different opinions of themselves):

Joyce Mujuru:
I am sure others call me a heroine because they have seen the determination, the courage, the commitment, the confidence, and also the lives that I saved during the most difficult times. The

leadership that I gave during those difficult and trying times. I wouldn't want to blow my own trumpet, but I am so grateful that, others have seen it, and seen it befitting that I am their heroine. I am sure that I will stand to live by it and make sure that I wont fail them. I am very grateful, I am very proud of the positions that they have given me in Zimbabwe, to continuously bestow on me. With what I have, you know the most pride that I derive from those positions, the appointments that His Excellency the President has been giving me ever since I joined the struggle. When I joined the struggle he wasn't there physically, but those commanders who were there had already seen this talent in me which I can't go out of my way to be proud of or see other people as useless people, and I pray that it is a god given gift. I must continue to pray to God that he continues to bestow that trust in me. To give me that courage.

Sekai:
I don't feel like a heroine because I have not been given the respect from others. I have got no medals to indicate that I am a hero. I feel empty, not a hero at all. I would appreciate to be shown love and appreciation for my sacrifice, but I don't know who will do this. Maybe the government, but at least the War Veterans Association is doing a good job, but I want my pay-out.

Monica:
I was very proud of my contribution, very proud and I have had no single day when I have regretted going to war. As much as we are going through a lot of problems during and after the war. As much as I felt I was being ill treated, simply because I am a former combatant, in this society in one time or another I am very proud that I fought for that war. You know there is one thing I always say, "what everybody did when I went to war, I have done it. What I did, what I did in the war, they would never do," so I will always be ahead. That gives me a lot of pleasure and happiness, I'm very proud that I fought in this war. But something has to be done to rehabilitate the ex-combatants. I know our economy is not that good but I really don't understand why things have to be

like that. Even if rural people hear about a program they can't afford the bus fare to come to the city.

Rudo:
How could I be called a terrorist then and today I can't be called a hero with my fellow comrades? The enemy called me a terrorist, and you can't call me a hero today, what does that mean? I totally condemn the selection of the heroes. If ever one crossed the border, going to join the struggle, and that person managed to fight during the war, or died during the war, or they survived, that person is a hero, because it's "Mission Accomplished!" It means we don't know the term, "What is a hero?" I can't explain, but the way that they are doing it now, I feel everybody that went to fight and came back, should be recognised.

These women ex-combatants should have the last word. Their voices demonstrate the contradictions not only in the position and status of women ex-combatants in Zimbabwe today, but in the representations of women as guerilla fighters. These are the women who went to war, were glorified, represented, reinscribed and silenced by the discourse of war. These same women experienced the war, suffered, survived and have stories to tell. In conclusion, as Nozipo Maraire has succinctly put it in her novel *Zenzele*:

But what is life, after all, but a story, some fiction and some truth? In the end, there are words. They are the very manifestations of our immortality. Your own life is a story yet to be told, and wisdom, when it comes, is simply to understand at last the beginning of the word and the story of our birth, death and rebirth.[3]

Endnotes

1. "Liberation The Real Reward, Says Nhongo," in *Sunday Mail*, November 29, 1981
2. Yvonne Vera, *Nehanda*, (Harare: Baobab, 1993), p. 111.
3. Nozipo Maraire, *Zenzele: A Letter For My Daughter*, p. 192.

Glossary of Terms

Boys in the bush	Term of endearment for the male guerilla fighters
Chef	Commander or leader
Chimbwido	Young female messenger or carrier
Chimurenga	Shona term for "war of liberation"
Frelimo	Front for the Liberation of Mozambique
Great Zimbabwe	Historical ruins, House of Stone
Harare	Capital city of Zimbabwe (was Salisbury)
Indaba	Meeting
Kraal	Village
Lobola	Bride-wealth. The prospective husband pays a negotiated fee to the father of the bride (from the Shona *roora*).
Mbuya	Grandmother, also used as respect for women.
Mhondoro	Chiefly or royal ancestor
Mujiba	Young male messenger or carrier
Nehanda	Well-known female *mhondoro*
Ndebele	Ethnic linguistic grouping and one of the three main official languages spoken in Zimbabwe (Shona, Ndebele and English)
Povo	The masses or people
Recce.stick	Reconnaissance group
Roora	Bride-wealth
Shona	Ethnic linguistic grouping and one of the three main official languages spoken in Zimbabwe (Shona, Ndebele and English)
Vashandi	Workers, used here to describe the members of ZIPA
Zvimbwido	Plural of *chimbwido*

Bibliography

Addis, Elisabetta, Valeria Russo and Lorenza Sebesta eds., *Women Soldiers: Images and Realities*, (New York: St. Martins Press, 1994).

Alcoff, Linda, "The Problem of Speaking for Others," in *Cultural Critique*, 20, Winter, 1991-92, pp. 5-32.

Armstrong, Alice, "Women and Rape in Zimbabwe," *Human and People's Rights Project*, Monograph No. 10, (Institute of Southern African Studies, National University of Lesotho, 1990).

Astrow, Andre, *Zimbabwe - A Revolution That Lost Its Way?* (London: Zed Press, 1983).

Banana, Canaan, "Opening Address by Canaan Banana, President of Zimbabwe," *Report of the Workshop on the Role of Women in Social, Economic and Cultural Reconstruction of Zimbabwe*, Harare, February 22 - March 4, 1982, organized by Pan-African Institute for Development East and Southern Africa, in collaboration with the Ministry of Community Development and Women's Affairs, 1982.

Barnes, Teresa and Everjoyce Win, *To Live a Better Life: An Oral History of Women in the City of Harare, 1930-70*, (Harare: Baobab, 1992).

Batezat, Elinor, et al., "Women and Independence: The Heritage and the Struggle," in Colin Stoneman ed., *Zimbabwe's Prospects: Issues of Race, Class, State and Capital in Southern Africa*, (London: Macmillan, 1988).

Beach, David "Chimurenga: The Shona Rising of 1896-97," *Journal of African History*, 20:3, 1979, pp.395-420.

Beach, David, *The Shona and Zimbabwe 900-1850: An Outline of Shona History*, (New York: Africana Publishing Company, 1980).

Beach, David, "An Innocent Woman, Unjustly Accused? Charwe, Medium of the Nehanda *Mhondoro* Spirit, and the 1896-7 Shona Rising in Zimbabwe," (University of Zimbabwe, Department of History Seminar Paper, No. 98, 1995).

Bergman, Arlene Eisen, *Women of Vietnam*, (C.A: People's Press, 1975).

Beverly, John, "Theses on subalternity, representations and politics", in *Postcolonial Studies*, 1:3, 1998, pp. 305-319.

Bhebe, Ngwabi, "The Nationalist Struggle, 1957-1962," in Canaan Banana ed., *Turmoil and Tenacity: Zimbabwe 1896-1990*, (Harare: College Press, 1989).

Bhebhe, Ngwabi, and Ranger, Terence eds., *Soldiers in Zimbabwe's Liberation War*, vol. 1, (Harare: University of Zimbabwe Publications, 1995).

Bhebhe, Ngwabi, and Ranger, Terence eds., *Society in Zimbabwe's Liberation War*, vol. 2, (Harare: University of Zimbabwe Publications, 1995).

Blake, Robert, *A History of Rhodesia*, (London, Eyre Methuen, 1977).

Bond-Stewart, Kathy, (Assisted by Leocardia Mudihu photos by Biddy Partridge), *Young Women in the Liberation Struggle: Stories and Poems from Zimbabwe*, (Harare: Zimbabwe Publishing House, 1984).

Bond-Stewart, Kathy, *Independence is Not Only for One Sex*, (Harare: Zimbabwe

Publishing House, 1987).

Bozzoli, Belinda, *Women of Phokeng: Consciousness, Life Strategy, and Migrancy in South Africa, 1900-1983*, with the assistance of Mmantho Nkotsoe, (Porstmouth: Heinemann; London: James Currey, 1994).

Chilla Bullbeck, *Re-Orienting Western Feminisms: Women's Diversity in a Postcolonial World*, (Cambridge: Cambridge University Press, 1996).

Caute, David, *Under the Skin: The Death of White Rhodesia*, (London: Allen lane, 1983).

Chatterjee, Partha, *Nationalist Thought and the Colonial World: A Derivative Discourse?* (London: Zed Books, 1986).

Chinodya, Shimmer, *Harvest of Thorns*, (Schools Edition), (Harare: Baobab, 1989).

Chowdhry, Geeta, "Engendering Development? Women in Development (WID) in International Regimes," in Marianne Marchand and Jane Parpart eds., *Feminism/Postmodernism/Development*, (London and New York: Routledge, 1995).

Cleaver, Tessa, and Wallace, Marion, *Namibia Women and War*, (London: Zed Books, 1990).

Clements, Barbara Evans, *Daughters of Revolution: A History of Women in the USSR*, (Illinois: Harlan Davidson, 1994).

Cobbing, Julian, "The Absent Priesthood: Another Look at the Rhodesian Risings of 1896-1897," in *Journal of African History*, 1:18, 1977, pp. 61-84.

Cock, Jacklyn, "Keeping the Fires Burning: Militarisation and the Politics of Gender in South Africa," in *Review of African Political Economy*, 45/46, 1989.

———. *Colonels and Cadres: War and Gender in South Africa*, (Oxford: Oxford University Press, 1991).

Cooke, Miriam, "Wo-man, Retelling the War Myth," in Miriam Cooke and Angela Woollacott *Gendering War Talk*, (New Jersey: Princeton University Press, 1993).

———, "Arab Women Arab Wars," *Cultural Critique*, Winter, 1994-95, pp. 5-29.

Cooke, Miriam and Woollacott, Angela, eds., *Gendering War Talk*, (New Jersey: Princeton University Press, 1993).

Dangarembga, Tsitsi, *Nervous Conditions*, (Harare: Zimbabwe Publishing House, 1988).

Davies, Miranda, ed., *Third World - Second Sex: Women's Struggles and National Liberation: Third World Women Speak Out*, (London: Zed Press, 1983).

DeVeaux, Alexis, "Zimbabwe Woman Fire!" in *Essence*, July 1981, p.111.

Drew, Allison, "Female Consciousness and Feminism in Africa," in *Theory and Society*, 24:1, 1995, pp. 1-33.

Elshtain, Jean Bethke, *Women and War*, (New York: Basic Book, 1987)

Enloe, Cynthia, *Does Khaki Become You? The Militarisation of Women's Lives*, (London: Pluto Press, 1983).

———, "Womenandchildren: Making Feminist Sense of the Persian Gulf Crisis," in *The Village Voice*, September 25, 1990.

Fanon, Frantz, "Algeria Unveiled," in *A Dying Colonialism*, translated by H. Chevalier, (New York: Grove Press, 1965) (original French 1959).

Flower, Ken, *Serving Secretly: An Intelligence Chief on Record, Rhodesia into Zimbabwe, 1964 to 1981,* (London: John Murray, 1987).

Frederikse, Julie, *None But Ourselves: Masses vs. Media in the Making of Zimbabwe,* (Harare: Otazi and Anvil, 1982).

Gabi, Ruth, "The Secret Cave," in Norma Kitson ed., *Zimbabwe Women Writers Anthology 1994,* (Harare: Zimbabwe Women Writers, 1994).

Gaidzanwa, Rudo, "Bourgeois Theories of Gender and Feminism and their Shortcomings with reference to Southern African Countries," in Ruth Meena ed., *Gender in Southern Africa: Conceptual and Theoretical Issues,* (Harare: SAPES Books, 1992).

Gaidzanwa, Ruth, *Images of Women in Zimbabwean Literature,* (Harare: College Press, 1995)

Geiger, Susan, "What is So Feminist About Doing Women's Oral History?" in Cheryl Johnson-Odim and Margaret Strobel eds., *Expanding The Boundaries of Women's History: Essays On Women in the Third World,* (Bloomington: Indiana University Press, 1992).

Geisler, Gisela, "Troubled Sisterhood: Women and Politics in Southern Africa: Case studies from Zambia, Zimbabwe and Botswana," *African Affairs,* 1995, 94, pp. 545-578.

Getecha, Ciru and Chipika, Jesimen eds., *Zimbabwe Women's Voices,* (Harare: Zimbabwe Women's Resource Centre and Network, 1995).

Gilliam, Angela and Bond, George, eds., *Social Construction of the Past: Representation as Power,* (London and New York: Routledge, 1994).

Godwin, Peter, *Mukiwa: A White Boy in Africa,* (London: MacMillan, 1996).

Godwin, Peter and Hancock, Ian, *Rhodesians Never Die: The Impact of War and Political Change on White Rhodesia, 1970-1980,* (Harare: Baobab Books, 1995).

Gordimer, Nadine, "Hanging on a Sunrise, Testimony and the Imagination in Revolutionary Writings, Part I and II," in *Southern African Review of Books,* 39/ 40, November/December, 1995.

Grant, Rebecca "The Quagmire of Gender and International Security," in V. Spike Petersen ed., *Gendered States: Feminist (Re)Visions of International Relations Theory,* (Boulder & London: Lynne Rienner Publishers, 1992).

Green, M., Lloyd, F., and Makwenda, Joyce, "Multi-Trouser Democracy! Clothes and Identity in Southern Africa," in *Women in Culture in Southern Africa,* Women in Culture in Southern Africa (WICSA), (Harare: WICSA Diary Notebook, 1996), pp. 55-7.

Haggard, Ryder, *King Solomon's Mines,* (London: Hamlyn Classics, 1986).

Heng, Geraldine, "A Great Way to Fly": Nationalism, the State, and the Varieties of Third-World Feminism," in Jacqui Alexander and Chandra Talpade Mohanty eds., *Feminist Genealogies, Colonial Legacies, Democratic Futures,* (New York and London: Routledge, 1997).

Higonnet, Margaret et al., *Behind the Lines: Gender and the Two World Wars,* (New Haven: Yale University Press, 1987).

Hoare, Quintin and Nowell, Geoffrey, eds., *Selections from the Prison Notebooks of Antonio Gramsci*, (London: Lawrence and Wishart, 1971/1986).

Hove, Chenjerai, *Bones*, (Harare: Baobab, 1988).

Jayawardena, Kumari, *Feminism and Nationalism in the Third World*, (London: Zed Books, 1986).

Jeater, Diana, *Marriage, Perversion and Power: The Construction of Moral Discourse in Southern Rhodesia 1894-1930*, (Oxford: Clarendon Press, 1993).

Kaarsholm, Preben, *Coming to terms with Violence: Literature and the Development of a Public Sphere in Zimbabwe*, Seminar Paper, University of Zimbabwe, January 1993.

Kachingwe, Sally, et al, eds., *Sally Mugabe: A Woman With a Mission,* (Harare: Department of Information and Publicity, Zanu(PF) Central Committee, 1994).

Kaler, Amy "Maternal Identity and War in Mothers of the Revolution" in *Journal of the National Women's Studies Association*, Spring 1997.

———, "Gender and Fertility in a post-colonial moment: the prohibition of Depo-Provera in Zimbabwe 1981," paper presented at *Gender and Colonialism in Southern Africa*, International Conference, University of Western Cape, South Africa, January 1997.

———, "Fertility, Gender and War: The 'Culture of Contraception' in Rhodesia," PhD Dissertation, University of Minnesota, 1998.

Kanengoni, Alexander, *Effortless Tears,* (Harare: Baobab, 1993).

———, *Echoing Silences*, (Harare: Baobab, 1997).

Kesby, Mike, *"Arenas for Control, Terrains of Gender Contestation: Guerrilla Struggle and Counter-Insurgency Warfare in Zimbabwe 1972-1980,"* in *Journal of Southern African Studies*, 22:4, December 1996, pp. 561-84.

Kriger, Norma, *Zimbabwe's Guerrilla War: Peasant Voices*, (Cambridge: Cambridge University Press, 1992; Harare: Baobab, 1995).

———, "The Politics of Creating National Heroes: The Search For Political Legitimacy and National Identity," in Ngwabi Bhebe and Terence Ranger, eds., *Soldiers in Zimbabwe's Liberation War*, (Harare: University of Zimbabwe Press, 1995).

Lake, Marilyn, and Damousi, Joy, *Gender and War: Australia at War in the Twentieth Century*, (Cambridge: Cambridge University Press, 1995).

Lal, Jayati, "Situating Locations: The Politics of Self, Identity, and "Other," in Living and Writing the Text," in Diane Wolf ed., *Feminist Dilemmas in Fieldwork*, (Boulder: Westview Press, 1996).

Lan, David, *Guns and Rain: Guerrillas and Spirit Mediums in Zimbabwe*, (London: James Currey, 1985).

Lapchick, Richard, and Urdang, Stephanie, *Oppression and Resistance: The Struggle of Women in Southern Africa*, Based on Materials prepared for the World Conference of the United Nations Decade for Women (Copenhagen, 1980), (Westport: Greenwood Press, 1982).

Lewis, Desiree, "Winnie Mandela: The Surveillance and Excess of 'Black Woman' as Signifier," in *Southern African Feminist Review,* 2:1, June 1996.

Reina Lewis Gendering Orientalism, Race Femininity and Representation, (London: Routledge, 1996).

Lyons, Tanya, "(Mis)representations of Africa and the Politics of Gender," (Honors Thesis, Department of Politics, University of Adelaide, 1994).

Lyons, Tanya and Moore, David, "Written in the Revolutions: (Mis)Representations, the Politics of Gender and the Zimbabwean National Liberation War," in Peter Alexander, et al., eds., *Africa Today: A Multidisciplinary Snapshot of the Continent in 1995,* (Canberra: Humanities Research Centre, Australian National University, 1996).

Lyons, Tanya, "African Women and Western Feminisms, and the Dilemmas of Doing Feminist Field Work in Africa," paper presented at the African Studies Association of Australasia and the Pacific (AFSAAP) 2nd Annual Postgraduate Workshop, ANU, Canberra, September 1997.

———, "Gender and Development: African Women and Western Feminisms, and the Dilemmas of Doing Feminist Field Work in Africa," in *Outskirts,* Online: http://mmc.arts.edu.au/chloe/outskirts/, University of Western Australia, August 1999.

———, "Nehanda" and "Zimbabwean Women in the Liberation Struggle," in Reina Pennington ed., *Amazons to Fighter Pilots: A Biographical Dictionary of Military Women,* (Westport, Greenwood Press, 2003).

———, "Women Ex-Combatants and the Zimbabwe Liberation War Veterans Scam: Prelude to a Crisis," paper presented at the African Studies Association of Australasia and the Pacific Annual Conference, La Trobe University, July 1998.

———, "Guerrilla Girls and Women in the Zimbabwean National Liberation War," in Jean Allman, Susan Geiger and Nakanyike Musisi eds., *Women in African Colonial Histories,* (Bloomington: Indiana University Press, 2002).

Macdonald, Eileen, *Shoot the Women First,* (London: Fourth Estate, 1991).

Macdonald, Sharon, "Drawing the Lines - Gender, Peace and War: An Introduction," in Sharon Macdonald, Pat Holden and Shirley Ardener eds., *Images of Women in Peace and War: Cross-Cultural Perspectives,* (Wisconsin: The University of Wisconsin Press, 1987).

Machel, Samora, *Sowing The Seeds of Revolution,* (Harare: Zimbabwe Publishing House, 1981).

Mahamba, Irene Ropa Rinopfuka, *Woman in Struggle,* (Harare: Mambo Press, 1984).

Maitland, Sara, *Women Fly When Men Aren't Watching,* (London: Virago, 1993).

Mama, Amina, "Sheroes and Villains: Conceptualizing Colonial and Contemporary Violence Against Women in Africa," in Jacqui Alexander and Chandra Talpade Mohanty eds., *Feminist Genealogies, Colonial Legacies, Democratic Futures,* (New York and London: Routledge, 1997).

Maraire, Nozipo, *Zenzele: A Letter For My Daughter,* (Johannesburg: Ad Donker, 1996).

Maramba, Petronella, *Tracer Study on Women Ex-combatants in Zimbabwe,* incomplete and unpublished, (Report for International Labour Office,

December 1995).

Martin, David and Johnson, Phyllis, *The Struggle for Zimbabwe: The Chimurenga War,* (London: Faber and Faber, 1981).

Maruma, Olly, "Flame: The Ownership of History," *Southern African Political Economy Monthly*, February, 1996, pp.30-31.

Maughan-Brown, David, "Myths on the March: The Kenyan and Zimbabwean Liberation Struggles in Colonial Fiction," *Journal of Southern African Studies,* 9:1, 1982 pp. 93-117.

Maxwell, David "Local Politics and the War of Liberation in North-East Zimbabwe," *Journal of Southern African Studies,* 19:3, September 1993.

May, Jean, *Zimbabwean Women in Customary and Colonial Law*, (Gweru: Mambo Press, 1983).

McCalman, (Coordinator and Compiler), "We Carry a Heavy Load: Rural Women in Zimbabwe Speak Out," Report of a Survey Carried out by the Zimbabwe Women's Bureau, December 1981.

McClintock, Anne, *Imperial Leather: Race, Gender and Sexuality in the Colonial Conquest*, (New York and London: Routledge, 1995).

McKenzie, Darlene, "Looking at Them, Looking at Us", in *Racism, Representation and Photography*, Sandra Phillips, ed., compiled by Andrew Dewsney, (Australia: Inner City Education Centre, 1994).

McLaughlin, Janice, *On the Frontline: Catholic Missions in Zimbabwe's Liberation War*, (Harare: Baobab Books, 1996).

Meredith, Martin, *The Past is Another Country, Rhodesia: 1890-1979,* (London Andre Deutsch, 1979).

Mikell, Gwendolyn, "African Feminism: Toward a New Politics of Representation," in *Feminist Studies*, 21:2 1995.

———, *African Feminism: The Politics of Survival in Su-Saharan Africa*, (Philadelphia: University of Pennsylvania Press, 1997).

Minh-ha, Trinh T., *Woman, Native, Other: Writing Postcoloniality and Feminism*, (Bloomington: Indiana University Press, 1989).

Misihairambwi, Priscilla "Where Patriarchy is Institutionalised," in *Southern African Feminist Review*, 1:2, 1995.

Mohanty, Chandra "Under Western Eyes: Feminist Scholarship and Colonial Discourses," in *Feminist Review*, 30, Autumn 1988, pp.61-88

Momeyer, Alison, "Inside the struggles: Voices of women coming of age in the war for Independence," (independent project, University of Zimbabwe, 1990).

Monaco, James, *How to Read a Film: The Art, Technology, Language, History and Theory of Film and Media*, (revised edition) (New York and London: Oxford University press, 1981).

Moorcraft, Paul and McLaughlin, Peter, *Chimurenga: The War in Rhodesia 1975-1980,* (Marshalltown: Sygma Collins, 1982).

Moore, David, "The Contradictory Construction of Hegemony in Zimbabwe: Politics, Ideology and Class in the Formation of a New African State," unpublished PhD Dissertation, York University, 1990.

Moore, David, "The Zimbabwe People's Army: Strategic Innovation or More of the

Same?," in N. Bhebe and T. Ranger, eds., *Soldiers in Zimbabwe's Liberation War*, (Harare: University of Zimbabwe Press, 1995).

Moore, David, "Democracy, Violence and Identity in the Zimbabwean War of National Liberation: Reflections from the Realms of Dissent, *Canadian Journal of African Studies*, 29:3, 1995.

Mudimbe, V.Y., *The Invention of Africa: Gnosis, Philosophy, and the Order of Knowledge*, (Bloomington: Indiana University Press, 1988).

Mudondo, Mabel, "The Emancipation of Women and Their Role Towards Liberation Struggles," in *Zimbabwe News*, 10:1, January/February, 1978.

Mugabe, Robert, "The Role and History of the Zimbabwean Women in the National Struggle," Opening Speech, Xai Xai, Mozambique, May 21, 1979, in Naomi Nhiwatiwa, *Women's Liberation in the Zimbabwean Revolution: Materials from the ZANU Women's Seminar*, Maputo, Mozambique, (San Francisco, California: John Brown Book Club, Prairie Fire Organizing Committee, May 1979).

————, *Our War of Liberation: Speeches, Articles, Interviews 1976-1979*, (Gweru: Mambo Press, 1983).

Musemwa, Muchaparara, "The Ambiguities of Democracy: The Demobilisation of the Zimbabwean Ex-combatants and the Ordeal of Rehabilitation 1980-93," in *Transformation*, 26, 1995, pp.31-46.

Muthoni, Liki Mani, *Passbook Number F47927: Women and Mau Mau in Kenya*, (London: Macmillan, 1985).

Nhiwatiwa, Naomi, *Women's Liberation in the Zimbabwean Revolution: Materials from the ZANU Women's Seminar*, Maputo, Mozambique, (San Francisco, California: John Brown Book Club, Prairie Fire Organizing Committee, May 1979).

————, "Interview: Women in the National Liberation Struggle in Zimbabwe," with an Introduction by Carol B. Thompson, *Women's Studies International Forum*, 5:3-4, 1982, pp. 247-252.

Nhongo-Simbanegavi, Josephine, *Zimbabwean Women in the Liberation Struggle: ZANLA and its Legacy, 1972-1985*, PhD Thesis, Faculty of Modern History, University of Oxford, 1997.

————, *For better or Worse? Women and ZANLA in Zimbabwe's Liberation Struggle* (Harare: Weaver Press, 2000).

Nichols, Bill, *Ideology and the Image: Social Representation in the Cinema and Other Media*, (Bloomington: Indiana University Press, 1981).

Nkomo, Joshua, *Nkomo: The Story of My Life*, (London: Methuen, 1984).

Nordstrum, Carolyn, "Rape: Politics and Theory in War and Peace," in *Australian Feminist Studies*, 11:23, 1996.

Nyagumbo, Maurice, *With the People*, (London: Graham Publishers, 1980).

Nyamubaya, Freedom, *On the Road Again: Poems During and After the National Liberation of Zimbabwe*, (Harare: Zimbabwe Publishing House, 1986).

————, *Dusk of Dawn*, (Harare: Zimbabwe Publishing House, 1995).

Nzenza, Sekai *Zimbabwean Woman: My Own Story,* (London: Karia Press, 1988).

————, "Who should Speak For Whom? African Women and Western Feminism," in Penny Van Toorn and David English eds., *Speaking Positions: Aboriginality, Gender and Ethnicity in Australian Cultural Studies*, (Melbourne: Department of Humanities, Victorian University of Technology, 1995).

Nzenza-Shand, Sekai, *Songs to an African Sunset: A Zimbabwean Story*, Lonely Planet, Melbourne, 1997, pp.10-171.

————, "Women in Postcolonial Africa: Between African Men and Western Feminists," in Phillip Darby ed., *At the Edge of International Relations: Postcolonialism, Gender and Dependency*, (London: Pinter, 1997).

Ona Jirira, Kwanele "Our Struggle Ourselves: Shaping Feminist Theory in our Context: The Zimbabwe Scenario," in *Southern African Feminist Review*, 1:1, 1995.

Parpart, Jane, *Women and Development in Africa*, (Lanham: University Press of America, 1989).

Parpart, Jane, and Marchand, Marianne, "Exploding the Canon: An Introduction/ Conclusion," in Marianne Marchand and Jane Parpart eds., *Feminism / Postmodernism / Development*, (London and New York: Routledge, 1995).

Pennington, Reina ed., *Military Women Worldwide: A Biographical Dictionary*, (Greenwood Press, forthcoming).

Peterson, V. Spike, and Runyan, Anne Sisson, *Global Gender Issues*, (Boulder: Westview Press, 1993).

Pettman, Jan Jindy, *Worlding Women: A Feminist International Politics*, (Sydney: Allen and Unwin, 1996).

Phimister, Ian, *An Economic and Social History of Zimbabwe: 1890-1948: Capital Accumulation and Class Struggle*, (London: Longman, 1988).

Pocock, J.G.A *The Machiavellian Moment: Florentine Political Thought and the Atlantic Republican Tradition*, (Princeton: Princeton University Press, 1975).

Pongweni, A.J., *Songs that Won the Liberation War*, (Harare: College Press, 1982).

Presley, Cora Anne, "The Mau Mau Rebellion, Kikuyu Women and Social Change," in *Canadian Journal of African Studies*, 22:3, 1988.

Qunta, Christine ed., *Women In Southern Africa*, (London: Allison and Busby, 1987)

Raeburn, Michael, *Black Fire! Accounts of the Guerrilla War in Rhodesia*, (London: Julian Friedman, 1978).

Raftopoulos, Brian, "Gender, Nationalist Politics and the Fight for the City: Harare 1940-1950s," in *Southern African Feminist Review*, 1:2, September/October, 1995, pp.30-43.

Raftopoulos, Brian and Phimister, Ian eds., *Keep On Knocking: A History of the Labour Movement in Zimbabwe 1900-97*, (Harare: Zimbabwe Congress of Trade Unions, Baobab, 1997).

Ranchod-Nilsson, Sita., "This, too, is a way of fighting": Rural Women's Participation in Zimbabwe's Liberation War," in Tétreault, M.A, ed., *Women and Revolution in Africa, Asia and the New World*, (Columbia: University of South Carolina Press, 1994).

Ranger, Terence, *The African Voice In Southern Rhodesia:1898-1930*, (London: Heinemann, 1970).

———, *Revolt in Southern Rhodesia:1896-7*, (London: Heinemann, 1967; second edition, 1979).

———, "Women in the Politics of Makoni District Zimbabwe 1890-1980," (unpublished manuscript, Department of History, University of Manchester, 1982).

———, *Peasant Consciousness and Guerrilla War in Zimbabwe: A Comparative Study*, (London: James Curry, 1985).

———, ed., *Violence and Memory: Zimbabwe, 1896 to 1996*, The Britain-Zimbabwe Society's Research Day Newsletter, June 8, 1996.

Razavi, Shahrashoub, and Miller, Carol, *From WID to GAD: Conceptual Shifts in Women and Development Discourse*, Fourth World Conference on Women, Beijing, 1995, United Nations Research Institute For Social Development, Geneva, February 1995.

Ridd, R., and Callaway, H., eds., *Caught up in Conflict: Women's Responses to Political Strife*, (Oxford: Macmillan, 1986).

Roberts, Pepe, "Feminism *In* Africa: Feminism *And* Africa," in *Review of African Political Economy*, 27/28 1983, pp. 175-84.

Ruddick, Sara, *Maternal Thinking: Towards a Politics of Peace*, (Boston: Beacon Press, 1989).

Said, Edward, *Orientalism*, (London: Routledge, 1978).

Samupindi, Charles, *Pawns*, (Harare: Baobab, 1992).

Schmidt, Elizabeth, *Peasants, Traders and Wives: Shona Women in the History of Zimbabwe 1870-1939*, (Harare: Baobab, 1992).

Shamuyarira, Nathan, *Crisis in Rhodesia*, (London: Trinity Press and Andre Deutsch, 1963).

Shenje-Peyton, Angeline, "Balancing Gender, Equality, and Cultural Identity: Marriage Payments in Post-Colonial Zimbabwe," in *Harvard Human Rights Journal*, 9, 1997, pp. 105-44.

Spivak, Gayatri, "Can The Subaltern Speak?," in Gary Nelson and Lawrence Grossberg eds., *Marxism and the Interpretation of Culture*, (Chicago: University of Illinois Press, 1988), pp. 271-313.

Staunton, Irene ed., *Mothers of the Revolution*, (Harare: Baobab, 1990).

———, quoted in "SADC Women Writers Coming into their Own," aiacan@web.net, Stephanie Wells, internet news, 1986, (960806).

Stott, Leda, *Women and the Armed Struggle for Independence in Zimbabwe (1964-1979)*, occasional paper no. 25, (Edinburgh University, Centre of African Studies, 1990).

Sylvester, Christine, "Simultaneous Revolutions: The Zimbabwean Case," *Journal of Southern African Studies*, 16:3, 1990, pp. 452-75.

———, "Simultaneous Revolutions and Exits: A Semi-Skeptical Comment," in Tétreault, M.A, ed., *Women and Revolution in Africa, Asia and the New World*, (Columbia: University of South Carolina Press, 1994).

———, "African and Western Feminisms: World Traveling the Tendencies and

Possibilities," in *Signs*, Summer 1995, pp. 941- 69

Tétreault, Mary Ann, "Women and Revolution: A Framework for Analysis," in Tétreault, Mary Ann ed., *Women and Revolution in Africa, Asia and the New World,* (Columbia: University of South Carolina Press, 1994).

————, ed. *Women and Revolution in Africa, Asia and the New World,* (Columbia: University of South Carolina Press, 1994).

Thompson, Dorothy, ed., *Over Our Dead Bodies: Women Against The Bomb*, (London: Virago, 1983).

Tichagwa, W. N., "Lobola and Women's Status and Role in Society," *Culture Survey, Zimbabwe Women's Resource Centre and Network*, (Harare: Zimbabwe Women's Resource Centre and Network, February, 1995).

Todd, Judith, *An Act of Treason: Rhodesia 1965*, (Zimbabwe: Longman, 1982; first published 1966).

————, *The Right To Say No: Rhodesia 1972*, (Zimbabwe: Longman, 1987).

Tongogara, Josiah, M., *Our Struggle For Liberation*, (Gweru: Mambo Press, 1984).

Turshen, Meredeth and Clotilde Twagiramariya eds., *What Women Do in War Time: Gender and Conflict in Africa*, (St. Martins: Zed Press, 1998).

Urdang, Stephanie, *Fighting Two Colonialisms: Women in Guinea-Bissau*, (New York and London: Monthly Review Press, 1979).

Urdang, Stephanie, *And Still They Dance: Women, War and the Struggle for Change in Mozambique*, (London: Earthscan, 1989).

Vaughan, Richard, and Murphy, Ian, *Zimbabwe: Africa's Paradise*, (London: CBC, 1994).

Veit-Wild, Flora, *Teachers, Preachers and Non-Believers: A Social History of Zimbabwean Literature*, (Harare: Baobab, 1993).

Vera, Yvonne, *Nehanda*, (Harare: Baobab, 1993).

————, *Without a Name*, (Harare: Baobab, 1994).

————, *Why Don't You Carve Other Animals*, (Harare: Baobab, 1994).

Wagner Decew, Judith, "The Combat Exclusion and the Role of Women in the Military," *Hypatia*, 10:3, Winter 1995, pp. 56-73.

Weinrich, A.K.H., *Women and Racial Discrimination in Rhodesia*, (Paris: Unesco, 1979).

Weiss, Ruth, *The Women of Zimbabwe*, (Harare: Nehanda Publishers, 1986).

Windrich, Elaine, *The Rhodesian Problem: A Documentary Record 1923-1973*, (London and Boston: Routledge and Kegan Paul, 1975).

Wolf, Diane ed., *Feminist Dilemmas in Fieldwork*, (Colorado: Westview Press, 1996).

Yuval Davis, Nira, *Gender and Nation*, (London: Sage, 1997).

Yuval-Davis, Nira and Anthias, Floya eds., *Women-Nation-State*, (London: Macmillan, 1987).

Zimbabwe Women Writers, eds., *Women of Resilience: The Voices of Women Ex-Combatants*, (Harare: Zimbabwe Women Writers, 2000).

Miscellaneous References

"African Women, Conflict and War," *African Woman*, Issue 10, March-September, 1995.

British South Africa Company, *The '96 Rebellions: the British South Africa Company Reports on the Native Disturbances in Rhodesia 1896-97*, (Bulawayo: Books of Rhodesia, 1975).

Central African Archives, *A Guide to the Public Records of Southern Rhodesia under the Regime of the British South Africa Company, 1890-1923*, (Cape Town, Longmans, Green and Co., 1956).

"Feminine Folios - Jill's Hat Trick," in *Outpost*, Magazine of the BSAP, February, 1975.

A Guide to the Heroes Acre: Zimbabwe, (Harare: Zimbabwe Ministry of Information Publication, June 1990).

"Pamberi neChimurenga," *ZANU Women in the Struggle*, Poster by Department of Information and Publicity, ZANU Headquarters, *The Year of the People's Storm*. Maputo, Mozambique, November 1979.

"The Right of Women to Equality with Men." *ZANU(PF) 1980 Election Manifesto*, (Maputo: Zimbabwe Printing and Publishing House, 1980).

Report of the Workshop on the Role of Women in Social, Economic and Cultural Reconstruction of Zimbabwe, Harare, February 22 - March 4, 1982, organized by Pan-African Institute for Development East and Southern Africa, in collaboration with the Ministry of Community Development and Women's Affairs.

"Sally Mugabe: Women's Struggle for Liberation" - Roland Buck interviews Sally Mugabe, wife of the Prime Minister of Zimbabwe in *West Africa*, 1981, no. 3336, pp. 1531-32.

Women For Rhodesia, *Extracts From the Rhodesia Herald and Sunday Mail*, 1978 (National Archives of Zimbabwe).

Zimbabwe National Archives Oral History Collection.

Zimbabwe Women' s Bureau, *Black Women in Zimbabwe*, (London: 1980)

Zimbabwe National Liberation War Veterans Association (ZNLWVA) *Re-Integration Programme for War Veterans in Zimbabwe: A Participatory Development Plan*, 7 Downie Avenue, Belgravia, P.O. Box 2793 Harare, August 1996.

Zimbabwean Government Gazette Extraordinary, Vol. LXXI, No.27, 27, April, 1993.

ZANU Archives Women's Affairs Files
(ordered chronologically)

Sarudzai Churucheminzwa 'Why I Joined ZANLA Women's Detachment," pamphlet, reprinted from June 1974, *Zimbabwe News*, 1974.

The Zimbabwe Revolution" A Political Education Handbook, produced by a team of ZANU Cadres during their detention (Kamwala, Lusaka Remand Prison), written before April 1976, one year after the imprisonment of all ZANU leaders and cadres stationed in Zambia after the Chitepo Assassination in accordance with Vorster's Detente initiative. This manuscript was smuggled out of prison and made available to the freedom fighters, 1976.

Z.A.N.U. (ZANU) Z.A.N.L.A. Headquarters, Chimoio, 14, November 1977, *Women Without Husbands*, 1977.

"The Role of Women Before and After Liberation," by the ZANU Department of Women's Affairs, no date supplied, possibly sometime in 1977 due to the references to ZIPA.

ZANU Defence Secretariat, Rally held at operational base on July 20, 1978 - Pfutskeke Base - present at rally were Teurai Ropa Nhongo plus thirty-six female comrades, six general staff and Field Commander E. Mhuru, 1978.

Comrade Catherine, ZANU Defence Secretariat HQ July 29, 1978 Department of Women's Affairs - REF DSWS/01, minutes of central committee, high command general staff meeting (female comrades) held July 27, 1978.

Nhando Dzekuroora, ZANU Commissariat Department H.Q. August 16, 1978. This document was translated for me by Albert Manuel a staff member at the ZANU Archives, Harare, 1978.

Teurai Ropa, ZANU, Department of Women's Affairs, "Report for the Year Ending 31st December 1978," 1978.

Teurai Ropa, "ZANU Women's Affairs (League)" undated but between March 1978 and May 1979.

"Zimbabwe African National Union Women's Affairs (League):" unsigned document by Teurai Ropa (Secretary for Women's Affairs) member of National Executive of Central Committee of ZANU, p. 2. The article was written before the first ZANU Women's Seminar held in 1979.

Zimbabwe African National Union (ZANU), Manpower, Planning and Labour Department, Circular, 12/5/79. This document was actually signed and stamped, 1979.

"On Marriage" Z.A.N.U. ZANU Commissariat Department H.Q. July 6, 1979. This document was actually unsigned by Urimbo, bur was possibly a copy and not the original, 1979.

Teurai Ropa, "ZANU Women's Affairs," 1979.

Z.A.N.U. Women's Affairs (League): Document unsigned by Cde Teurai Ropa (Secretary for Women's Affairs) member of National Executive of Central Committee of ZANU (no date supplied).

"The Role of Women in the Liberation Struggle," by ZANU Archivist Tsatsayi Constantino, (unpublished notes, 1996).

Zimbabwean and Rhodesian Newspapers and Magazines

The *African Daily News Bulletin*

- The *African Daily News Bulletin,* Monday, September 17, 1956.

- "A number of girls at Carter Girls' Hostel were raped, and one criminally assaulted 5 times," The *African Daily News Bulletin,* Tuesday, September 18, 1956.

- "Aftermath of Riot - Danger Signs," The *African Daily News Bulletin*, Thursday, September 20, 1956.

- "Fewer Girls," The *African Daily News Bulletin*, Saturday, September 22, 1956.

Bibliography

The *African Times*

- "They are teaching our women how to murder," *The African Times*, February 15, 1978.

- *The African Times*, January 25, 1978, p.12

The *Chronicle* (Bulawayo)

- "Salisbury Fuel Depot Blown Up on Wednesday," The *Chronicle*, December 14, 1978.

- Edson Zvobgo, "Oppression of Women is Dead," in The *Chronicle*, May 22nd, 1980.

- *The Chronicle*, January 31st, 1981, p.1.

- "Army Officers told: We wont look for scapegoats," The *Chronicle*, February 4, 1981, p.1.

- "Girls Abandon Guns to Fight Peacetime Battle," The *Chronicle*, November 30, 1981.

- The *Chronicle*, December 4, 1981.

The Daily Gazette

- The *Daily Gazette*, August 15, 1994.

The Financial Gazette

- The *Financial Gazette*, May 1st 1997, p.12.

- Nevanji Madanhire, "Liberation History much more complex than hitherto portrayed," The *Financial Gazette*, July 7, 1994.

- "Shocking Revelations of War time rape emerge as War vets Fund Scam Turns Ugly: Female beneficiaries threaten to sing," The *Financial Gazette*, April 24, 1997, p.1.

- "Female Combatants: Raped or Consented," The *Financial Gazette*, May 15, 1997.

- "Ex-combatants cry foul as inquiry unfolds," in The *Financial Gazette*, August 28, 1997.

- The *Financial Gazette*, August 20, 1998.

- The *Financial Gazette*, August 27, 1998.

Focus on Rhodesia

- "Progress By the Feminine Task Force," in *Focus on Rhodesia*, 2:2, 1977.

- "Petticoat Power Backs Men in the Bush," *Focus on Rhodesia*, 2:6, 1977.

- "Massive Raids were Enormously Successful," in *Focus on Rhodesia*, 3:7, 1978.

- "Unwanted Burdens of the Revolution," *Focus on Rhodesia*, 3:3, 1978.

- "Food to feed the fighters," *Focus on Rhodesia*, 4:2, 1979.

- The *Herald* (Rhodesia and Zimbabwe)

The *Rhodesian Herald*, December 9, 11, 13,, 14, and 15, 1961.

- "City disturbances: 80 women fined," The *Rhodesian Herald*, Tuesday, December 12, 1961.

- "Women to Serve in Army and Air Force" The *Herald*, Saturday June 28, 1975.

- "Women Anxious to Join The Forces," The *Herald*, Wednesday, July 2, 1975.

- "Women Urged to Help Men's Morale," The *Herald*, Monday, August 23, 1976.

- "A Long Wait for Victory of Zimbabwe," The *Herald*, March 7, 1980.

- "National Dress Makes its Debut," The *Herald*, March 28, 1980.

- Letter to the Editor by L.E. Chisiri - Seke, in The *Herald*, Monday, June 2, 1980, p.8.

- "Confidence the Key to Women's Future Hopes," The *Herald*, March 6, 1981.

- "Hospitals to be renamed after Heroes," in The *Herald*, April 15, 1981, p.7.

- "National Dress Not A Priority," The *Herald*, September 6, 1996.

- The *Herald*, Monday, March 10, 1997, p.1.

- Davison Maruziva, "Brutalities of the war as seen by a former combatant," The *Herald*, Monday December 29, 1997, p.8.

Mail and Guardian (South Africa)

- Matambanadzo, Isabella, "Women's War Story Causes a Stir," *Mail and Guardian*, (South Africa), December 8, 1995.

Moto (Magazine)

- *Moto*, 1:2, June, 1982.

- Mattarozzi, Madaleine, "What About Women," Letters To *Moto*, 1:4, August 1982.

- "Fay Chung: Educator for Change," *Moto*, 1:4, August 1982, pp.41-42.

- "Another Battle for Women Ex-Combatants," *Moto*, March 1983, p.31.

- "Enraged By Police Blitz," letters to *Moto*, No.19 December 1983/ January 1984.

- "Operation Clean-Up Takes Women's Lib One Step Back," *Moto*, No.19, December 1983/January 1984, pp. 5-9.

- Mafukidze, G., "In Support of Operation Clean-Up," Letter to *Moto*, March 1984, p.3.

- Letters to the Editor, *"Women's Lib Threatens Humanity" in Moto,* May 1984

- Myo, B., "Blitz on Women Retrogressive," Letter to *Moto*, May 1984, p.3.

- "A Luta Continua," in *Moto*, No.94, November, 1990, p.4.

- "Gremerina Zembbiti," *Moto*, No.94, November, 1990, pp.4-5.

- "Joyce Teurai Ropa Mujuru: Zimbabwe's Own Woman of Substance," *Moto*, No.94, November, 1990, pp. 7-8.

The *People's Voice*

- "Rudo Hondo: Heroine of Liberation Struggle," The *People's Voice*, March 13-19, 1994, p.13.

Social Change and Development

- "Ambuya Nehanda: Fighter for Justice," in *Social Change and Development*, Special supplement: "Religion for Liberation," no.21, September-November 1985, pp. 3-4.

- Focus on: Sexual Violence and War: When will we tell our own Story?: A woman called 'Sarah,'" in *Social Change and Development*, No.40, July, 1996, pp. 25-6.

The *Sunday Mail*

- "Big Welcome for Women's Forces Plan," The *Sunday Mail*, June 29, 1975.

- The *Sunday Mail*, December 7, 1975.

- The *Sunday Mail*, September 25, 1977.

- "Tough, Disciplined ... they're eager for a role in the new society," The *Sunday Mail*, May 17, 1981, p.15.

- The *Sunday Mail*, May 31, 1981, p.15.

- "Nhongo Calls for ban on Beauty Contest," The *Sunday Mail*, September 27, 1981.

- "Sex Barriers Have Stood Too Long," in The *Sunday Mail* (Harare), October 11, 1981.

- "Guerrilla TV Film Dropped," The *Sunday Mail*, October 11, 1981.

- "Be Realistic. Mrs. Nhongo Tells Women," The *Sunday Mail* (Harare), November 15, 1981, p.2.

- Michelle Faul, "Are men Fighting Shy of Marrying the Guerrilla Girls?," The *Sunday Mail*, November 22nd, 1981.

- "Liberation the real reward Says Nhongo," The *Sunday Mail*, November 29, 1981.

- The *Sunday Mail*, Harare, December 24, 1995.

- The *Sunday Mail*, July 14, 1996.

The *Sunday News*

- "The Angel of Mercy Who left Rhodesia With A Dark Secret," in *Sunday News*, February 12, 1978.

- "Sergeant Beryl and the Dogs with a nose for Danger," in *Sunday News,* April 23, 1978.

- The *Sunday News*, June 25, 1978.

- "Minister Urges Women: Help End the War," in *Sunday News*, August 20, 1978, p. 7.

Zimbabwe Independent

- "Muckraker," The *Zimbabwe Independent On Line*, www.samara.co.zw/zimin November 28, 1997.

The *Zimbabwe News (ZANU)*

- The *Zimbabwe News*, July -December, 1977, p.46.

- "Our Women are Women of Action," in *Zimbabwe News*, Vol. 10, No.1, Jan- Feb 1978

- Mabel Mudondo, "The Emancipation of Women and their Role Towards Liberation Struggle," *Zimbabwe News*, 10:1, 1978, p.23.

- "Comrade Teurai Ropa: Women have Total Involvement in Struggle," in *Zimbabwe News,* 10:2, May-June 1978, p.30.

- "Chimurenga is Now Liberating Our Country," *Zimbabwe News*, 10:4, July-August 1978.

- "Murder," The *Zimbabwe News*, 10:5, September - October, 1978, p.23.

- Comrade Zvisinei, "We Women Have The Right To Fight," in *Zimbabwe News*, 11:3, September/October, 1979.

- "The Trial of Mbuya Nehanda and other Chimurenga Revolutionaries," *Zimbabwe News*, 13:1, 1982, p. 14.

- "The Policies and Programmes of ZANU(PF), A Proud Record of Achievement," in *Zimbabwe News*, 16:5, May/June 1985, p. 14.

- "The Nairobi '85 Manifesto and Women's Decade 1075-1985: What women must do": special issue of *Zimbabwe News*, 17:3 March, 1986, p. 1.

- "Women should be advanced, says the Beijing Platform for Action," *Zimbabwe News*, April 1996, 27:5, p.8.

The *Zimbabwe People's Voice (ZAPU)*

- "Massacre of defenceless Girls at Mkushi," *Zimbabwe People's Voice*, October 28, 1978.

- "Women are Breastfeeding the Revolution," The *Zimbabwe People's Voice*, March 3, 1979.

- "Women Indispensible in Struggle," in *Zimbabwe People's Voice*, March 17, 1979.

- "The Role of the Zimbabwe Women in the Liberation Struggle," in *Zimbabwe People's Voice*, UK Edition, 1979, pp.10-12.

- "Rhodesia Forms Mummies Army," *Zimbabwe People's Voice*, September 29, 1979.

The *Zimbabwe Review (ZAPU)*

- The *Zimbabwe Review*, The Official Organ of ZAPU, October 20, 1973

- "The role of the Zimbabwe Women in our struggle," The *Zimbabwe Review*, October 20, 1973.

- Sikhubekiso Madeya and Angela Mhlanga, in "Young Women's Conference," The *Zimbabwe Review*, September, October, 4:5, 1975.

- The *Zimbabwe Review,* 4:6, 1975.

- "Girls Role in the Struggle," by Thokozile Ushe, in The *Zimbabwe Review*, October, 6:10, 1977.

- "Come Forward and Feed the Children," The *Zimbabwe Review*, official organ of ZAPU, June 5, 1978.

The *Zimbabwe Standard*

- "Brace Up For Stunning Revelations from War Victims Compensation Scam," in *Zimbabwe Standard*, May 4-10, 1997, p.11

Interviews

Women Ex-Combatants interviewed in Harare 1996 and 1997.

Most names have been changed to protect their anonymity, unless otherwise stated.

anon. ex-ZIPA combatant, Harare, July 1996.
Monica, woman ex-combatant, Harare, August, 1996.
Nyarai, woman ex-combatant, Harare, August, 1996.
Teresa, woman ex-combatant Harare, September, 1996 and October, 1996.
Rufaro, woman ex-combatant, Harare, September, 1996.
Maria, woman ex-combatant, Harare, September, 1996.
Rudo, woman ex-combatant, Harare, September, 1996.
Shupikai, woman ex-combatant, Harare, September, 1996.
Sekai, woman ex-combatant, Harare, September, 1996.
Honour, woman ex-combatant, Harare, August and September, 1996.
Ruth, woman ex-combatant, Harare, September, 1996.
Anon. woman ex-combatant, Harare, September, 1996.
Nhamo, woman ex-combatant, Harare, October, 1996.
Tsi Tsi, woman ex-combatant, Harare, October, 1996.
Sylvia, woman ex-combatant, Marondera, October, 1996

Joyce Mujuru, The Minister for Information Posts and Telecommunications, October 30, 1996 and March 5, 1997.

Freedom Nyamubaya, author, poet, and outspoken woman ex-combatant, in Marondera, October 6, 1996.

Margaret Dongo, Independent Member of Parliament for Harare South, and woman ex-combatant, interviewed in conjunction with Joyce Makwenda, Harare, November 19, 1996.

Other Interviews

Chenjerai Hove, interviewed by David Moore, Harare, July, 1991.

Anon. woman ex-combatant interviewed by David Moore, Canada, 26, April, 1994.

Julian Cobbing, interviewed in Adelaide, May 1995.

Ingrid Sinclair, Director of *Flame*, Harare, July 18, 1996.

Zimbabwe National Heroes Acre Army Guide, Harare, July 1996.

Dzino, male ex-combatant, Harare, August 1996 and December 30, 1996.

John Gwitira, Executive Director of the ZNLWVA, August 29, 1996, (and September 1996).

Martin Mhando, Tanzanian film-maker, Southern African Film Festival, Harare, September, 1996.

Jill, ex-section leader, Rhodesian police reserves, Borrowdale, Harare, March 1998.

Personal Correspondence
Letter from Judith Todd to author, September 28, 1996.
Letter from Ingrid Sinclair to author, August 30, 1996.

INDEX

H